1995
Dor.

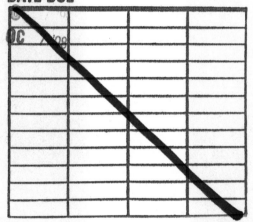

The Sporting News

THE

ALL-STAR GAME

"A PICTORIAL HISTORY, 1933 TO PRESENT"

The Sporting News

THE
ALL-STAR GAME

"A PICTORIAL HISTORY, 1933 TO PRESENT"

BY DONALD HONIG

Published in the United States by THE SPORTING NEWS
Publishing Co., 1212 North Lindbergh Boulevard,
St. Louis, Missouri 63132.

Library of Congress Catalog Card Number: 87-61059

ISBN: 0-89204-261-3
10 9 8 7 6 5 4 3 2 1

First Edition

ACKNOWLEDGMENTS

I am deeply indebted to a number of people for their generous support and encouragement during the writing of this book. I would most especially like to thank Richard Waters, President and Chief Executive Officer of The Sporting News, and the following members of his crackerjack staff: Maurine Herron, James Booth, Ron Smith, Tom Barnidge, Joe Hoppel, Craig Carter, Bill Perry, Mike Bruner, Rich Pilling, Steve Gietschier and Sandy Dupont. Also, for their good advice and wise counsel, I am grateful to these keen students of baseball history: Stanley Honig, David Markson, Lawrence Ritter, Andrew Aronstein, Allan J. Grotheer, Douglas Mulcahy, Louis Kiefer and Thomas Brookman.

Most of the photo research was done in the incomparable archives of The Sporting News.

Other Baseball Books
By Donald Honig

BASEBALL WHEN THE GRASS WAS REAL

BASEBALL BETWEEN THE LINES

THE MAN IN THE DUGOUT

THE OCTOBER HEROES

THE IMAGE OF THEIR GREATNESS (WITH LAWRENCE RITTER)

THE 100 GREATEST BASEBALL PLAYERS OF ALL TIME (WITH LAWRENCE RITTER)

THE BROOKLYN DODGERS: AN ILLUSTRATED TRIBUTE

THE NEW YORK YANKEES: AN ILLUSTRATED HISTORY

BASEBALL'S TEN GREATEST TEAMS

THE LOS ANGELES DODGERS: THE FIRST QUARTER CENTURY

THE NATIONAL LEAGUE: AN ILLUSTRATED HISTORY

THE AMERICAN LEAGUE: AN ILLUSTRATED HISTORY

THE BOSTON RED SOX: AN ILLUSTRATED TRIBUTE

BASEBALL AMERICA

THE NEW YORK METS: THE FIRST QUARTER CENTURY

THE WORLD SERIES: AN ILLUSTRATED HISTORY

CONTENTS

For my daughter Catherine

INTRODUCTION

The idea seemed so logical, so natural, that the only question was: Why hadn't anyone thought of it before? The fact was, baseball's two-league structure had been in place for a third of a century before anyone succeeded in bringing the respective stars together for a "dream game."

The All-Star Game that was to become a tradition in baseball (and, in later years, every major sport) was conceived in 1933 by a gentleman named Arch Ward, at the time sports editor of the Chicago Tribune. Ward saw the game as a one-time-only pageant, to be played as part of Chicago's Century of Progress Exposition. The notion of putting baseball's reigning princes on the field at one time and having a cosmic shootout must have been irresistible.

When Ward secured the approval for the game from Commissioner Kenesaw Mountain Landis, in those days baseball's stern and supreme overlord, plans went ahead to play the game at Chicago's Comiskey Park on July 6. The proceeds would go into the Players' Pension Fund, which had been created to help needy former players.

It was Ward's contention that the stars representing each league should be selected by a vote of the fans, and this was the way it was done for the first two years. Those first teams were limited to 18 players, with the size of the squads being gradually increased, to 20 in 1934, 21 in 1936, 23 in 1937, 25 in 1939 and 28 in 1969, the current limit.

The selection system was changed in 1935 when it was decided to have the rival managers choose the players. Then, starting in 1938, the eight managers from each league picked the teams. From 1947 through 1957, the makeup of the teams was returned to the fans, with balloting being nationwide. (Then as now, pitchers were excluded from the voting, being named by the managers.) When a vigorous get-out-the-vote campaign in Cincinnati in 1957 ended with the National League All-Star team being overloaded with Reds, the fans were disenfranchised and the responsibility for choosing the teams was given over to managers, coaches and players (each, of course, voting only for players in his own league, but not any from his own team). There are many people who maintain that this is still the best way to select the truest All-Star teams. In 1970, the voting was returned to the fans, a system that still prevails.

The managers for the teams each year would be the skippers who had met in the previous World Series, when possible, for not every manager who had won the pennant the year before survived in the job until the next All-Star Game.

The managers selected for that first game back in 1933 were choices at once sentimental and apt—Connie Mack for the American League and John McGraw for the National. Mack, 70 years old, had been managing his Philadelphia Athletics for 33 years (and had another 17 to go). McGraw had retired as manager of the New York Giants the previous June after 30 years of bitter and sweet. (It also proved to be John J.'s final farewell to baseball; he died seven months later.)

The "one-time-only dream game" caught the public imagination so completely that it immediately became a yearly institution, a perfect pause in the midst of baseball's summer-long pennant races. It even became, for a time, a twice-a-year event, from 1959 through 1962. Though some people felt that an encore game each year would dilute the product, all of these games were strongly supported and provided additional revenue for the Players' Pension Fund, aided needy old-time players and helped youth baseball. The second All-Star Game was discontinued after 1962 because, among other reasons, the newly expanded schedule of 162 games made a second interlude in the tightly packed season impractical to maintain.

After more than half a century, the All-Star Game remains one of the jewels in baseball's crown, its own act of self-renewal, ever fresh and eagerly awaited, an annual roll call of the game's top shelf. The very name of the game implies its magic and assures its excitement and vitality.

1933

ONE TO

1939

A Brand
New Idea

The Beginning

Nationals	AB.	R.	H.	RBI.	PO.	A.
Martin (Cardinals), 3b	4	0	0	1	0	3
Frisch (Cardinals), 2b	4	1	2	1	5	3
Klein (Phillies), rf	4	0	1	0	3	0
P. Waner (Pirates), rf	0	0	0	0	0	0
Hafey (Reds), lf	4	0	1	0	0	0
Terry (Giants), 1b	4	0	2	0	7	2
Berger (Braves), cf	4	0	0	0	4	0
Bartell (Phillies), ss	2	0	0	0	0	3
cTraynor (Pirates)	1	0	1	0	0	0
Hubbell (Giants), p	0	0	0	0	0	0
eCuccinello (Dodgers)	1	0	0	0	0	0
Wilson (Cardinals), c	1	0	0	0	2	0
aO'Doul (Giants)	1	0	0	0	0	0
Hartnett (Cubs), c	1	0	0	0	2	0
Hallahan (Cardinals), p	1	0	0	0	1	0
Warneke (Cubs), p	1	1	1	0	0	0
dEnglish (Cubs), ss	1	0	0	0	0	0
Totals	34	2	8	2	24	11

Americans	AB.	R.	H.	RBI.	PO.	A.
Chapman (Yankees), lf-rf	5	0	1	0	1	0
Gehringer (Tigers), 2b	3	1	0	0	1	3
Ruth (Yankees), rf	4	1	2	2	1	0
West (Browns), cf	0	0	0	0	0	0
Gehrig (Yankees), 1b	2	0	0	0	12	0
Simmons (W. Sox), cf-lf	4	0	1	0	4	0
Dykes (White Sox), 3b	3	1	2	0	2	4
Cronin (Senators), ss	3	1	1	0	2	4
R. Ferrell (Red Sox), c	3	0	0	0	4	0
Gomez (Yankees), p	1	0	1	1	0	0
Crowder (Senators), p	1	0	0	0	0	0
bAverill (Indians)	1	0	1	1	0	0
Grove (Athletics), p	1	0	0	0	0	0
Totals	31	4	9	4	27	11

```
National League ...............0 0 0  0 0 2  0 0 0—2
American League ..............0 1 2  0 0 1  0 0 x—4
```

Nationals	IP.	H.	R.	ER.	BB.	SO.
Hallahan (L)	2*	2	3	3	5	1
Warneke	4	6	1	1	0	2
Hubbell	2	1	0	0	1	1

Americans	IP.	H.	R.	ER.	BB.	SO.
Gomez (W)	3	2	0	0	0	1
Crowder	3	3	2	2	0	0
Grove	3	3	0	0	0	3

*Pitched to three batters in third.

aGrounded out for Wilson in sixth. bSingled for Crowder in sixth. cDoubled for Bartell in seventh. dFlied out for Warneke in seventh. eStruck out for Hubbell in ninth. E—Gehrig. DP—Nationals 1, Americans 1. LOB—Nationals 10, Americans 5. 2B—Traynor. 3B—Warneke. HR—Ruth, Frisch. SB—Gehringer. SH—Ferrell. U—Dinneen and McGowan (A.L.), Klem and Rigler (N.L.). T—2:05. A —47,595.

Baseball's sparkling new contribution to the glamour and romance of American sports, the All-Star Game, made its debut at 1:15 on the sweltering afternoon of July 6, 1933, at Chicago's Comiskey Park. There were 47,595 fans in the stands, all eager to see a novel concept in action—action that would be performed by the most glittering assemblage of ballplaying talent ever brought together on a single diamond at the same time.

Exhibition game or not, American League Manager Connie Mack was out to win. Unlike later years, when managers tried to accommodate as many players as possible, Mack made just one change in his starting lineup (excluding pitching), using a total of 13 players. The National League's John McGraw used 17, including four pinch-hitters.

Not all the fans were in the stands (where a reserved seat set one back all of $1.10 in those hard-bottom years of the Great Depression); a few were sitting in the National League dugout, watching the American Leaguers take batting practice. There were some formidable thumpers on the A.L. side—including Lou Gehrig, Jimmie Foxx and Al Simmons. They were special. But one among the American League contingent was unique, then and always, and those National Leaguers, those All-Stars, knew it. And when he stepped into the batting cage, the National Leaguers were fans again, as many of them had been a decade before when the Big Man become the embodiment of baseball and stirred their youthful imaginations.

"We wanted to see the Babe," said Wild Bill Hallahan of the St. Louis Cardinals, a hard-throwing lefthander who started for the Nationals. "Sure, he was old and had a big waistline, but that didn't make any difference. We were on the same field as Babe Ruth."

Nor did Ruth disappoint. Fittingly, the man who seemed to have invented the home run, who had virtually made the national game over in his own image, was to anoint this new spectacle and leave his trademark on it like the mark of a branding iron.

Hallahan, who had pitched a complete-game victory only two days before, started against the Yankees' Lefty Gomez, a 24-year-old lefthander who also was working on one day's rest (Gomez, in fact, had gone 9⅓ innings in a July 4 loss). Hallahan had the thrill of striking out Ruth in the first inning. "That was quite a kick for me," Wild Bill recalled in an interview four decades after the fact.

The American League scored the first run in All-Star Game history in the bottom of the second, and it pointed up once again the vagaries that shape baseball into the most entertaining of all games. With one out, Hallahan, who walked five batters in his two-plus innings of work, walked the White Sox's Jimmie Dykes and the Senators' Joe Cronin. Bill seemed clear of the woods when he retired the Red Sox's Rick Ferrell, with the notoriously weak-hitting Gomez coming to bat. But Lefty, a .113 hitter that year, stunned everyone by lining a single to center, scoring Dykes.

An inning later, Ruth put things back in perspective. After Hallahan had walked Detroit's Charlie Gehringer, the 38-year-old colossus of Yankee Stadium came to bat and gave each fan his buck-ten's worth. The Babe uncoiled on a Hallahan delivery and drove it on a low, scorching, one-way journey just inside the right-field foul line and into the lower stands. The crowd, according to one newspaper account, "roared in acclamation." Believe it. There was no home run like a Babe Ruth home run, and the occasion was festive to begin with.

Hallahan then walked Gehrig and departed in favor of the Cubs' Lon Warneke. The tall righthander restored order and shut down the American Leaguers through the fifth inning, matched now by Washington's Alvin Crowder.

The National League finally emerged from the darkness in the top of the sixth. With one out, Warneke looped a fly ball down the right-field line, into Ruth's sector. The Babe was unable to get to it and the ball rolled past him. Warneke wound up on third with a triple (charitably scored, some thought). When the Cardinals' Pepper Martin grounded out, Warneke scored. A moment later,

Frankie Frisch, the Cardinals' player-manager, drove one into the right-field customers and the score was 3-2, American League.

The Americans retrieved one of those runs in their sixth on a Cronin single, Ferrell's sacrifice and a pinch-hit single by Cleveland's Earl Averill (batting for Crowder). That was the end of the scoring, but not of the suspense.

Two of baseball's all-time-best lefthanders took over in the seventh, the Athletics' Lefty Grove for the Americans and the Giants' Carl Hubbell for the Nationals. (Four days before, Hubbell had pitched a classic 18-inning, 1-0 shutout against the Cardinals.)

The Nationals ruffled the dour Grove's feathers in the seventh when the Giants' Bill Terry singled and Pittsburgh's Pie Traynor rapped a pinch double, putting runners on second and third with one out. Grove then accelerated what had become, in the post-Walter Johnson years, America's fastest fastball, a pitch that seemed to vaporize on its way to the plate. With it, he fanned the Cubs' Gabby Hartnett and got Gabby's Chicago teammate, Woody English, on a fly ball.

"Told myself I had to do it," Grove said. "Didn't want to be embarrassed out there in front of everybody." (By "everybody," he meant that first congress of All-Stars.)

In the eighth, Frisch singled and the Reds' Chick Hafey, swinging late on a Grove smoker, sent Ruth to the right-field wall, where the Babe corraled the ball, ending the Nationals' final threat.

That first All-Star Game, taken by the American League, 4-2, on the strength of Ruth's homer, was a resounding success, financially and artistically. And more than that, it had caught the public imagination as a "natural." It was soon apparent that Arch Ward's finely conceived, splendidly motivated "game of the century" would become an annual event, as uniquely a part of the baseball mosaic as opening day and the World Series.

Babe Ruth gets five from the batboy after slamming the first home run in All-Star competition.

N.L. Manager John McGraw.

A.L. Manager Connie Mack.

Frankie Frisch swats the National League's first All-Star homer as catcher Rick Ferrell looks on.

National Leaguers (left to right) Chuck Klein of the Phillies, Chick Hafey of the Reds and Wally Berger of the Braves in their specially made All-Star uniforms.

Lefty Gomez.

Jimmie Dykes scores the first run in All-Star history.

Carl Is King

Americans	AB.	R.	H.	RBI.	PO.	A.
Gehringer (Tigers), 2b	3	0	2	0	2	1
Manush (Senators), lf	2	0	0	0	0	0
Ruffing (Yankees), p	1	0	1	2	0	0
Harder (Indians), p	2	0	0	0	1	0
Ruth (Yankees), rf	2	1	0	0	0	0
Chapman (Yankees), rf	2	0	1	0	0	1
Gehrig (Yankees), 1b	4	0	0	0	11	1
Foxx, (Athletics), 3b	5	1	2	1	1	2
Simmons (W. Sox), cf-lf	5	3	3	1	3	0
Cronin (Senators), ss	5	1	2	2	2	8
Dickey (Yankees), c	2	1	1	0	4	0
hCochrane (Tigers), c	1	0	0	0	1	1
Gomez (Yankees), p	1	0	0	0	0	0
bAverill (Indians), cf	4	1	2	3	1	0
West (Browns), cf	0	0	0	0	1	0
Totals	39	9	14	9	27	14

Nationals	AB.	R.	H.	RBI.	PO.	A.
Frisch (Cardinals), 2b	3	3	2	1	0	1
aHerman (Cubs), 2b	2	0	1	0	0	1
Traynor (Pirates), 3b	5	2	2	1	1	0
Medwick (Cardinals), lf	2	1	1	3	0	0
dKlein (Cubs), lf	3	0	1	1	1	0
Cuyler (Cubs), rf	2	0	0	0	2	0
eOtt (Giants), rf	2	0	0	0	0	1
Berger (Braves), cf	2	0	0	0	0	0
fP. Waner (Pirates), cf	2	0	0	0	1	0
Terry (Giants), 1b	3	0	1	0	4	0
Jackson (Giants), ss	2	0	0	0	0	1
gVaughan (Pirates), ss	2	0	0	0	4	0
Hartnett (Cubs), c	2	0	0	0	9	0
Lopez (Dodgers), c	2	0	0	0	5	1
Hubbell (Giants), p	0	0	0	0	0	0
Warneke (Cubs), p	0	0	0	0	0	0
Mungo (Dodgers), p	0	0	0	0	0	0
cMartin (Cardinals)	0	1	0	0	0	0
Dean (Cardinals), p	1	0	0	0	0	0
Frankhouse (Braves), p	1	0	0	0	0	0
Totals	36	7	8	6	27	5

American League ...... 0 0 0 2 6 1 0 0 0—9
National League ...... 1 0 3 0 3 0 0 0 0—7

Americans	IP.	H.	R.	ER.	BB.	SO.
Gomez	3	3	4	4	1	3
Ruffing	1†	4	3	3	1	0
Harder (W)	5	1	0	0	1	2

Nationals	IP.	H.	R.	ER.	BB.	SO.
Hubbell	3	2	0	0	2	6
Warneke	1*	3	4	4	3	1
Mungo (L)	1	4	4	4	2	1
Dean	3	5	1	1	1	4
Frankhouse	1	0	0	0	1	0

*Pitched to two batters in fifth.
†Pitched to four batters in fifth.

aPopped out for Hubbell in third but was permitted to replace Frisch in seventh. bTripled for Gomez in fourth. cWalked for Mungo in fifth. dSingled for Medwick in fifth. eForced runner for Cuyler in fifth. fStruck out for Berger in fifth. gForced runner for Jackson in fifth. hRan for Dickey in sixth. E—Gehrig, Berger. DP—Nationals 1. LOB—Americans 12, Nationals 5. 2B—Foxx, Simmons 2, Cronin, Averill, Herman. 3B—Chapman, Averill. HR—Frisch, Medwick. SB—Gehringer, Manush, Traynor, Ott. U—Pfirman and Stark (N.L.), Owens and Moriarty (A.L.). T—2:44. A—48,363.

After Babe Ruth had embossed the imprimatur of the slugger on the first All-Star Game, Carl Hubbell returned a year later and on behalf of the pitching fraternity made the second mustering of the stars perhaps the most memorable of them all. What Hubbell did on the afternoon of July 10—appropriately enough, on the mound of his home park, New York's Polo Grounds—was turn in perhaps the most spellbinding bit of pitching wizardry ever seen in baseball.

What the New York Giants' screwballing lefthander accomplished, in fact, could only have been done in an All-Star Game, for only in a contest of this nature was it possible to face so many of baseball's landmark names in a row—and dispose of them in a performance of remarkable purity.

American League Manager Joe Cronin sent up a lineup that in all of baseball history is difficult to match: Charlie Gehringer, Heinie Manush, Babe Ruth, Lou Gehrig, Jimmie Foxx, Al Simmons, Cronin himself and Bill Dickey, followed by starting pitcher Lefty Gomez. (Aside from Gomez, the lineup batted a composite .333 that year.)

National League Manager Bill Terry was able to send up some high-caliber hitters of his own—most notably Joe Medwick, Chuck Klein, Mel Ott, Paul Waner, Pie Traynor and Terry himself—but not even this array of estimable swingers could match the thunderous power packed into Cronin's lineup.

Interestingly enough, in that age of the playing manager, the game saw no less than five of that now-all-but-vanished breed in action: the Senators' Cronin, the Giants' Terry, the Pirates' Traynor, the Cardinals' Frankie Frisch and the Tigers' Mickey Cochrane.

Enhancing the drama of what was to come, Hubbell began the top of the first inning by getting into hot water. Very hot water. Detroit's Gehringer led off with a single and moved to second on an outfield bobble. Washington's Manush then drew a walk. Men on first and second, none out, and King Carl looking down the menacing gun barrels of Ruth, Gehrig, Foxx.

Hubbell then began turning over his screwball with uncanny precision. It was a delivery designed to break the backs of free-swingers. The Great Man, Ruth himself (who three days later would hit his 700th big-league home run), was the first to go. The Babe took a called third strike, looking "decidedly puzzled," according to one contemporary account, as Hubbell's screwball darted back and sliced the outside corner. Then Gehrig went down swinging mightily at the low-breaking twisters. (Gehringer and Manush pulled a double steal on the third strike.) As Gehrig passed Foxx on his way back to the dugout, he warned Jimmie (who was playing third base in this game), "You might as well cut. It won't get any higher." The tip didn't help; Foxx went down on strikes, ending the threat.

Frisch put the Nationals ahead, 1-0, with a leadoff homer in the bottom of the first, and then Hubbell returned to the mound. The first man he faced was the White Sox's Al Simmons (who went into the 1934 season with a 10-year major league batting average of .355), and this feared slugger, too, struck out. Hubbell then made it five in a row when he fanned Cronin, and the 48,363 spectators knew right then and there that they were sitting in on a moment of baseball history of no small proportions.

It was the Yankees' Bill Dickey who finally broke the spell by lining a single to left. "I was happy to see that," Gehringer said. "It was starting to get embarrassing."

After the Dickey single, Hubbell concluded the second inning by making Gomez his sixth strike-out victim.

In the third, the Giants' standout retired the side on two fly balls and a grounder and headed across the field to the center-field clubhouse, his ears ringing from a tremendous ovation.

It began to look like a National League day all the way when, in the third, the home team scored three runs on a homer by the Cardinals' Joe Medwick, just beginning to emerge as the National League's most fearsome hitter.

Hubbell's successors, however, were unable to handle that awesome American League lineup as deftly as he had. The Cubs' Lon Warneke and Brooklyn's Van Lingle Mungo soon found themselves cringing in a hailstone of hits. The American behemoths reached Warneke for two runs in the fourth and then roared for six more in the fifth (two off Warneke, four against Mungo).

After Warneke opened the fifth by walking Ruth and Gehrig, he was replaced by Mungo, the hard-throwing ace of Casey Stengel's Dodger staff. Foxx and Simmons hit run-scoring singles, Dickey walked and Cleveland's Earl Averill, who had pinch-hit a tremendous triple the inning before and then remained in the game, doubled in two more runs. Gehringer was walked to get to Yankee pitcher Red Ruffing. Ruffing, one of the game's great hitting pitchers, thwarted the strategy by singling in the inning's fifth and sixth runs.

Behind 8-4 now, the Nationals came back with three runs of their own in the bottom of the fifth on a walk and a row of three singles, plus a double steal. The Americans added the game's final run against Dizzy Dean in the sixth and then sat back as Mel Harder, Cleveland's fine curve-baller, handled the Nationals with little trouble. Harder, in fact, pitched the final five innings and allowed just one hit.

It is ironic that a game that ended with a 9-7 score and saw 10 extra-base hits should be remembered for an exhibition of pitching artistry, but it is Carl Hubbell's feat of striking out, in succession, five of baseball's greatest hitters that will always be the glowing memory of the 1934 All-Star Game. And for Hubbell himself, the achievement remains the capstone of a major league career that saw him win 253 games and log five straight seasons of more than 20 victories. Nothing else that the elegant lefthander ever did came close to capturing the imaginations of baseball fans as his performance in New York on the sunny afternoon of July 10, 1934, at the old Polo Grounds in the second All-Star Game.

Four of Carl Hubbell's victims were (left to right) Al Simmons, Lou Gehrig, Babe Ruth and Jimmie Foxx.

Joe Medwick.

Joe Cronin.

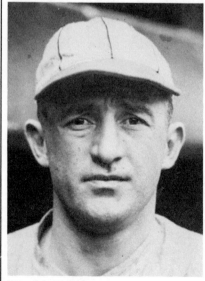

Frankie Frisch.

Carl Hubbell.

Mel Harder.

Earl Averill.

Al Simmons slides safely into second base in the sixth inning. Waiting for the throw is the Cubs' Billy Herman.

19

The Foxx Hunt

Nationals	AB.	R.	H.	RBI.	PO.	A.
Martin (Cardinals), 3b	4	0	1	0	0	0
Vaughan (Pirates), ss	3	1	1	0	2	2
Ott (Giants), rf	4	0	0	0	1	0
Medwick (Cardinals), lf	3	0	0	0	0	0
Terry (Giants), 1b	3	0	1	1	5	1
Collins (Cardinals), 1b	1	0	0	0	2	0
Berger (Braves), cf	2	0	0	0	1	0
bMoore (Giants), cf	2	0	0	0	1	0
Herman (Cubs), 2b	3	0	0	0	1	4
Wilson (Phillies), c	3	0	1	0	8	0
cWhitehead (Cardinals)	0	0	0	0	0	0
Hartnett (Cubs), c	0	0	0	0	3	0
Walker (Cardinals), p	0	0	0	0	0	0
aMancuso (Giants)	1	0	0	0	0	0
Schmuacher (Giants), p	1	0	0	0	0	1
dP. Waner (Pirates)	1	0	0	0	0	0
Derringer (Reds), p	0	0	0	0	0	0
Dean (Cardinals), p	0	0	0	0	0	0
Totals	31	1	4	1	24	8

Americans	AB.	R.	H.	RBI.	PO.	A.
Vosmik (Indians), rf	4	1	1	0	1	0
Gehringer (Tigers), 2b	3	0	2	0	1	3
Gehrig (Yankees), 1b	3	1	0	0	12	0
Foxx (Athletics), 3b	3	1	2	3	0	0
Bluege (Senators), 3b	0	0	0	0	0	0
Johnson (Athletics), lf	4	0	0	0	4	0
Chapman (Yankees), lf	0	0	0	0	0	0
Simmons (White Sox), cf	4	0	2	0	2	0
Cramer (Athletics), cf	0	0	0	0	0	0
Hemsley (Browns), c	4	1	1	0	6	0
Cronin (Red Sox), ss	4	0	0	1	1	4
Gomez (Yankees), p	2	0	0	0	0	2
Harder (Indians), p	1	0	0	0	0	1
Totals	32	4	8	4	27	10

National League	0	0	0	1	0	0	0	0 0	—1
American League	2	1	0	0	1	0	0	0 x	—4

Nationals	IP.	H.	R.	ER.	BB.	SO.
Walker (L)	2	2	3	3	1	2
Schumacher	4	4	1	1	1	5
Derringer	1	1	0	0	0	1
Dean	1	1	0	0	1	1

Americans	IP.	H.	R.	ER.	BB.	SO.
Gomez (W)	6	3	1	1	2	4
Harder	3	1	0	0	0	1

aFlied out for Walker in third. bFlied out for Berger in seventh. cRan for Wilson in seventh. dGrounded out for Schumacher in seventh. E—Martin. LOB—Nationals 5, Americans 7. 2B—Vaughan, Wilson, Gehringer, Simmons. 3B—Hemsley. HR—Foxx. U—Ormsby and Geisel (A.L.), Magerkurth and Sears (N.L.). T—2:06. A—69,831.

The third edition of what was soon to become known as baseball's "midsummer classic" was played at Cleveland Stadium on July 8, 1935. One of the game's monster ball yards, the stadium totaled 69,831 admissions for this game, an All-Star Game record that prevailed until 1981, when more than 72,000 fans attended the 52nd game of the series in the same park.

After the exciting novelty of the first game and Hubbell's compelling performance in 1934, the 1935 affair was rather mundane. The American League won for the third year in a row, this time by a 4-1 score, and it was pretty much a Jimmie Foxx show. The Athletics' slugger, again playing third base in deference to Lou Gehrig, belted a two-run homer in the bottom of the first inning, sending his club off to a lead it never relinquished.

In the second inning, St. Louis Browns catcher Rollie Hemsley tripled and scored on a fly ball by Joe Cronin (who was now the playing manager of the Boston Red Sox).

These runs were scored off left-hander Bill Walker of the Cardinals, the starter and loser for the Nationals. Walker was followed to the mound by the Giants' Hal Schumacher, who worked four creditable innings, yielding just one run (which was driven in by Foxx in the fifth, giving Jimmie his third RBI).

The National League scored its lone run in the fourth. Pittsburgh's Arky Vaughan, the league's premier shortstop of the '30s, led off with a double and scored on Bill Terry's single. These hits amounted to half of the Nationals' game total.

Applying the silencer to the National League bats were Lefty Gomez, starting for his league for the third straight year, and Mel Harder, who had pitched so effectively the year before. Over the two games, Harder showed eight innings of work in which he yielded just two hits and no runs.

Gomez went the first six innings in the '35 game, giving up three hits and one run. The longevity of Lefty's stint prompted a change—at the Nationals' behest—in All-Star rules, prohibiting a pitcher from going more than three innings unless a game goes into extra innings.

The managers (who for the first time had chosen the squads) were still playing tight baseball. Accordingly, A.L. skipper Mickey Cochrane used just 13 players, including pitchers, while his counterpart, Frankie Frisch, used 18, including pitchers and pinch-hitters.

Of the players participating in all three All-Star Games to date, the White Sox's Al Simmons was the event's top hitter with a 6-for-13 showing at the plate and a .462 batting average. Simmons, though, never appeared in another All-Star Game. Oddly, the game's most frustrated hitter was the man who at the time was, arguably, baseball's premier belter, Gehrig. The Yankee star, a Triple Crown winner in 1934, was hitless in nine at-bats in All-Star competition.

Jimmie Foxx.

Bill Terry.   **Lefty Gomez.**

Arky Vaughan.

Joe Vosmik.

Lou Gehrig crosses the bag after hitting into a forceout. Bill Terry takes the throw as pitcher Bill Walker looks on.

19 36

An N.L. Breakthrough

Americans	AB.	R.	H.	RBI.	PO.	A.
Appling (White Sox), ss	4	0	1	2	2	2
Gehringer (Tigers), 2b	3	0	2	0	2	1
DiMaggio (Yankees), rf	5	0	0	0	1	0
Gehrig (Yankees), 1b	2	1	1	1	7	0
Averill (Indians), cf	3	0	0	0	3	1
Chapman (Senators), cf	1	0	0	0	0	0
Ferrell (Red Sox), c	2	0	0	0	4	0
aDickey (Yankees), c	2	0	0	0	2	0
Radcliff (White Sox), lf	2	0	1	0	2	0
Goslin (Tigers), lf	1	1	1	0	1	0
Higgins (Athletics), 3b	2	0	0	0	0	1
bFoxx (Red Sox), 3b	2	1	1	0	0	1
Grove (Red Sox), p	1	0	0	0	0	0
Rowe (Tigers), p	1	0	0	0	0	0
cSelkirk (Yankees)	0	0	0	0	0	0
Harder (Indians), p	0	0	0	0	0	1
fCrosetti (Yankees)	1	0	0	0	0	0
Totals	32	3	7	3	24	7

Nationals	AB.	R.	H.	RBI.	PO.	A.
Galan (Cubs), cf	4	1	1	1	1	0
Herman (Cubs), 2b	3	1	2	0	3	4
Collins (Cardinals), 1b	2	0	0	0	9	1
Medwick (Cardinals), lf	4	0	1	1	0	0
Demaree (Cubs), rf	3	1	1	0	1	0
dOtt (Giants), rf	1	0	1	0	0	0
Hartnett (Cubs), c	4	1	1	1	7	0
Whitney (Phillies), 3b	3	0	1	1	0	2
eRiggs (Reds), 3b	1	0	0	0	0	0
Durocher (Cardinals), ss	3	0	1	0	4	0
J. Dean (Cardinals), p	1	0	0	0	0	2
Hubbell (Giants), p	1	0	0	0	2	1
Davis (Cubs), p	0	0	0	0	0	1
Warneke (Cubs), p	1	0	0	0	0	0
Totals	31	4	9	4	27	11

American League ...... 0 0 0 0 0 0 3 0 0—3
National League .... 0 2 0 0 2 0 0 0 x—4

Americans	IP.	H.	R.	ER.	BB.	SO.
Grove (L)	3	3	2	2	2	2
Rowe	3	4	2	1	1	2
Harder	2	2	0	0	0	2

Nationals	IP.	H.	R.	ER.	BB.	SO.
J. Dean (W)	3	0	0	0	2	3
Hubbell	3	2	0	0	1	2
Davis	⅔	4	3	3	1	0
Warneke	2⅓	1	0	0	3	2

aGrounded out for Ferrell in seventh. bSingled for Higgins in seventh. cWalked for Rowe in seventh. dSingled for Demaree in eighth. eStruck out for Whitney in eighth. fStruck out Harder in ninth. E—DiMaggio. DP—Americans 1, Nationals 1. LOB —Americans 9, Nationals 6. 2B—Gehringer. 3B— Hartnett. HR—Galan, Gehrig. WP—Hubbell. U— Reardon and Stewart (N.L.), Summers and Kolls (A.L.). T—2:00. A—25,556.

The National League finally came in out of the cold in the 1936 All-Star Game, played at Braves Field, Boston, on July 7. The senior league achieved its breakthrough primarily on the pitching of its two widely contrasting aces—the ebullient, hard-throwing Dizzy Dean and the self-effacing, screwballing Carl Hubbell, winners of 50 games between them that year.

Dean, the Cardinals' garrulous showman, worked the first three innings and gave neither a hit nor a run. Hubbell poker-faced his way through the next three and, though not as breathtaking as he had been in 1934, gave just two hits and no runs.

The American League, managed by the Yankees' Joe McCarthy (a replacement for Detroit's Mickey Cochrane, who had suffered a nervous breakdown that season), started 36-year-old Lefty Grove of the Red Sox. With his once-intimidating fastball no longer at peak velocity, Lefty was getting by on curves and guile (enough so to lead the league that year in shutouts, with six, and earned-run average, with a 2.81 mark). The Nationals, however, peppered him for two runs in the bottom of the second. The Cubs' Frank Demaree singled and then scored on Chicago teammate Gabby Hartnett's triple, with Hartnett in turn scoring on a fly ball.

Hartnett's triple was the result of a missed shoestring-catch attempt by the American League's rookie right fielder, the Yankees'

Joe DiMaggio. A rookie starting in the All-Star Game was without precedent; this, though, was no ordinary freshman. After just two months in the big leagues (an injury delayed his debut until May 3), the 21-year-old Yankee was doing it all, with grace, power and splendor (and a .358 batting average). McCarthy had no qualms about putting him in there with the reigning lions. Joe, however, for one of the few times in his career, disappointed. Playing the entire game in right field (Cleveland's Earl Averill and Washington's Ben Chapman shared center), Joe not only missed the shoestring catch on Hartnett, but later committed an error that set up the winning run. To make his day entirely forgettable, the youngster took the collar in five at-bats.

Taking advantage of the luxury

of picking his team, National League Manager Charley Grimm started four of his own Chicago Cubs—center fielder Augie Galan, second baseman Billy Herman, right fielder Demaree and catcher Hartnett. The Cubs connection came through for the skipper, being instrumental in all of the Nationals' runs.

In the fifth, Galan, facing Detroit's Schoolboy Rowe, hoisted a high drive down the right-field line that dropped into the bleachers for a home run (McCarthy argued vehemently that the smash was foul). Herman then singled to right and went to second when DiMaggio fumbled the ball. A few moments later, Billy scored what proved the winning run on Joe Medwick's single. It was now 4-0, Nationals.

When Cubs righthander Curt Davis took over the pitching in the top of the seventh, the American Leaguers pounced. Lou Gehrig finally threw off his All-Star shackles by sending a Davis pitch well out into the right-field bleachers. Davis retired the next two batters, but that was as far as he got. Detroit veteran Goose Goslin singled. Jimmie Foxx scorched a base hit off the glove of Cardinals shortstop Leo Durocher. The Yankees' George Selkirk hit for Rowe and drew a walk, loading the bases. The White Sox's Luke Appling (a .388 hitter that year) singled in a pair, making it 4-3.

Appling's hit sent Davis to the showers and brought in another Cubs righthander, Lon Warneke.

24

Warneke walked Charlie Gehringer, again filling the bases and bringing up DiMaggio. With a chance to redeem a wretched day, Joe ripped a line drive just to the right of Durocher, who made a fine play to snare the liner and retire the side.

Warneke held tough through the final two innings and wrapped up a one-run triumph for the Nationals. Mel Harder pitched the last two for the Americans and continued his mastery of the National League with another scoreless effort, giving him 10 unblemished innings of All-Star Game work.

Ironically, the National League's first victory was witnessed by the smallest crowd ever assembled for an All-Star Game. A series of newspaper stories had assured Bostonians that the game was a sellout; consequently, many normally interested fans didn't bother going out to the park. The attendance was only 25,556, with some 15,000 seats remaining empty.

Carl Hubbell.

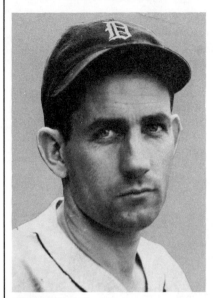

Charlie Gehringer.

Augie Galan.

Luke Appling.

Gabby Hartnett.

Lou Gehrig's Yankee manager, Joe McCarthy, generally disapproved of pipe smoking. But Lou, McCarthy said, "was all right." Gehrig was, in fact, McCarthy's all-time favorite player.

Joe DiMaggio.

Dizzy Dean.

Players (left to right) Jimmie Foxx, Lou Gehrig, Arky Vaughan and Charlie Gehringer meeting with sportswriter Fred Lieb before the 1936 All-Star Game.

The big story of the 1937 All-Star Game, played July 7 at Griffith Stadium in Washington, D.C., was not the fact that President Franklin D. Roosevelt and a battalion of government nabobs were in attendance. Neither was the slugging of Lou Gehrig the big story; nor the rat-a-tat-tat bat of Joe Medwick, whose line drives singed the already broiling air all afternoon. In fact, at the time no one even knew which story was the *big* story; after all, it turned out to be an infield play, an out which merely ended the bottom of the third inning for the American League.

That innocuous-appearing play, however, marked the beginning of the end of one of major league baseball's most spectacular careers. The batter was Cleveland's Earl Averill, the pitcher the Cardinals' flamboyant Dizzy Dean, a 30-game winner in 1934, a 28-game winner in 1935, a 24-game winner in 1936 and well on his way to another big season in 1937 with a 12-7 record. Tall and lean and armed with a sizzling fastball and a crackling curve that he called his "crooky," Dean had become, with the retirement of Babe Ruth, baseball's most magnetic performer, its biggest drawing card.

The moment Dizzy fired to Averill and Averill cracked a low screamer that hit Dean on the foot, the baseball sun began to set for the self-styled "Great One." Averill was thrown out (second baseman Billy Herman making the play), and Dean headed for

Dean's Demise

Nationals	AB.	R.	H.	RBI.	PO.	A.
P. Waner (Pirates), rf	5	0	0	1	0	0
Herman (Cubs), 2b	5	1	2	0	1	4
Vaughan (Pirates), 3b	5	0	2	0	3	0
Medwick (Cardinals), lf	5	1	4	1	1	0
Demaree (Cubs), cf	5	0	1	0	3	1
Mize (Cardinals), 1b	4	0	0	1	7	0
Hartnett (Cubs), c	3	1	1	0	6	0
bWhitehead (Giants)	0	0	0	0	0	0
Mancuso (Giants), c	1	0	0	0	1	0
Bartell (Giants), ss	4	0	1	0	2	3
J. Dean (Cardinals), p	1	0	0	0	0	1
Hubbell (Giants), p	0	0	0	0	0	0
Blanton (Pirates), p	0	0	0	0	0	0
aOtt (Giants)	1	0	1	0	0	0
Grissom (Reds), p	0	0	0	0	0	0
cCollins (Cubs)	1	0	1	0	0	0
Mungo (Dodgers), p	0	0	0	0	0	1
eMoore (Giants)	1	0	0	0	0	0
Walters (Phillies), p	0	0	0	0	0	0
Totals	41	3	13	3	24	10

Americans	AB.	R.	H.	RBI.	PO.	A.
Rolfe (Yankees), 3b	4	2	2	2	0	1
Gehringer (Tigers), 2b	5	1	3	1	2	5
DiMaggio (Yankees), rf	4	1	1	1	1	1
Gehrig (Yankees), 1b	4	1	2	4	10	1
Averill (Indians), cf	3	0	1	0	2	0
Cronin (Red Sox), ss	4	1	1	0	4	3
Dickey (Yankees), c	3	1	2	1	2	0
West (Browns), lf	4	1	1	0	5	0
Gomez (Yankees), p	1	0	0	0	0	0
Bridges (Tigers), p	1	0	0	0	0	1
dFoxx (Red Sox)	1	0	0	0	0	0
Harder (Indians), p	1	0	0	1	1	1
Totals	35	8	13	8	27	13

National League	0 0 0	1 1 1	0 0 0—3
American League	0 0 2	3 1 2	0 0 x—8

Nationals	IP.	H.	R.	ER.	BB.	SO.
J. Dean (L)	3	4	2	2	1	2
Hubbell	⅔	3	3	3	1	1
Blanton	⅓	0	0	0	0	1
Grissom	1	2	1	1	0	2
Mungo	2	2	2	2	2	1
Walters	1	2	0	0	0	0

Americans	IP.	H.	R.	ER.	BB.	SO.
Gomez (W)	3	1	0	0	0	0
Bridges	3	7	3	3	0	0
Harder	3	5	0	0	0	0

aDoubled for Blanton in fifth. bRan for Hartnett in sixth. cSingled for Grissom in sixth. dGrounded out for Bridges in sixth. eForced runner for Mungo in eighth. E—Rolfe 2. DP—Nationals 1. LOB—Nationals 11, Americans 7. 2B—Gehrig, Dickey, Cronin, Ott, Medwick 2. 3B—Rolfe. HR—Gehrig. U—McGowan and Quinn (A.L.), Barr and Pinelli (N.L.) T—2:30. A—31,391.

the clubhouse, his three-inning stint over. In the clubhouse, it was determined that Dean had suffered a broken toe. Hardly a serious injury, but one which he (and Cardinal management) took a bit too nonchalantly. Dean returned to the mound before the toe was healed, and in favoring the injured digit began pitching with an unnatural motion. The strain of the delivery caused an injury to his arm and the glory days of Dizzy Dean—just 26 years old—turned into one long, gray, wistful twilight.

Starting for the fourth time in five years for the American League—and winning his third game—was Lefty Gomez. The Yankee lefthander held the Nationals to one hit over his three innings and was the beneficiary of a booming two-run homer in the third off the bat of New York

teammate Lou Gehrig. The entire game, in fact, was symbolic of existing Yankee dominance (McCarthy's club was in the midst of a roll of four straight World Series championships from 1936 through 1939). New York third baseman Red Rolfe singled and tripled and drove in two runs, right fielder Joe DiMaggio singled before Gehrig's homer, catcher Bill Dickey singled and doubled, Gehrig added a double to his home run and drove in four runs overall and Gomez pitched superbly.

Leading 2-1 in the fourth, the Americans iced the game in that inning by roughing up no less than Carl Hubbell for three more runs and, in fact, driving out the Giants' ace after just two-thirds of an inning. The junior league went on to an 8-3 triumph.

McCarthy played every one of his eight "position" starters the full game, using Detroit's Tommy Bridges (possessor of baseball's finest curveball, it was said) and Cleveland's Mel Harder on the mound after Gomez. Harder, making his final All-Star Game appearance, pitched three more innings of shutout ball (although yielding five hits), giving him 13 scoreless innings in All-Star competition.

Bill Terry's Nationals did their scoring against Bridges, building a picket fence on the scoreboard with single runs in the fourth, fifth and sixth innings. The National League's principal basher was Medwick, and appropriately so, for the Cardinals' irascible mass of muscles was in the middle of a Triple Crown season inlaid with the glitter of a .374 batting average, 154 runs batted in, 31 home runs, 237 hits, 56 doubles, and on and on. The dour Joseph led the league in virtually everything but smiles that year. In this game, he tattooed American League pitching for two singles and two doubles in five at-bats.

The post-game stories dwelled on President Roosevelt throwing out the first ball, on the slugging of Gehrig and his Yankee mates,

on the suffocating pitching of Gomez and Harder and on Medwick's four hits (the first time anyone had collected that many in an All-Star Game). There were wisecracks about the existence of three major leagues: the American, the National and the Yankees.

But the biggest story to evolve from the 1937 All-Star Game was that small, painful, broken toe on the foot of Dizzy Dean.

Years later, when he was about to be inducted into the Hall of

Fame at Cooperstown, the man who had become forever linked to Dean the way Tony Lazzeri was to Grover Cleveland Alexander and Ralph Branca was to Bobby Thomson, reminisced in the lobby of the staid old Otesaga Hotel.

"I batted .378 in 1936, I got over 2,000 hits in my career," said a bemused Earl Averill. "But the thing I'll always be most remembered for is breaking a guy's toe."

Well, yes. But not just any guy, and not just any toe.

Dizzy Dean.

Earl Averill.

Lefty Gomez fires the first pitch of the game to Pittsburgh's Paul Waner.

President Franklin D. Roosevelt greets National League President Ford Frick before the start of the 1937 All-Star Game. Commissioner Kenesaw Mountain Landis is in the middle, while President Roosevelt's son James is at his father's left.

Joe Medwick.

Billy Herman.

Obliging the photographer before the start of the 1937 game are the stars of the American League (left to right): Lou Gehrig, Joe Cronin, Bill Dickey, Joe DiMaggio, Charlie Gehringer, Jimmie Foxx and Hank Greenberg.

Terry Learns Fast

Americans	AB.	R.	H.	RBI.	PO.	A.
Kreevich (White Sox), lf ...	2	0	0	0	1	0
cCramer (Red Sox), lf.......	2	0	0	0	0	0
Gehringer (Tigers), 2b.......	3	0	1	0	2	2
Averill (Indians), cf...........	4	0	0	0	5	0
Foxx (Red Sox), 1b-3b.......	4	0	1	0	5	1
DiMaggio (Yankees), rf	4	1	1	0	2	0
Dickey (Yankees), c	4	0	1	1	8	0
Cronin (Red Sox), ss.........	3	0	2	0	0	2
Lewis (Senators), 3b.........	1	0	0	0	0	1
bGehrig (Yankees), 1b......	3	0	1	0	1	0
Gomez (Yankees), p	1	0	0	0	0	0
Allen (Indians), p............	1	0	0	0	0	0
dYork (Tigers)..................	1	0	0	0	0	0
Grove (Red Sox), p	0	0	0	0	0	0
eJohnson (Athletics)	1	0	0	0	0	0
Totals.....................	34	1	7	1	24	6

Nationals	AB.	R.	H.	RBI.	PO.	A.
Hack (Cubs), 3b	4	1	1	0	1	2
Herman (Cubs), 2b...........	4	1	0	0	3	4
Goodman (Reds), rf	3	0	0	0	2	0
Medwick (Cardinals), lf.....	4	0	1	1	2	0
Ott (Giants), cf................	4	1	1	0	3	0
Lombardi (Reds), c	4	0	2	1	5	0
McCormick (Reds), 1b......	4	1	1	0	11	0
Durocher (Dodgers), ss.....	3	1	1	0	0	3
Vander Meer (Reds), p......	0	0	0	0	0	3
aLeiber (Giants)..............	1	0	0	0	0	0
Lee (Cubs), p...................	1	0	0	0	0	0
Brown (Pirates), p............	1	0	0	0	0	1
Totals.....................	33	4	8	2	27	13

American League	0 0 0	0 0 0	0 0 1—1			
National League	1 0 0	1 0 0	2 0 x—4			

Americans	IP.	H.	R.	ER.	BB.	SO.
Gomez (L).......................	3	2	1	0	0	1
Allen.............................	3	2	1	1	0	3
Grove............................	2	4	2	0	0	3

Nationals	IP.	H.	R.	ER.	BB.	SO.
Vander Meer (W)	3	1	0	0	0	1
Lee...............................	3	1	0	0	1	2
Brown...........................	3	5	1	1	1	2

aLined out for Vander Meer in third. bGrounded out for Lewis in fifth. cGrounded out for Kreevich in sixth. dStruck out for Allen in seventh. eStruck out for Grove in ninth. E—Foxx, DiMaggio, Dickey, Cronin. LOB—Americans 8, Nationals 6. 2B—Dickey, Cronin. 3B—Ott. SB—Goodman, DiMaggio. HBP—By Allen (Goodman). U—Ballanfant and Klem (N.L.), Basil and Geisel (A.L.). T—1:58. A—27,067.

When Joe McCarthy and Bill Terry returned to head the squads for the 1938 All-Star Game, played on July 6 at Cincinnati's Crosley Field, Terry showed that he had learned something from the Yankee skipper. Terry started his eight best players and stayed with them. Overall, Bill employed just 12 men, including three pitchers and one pinch-hitter. McCarthy used 15, and in this instance more was less.

Major league baseball had a glamorous new hero that summer. His name was Johnny Vander Meer. The Cincinnati lefthander was extremely fast and a bit wild. Never a big winner, Johnny had earlier that summer (on June 11 and 15) electrified the baseball world by firing back-to-back no-hitters against the Boston Bees and Brooklyn Dodgers, a feat unprecedented and since unmatched. ("An unbreakable record, I think," Johnny said with a wry smile years later. "You'd have to pitch three in a row to top it.")

With the game being played in Cincinnati, Terry made the proper public relations gesture by starting Vander Meer. After Johnny's two no-hitters, the Americans really gave him a scuffing— one hit in three innings. The American League starter, for the fifth time in six years, was the Yankees' Lefty Gomez. With Gomez on the mound, this made it six consecutive times that a lefthander had opened for the Americans, Lefty Grove having started in 1936. With Vander Meer, the Nationals were starting a lefthander for the fourth time in six games, Johnny's lefthanded-throwing predecessors being Bill Hallahan, Carl Hubbell and Bill Walker. Dizzy Dean (twice) was thus far the only righthander on either team to start an All-Star Game.

Gomez gave up an unearned run in the bottom of the first, an error by Red Sox shortstop Joe Cronin paving the way. The American League never caught up and Gomez took the loss, his first after three All-Star victories (a total still unequaled).

The Nationals scored a second run in the fourth inning against Johnny Allen, Cleveland's gifted but tempestuous righthander, and then tied the ribbon around the game in the seventh as the Americans, who committed four errors in the game, put on a clinic of untidy baseball.

After Cubs righthander Bill Lee shut down the American League through the middle innings, the score was still 2-0 when Leo Durocher came to bat and bunted a "home run."

Cincinnati first baseman Frank McCormick had opened the Nationals' half of the seventh with a single off the 38-year-old Grove, whose fastball was now history but who was still effective throwing slow curlers out of what Ted Williams once described as "the most beautifully coordinated motion I ever saw."

With McCormick at first, Durocher, the next batter, was ordered to sacrifice. Leo, an adroit bunter, laid one down and then began a gallop into the banjo hitters' Hall of Fame. Third baseman Jimmie Foxx charged in, made his scoop and peg—and suddenly this baseball took on a life of its own, sailing into right field. Joe DiMaggio, still an All-Star right fielder in deference to Earl Averill, raced in, picked up the ball and fired home. This time, the rogue pellet flew over catcher Bill Dickey's head, allowing McCormick to score. Meanwhile, the ever-aggressive Durocher never stopped running until he had circled the bases. That made it 4-0, Nationals, with Durocher credited with a single and Foxx and DiMaggio charged with errors.

Shut out until the ninth, the American Leaguers suddenly made a run at Pittsburgh right-hander Mace Brown, who near the end of the season would throw a home run ball to Chicago's Gabby Hartnett that proved pivotal as the Cubs slipped around the Pirates for the pennant.

Mace yielded some long balls in the final inning, but his outfield saved him embarrassment. After DiMaggio opened the ninth with a single, Dickey drove one deep to left that Joe Medwick hauled in after a long run. Cronin doubled in DiMaggio. Lou Gehrig then bashed one of his patented rockets that Cincinnati right fielder Ival Goodman finally outran. Thus reprieved, Brown struck out the Athletics' Indian Bob Johnson and the National League had its second All-Star triumph in six games, a 4-1 victory highlighted by Leo Durocher's classically misplayed bunt.

Johnny Vander Meer.

Ernie Lombardi.

Leo Durocher.

Joe Cronin.

Joe McCarthy.

Joe DiMaggio.

Bill Lee.

New York, New York

Nationals	AB.	R.	H.	RBI.	PO.	A.
Hack (Cubs), 3b	4	0	1	0	1	1
Frey (Reds), 2b	4	0	1	1	0	4
Goodman (Reds), rf	1	0	0	0	0	0
cHerman (Cubs)	1	0	0	0	0	0
Moore (Cardinals), cf	1	0	0	0	0	0
McCormick (Reds), 1b	4	0	0	0	7	1
Lombardi (Reds), c	4	0	2	0	6	0
Medwick (Cardinals), lf	4	0	0	0	1	0
Ott (Giants), cf-rf	4	0	2	0	4	0
Vaughan (Pirates), ss	3	1	1	0	4	1
Derringer (Reds), p	1	0	0	0	0	0
bCamilli (Dodgers)	1	0	0	0	0	0
Lee (Cubs), p	0	0	0	0	0	0
dPhelps (Dodgers)	1	0	0	0	0	0
Fette (Braves), p	0	0	0	0	1	0
eMize (Cardinals)	1	0	0	0	0	0
Totals	34	1	7	1	24	7

Americans	AB.	R.	H.	RBI.	PO.	A.
Cramer (Red Sox), rf	4	0	1	0	3	0
Rolfe (Yankees), 3b	4	0	1	0	1	0
DiMaggio (Yankees), cf	4	1	1	1	1	0
Dickey (Yankees), c	3	1	0	0	10	0
Greenberg (Tigers), 1b	3	1	1	0	7	1
Cronin (Red Sox), ss	4	0	1	0	2	3
Selkirk (Yankees), lf	2	0	1	1	0	0
Gordon (Yankees), 2b	4	0	0	0	2	5
Ruffing (Yankees), p	0	0	0	0	0	0
aHoag (Browns)	1	0	0	0	0	0
Bridges (Tigers) p	1	0	0	0	1	0
Feller (Indians), p	1	0	0	0	0	0
Totals	31	3	6	2	27	9

National League	0 0 1	0 0 0	0 0 0—1
American League	0 0 0	2 1 0	0 0 x—3

Nationals	IP.	H.	R.	ER.	BB.	SO.
Derringer	3	2	0	0	0	1
Lee (L)	3	3	3	2	3	4
Fette	2	1	0	0	1	1

Americans	IP.	H.	R.	ER.	BB.	SO.
Ruffing	3	4	1	1	1	4
Bridges (W)	2⅓	2	0	0	1	3
Feller	3⅔	1	0	0	1	2

aStruck out for Ruffing in third. bStruck out for Derringer in fourth. cStruck out for Goodman in fifth. dGrounded out for Lee in seventh. eStruck out for Fette in ninth. E—Vaughn, Cronin. DP—Americans 1. LOB—Nationals 9, Americans 8. 2B—Frey. HR—DiMaggio. U—Hubbard and Rommel (A.L.), Goetz and Magerkurth (N.L.). T—1:55. A—62,892.

In 1939, Joe McCarthy, once more managing the American League in the All-Star Game and perhaps smarting from the previous year's loss, decided to take no chances. McCarthy bought what was then baseball's soundest insurance policy: He started six of his World Series champion Yankees in the game against Gabby Hartnett's Nationals. Joe then turned the screws just a little tighter, letting all of his "position" starters go the distance.

Along with right fielder Doc Cramer and shortstop Joe Cronin of the Red Sox and first baseman Hank Greenberg of the Tigers, the Americans' lineup consisted of the following Yankees: Red Rolfe at third base, Joe DiMaggio in center field, George Selkirk in left, Joe Gordon at second, Bill Dickey catching and Red Ruffing pitching.

"Wasn't that favoritism?" a writer asked McCarthy in an interview many years later.

The old gentleman smiled mischievously and said, "You have to play your best men."

Actually, McCarthy wasn't supposed to be the American League's man-in-charge. Because it was baseball's centennial year, the junior league sought to honor its senior manager, Connie Mack, by naming the Philadelphia pilot to guide the Americans. But Mack, 76 years old and manager of the A's since the American League's inception in 1901, was unable to handle the Americans because of illness. McCarthy, who under normal circumstances would have been at the Americans' helm based on his pennant-winning record of 1938, thus wound up managing the American Leaguers after all. And manage he did.

After using Ruffing for three innings, McCarthy came on with Detroit veteran Tommy Bridges and closed out with—and this was really laying it on—Cleveland's 20-year-old Robert William Andrew Feller, already in his fourth big-league season, possessor of a frightening Johnsonian fastball and a frightening curve for which there seemed no precedent.

"I faced Tommy Bridges in that game," Cincinnati first baseman Frank McCormick recalled, "and I said to myself, 'That's the greatest curveball I've ever seen.' A few innings later, I faced Feller and I said to myself, 'No, *that's* the greatest curveball I've ever

seen.' "

Hartnett's starter was himself no mere pittance—Cincinnati's splendid, high-kicking Paul Derringer, in the midst of carving out a 25-7 season. Derringer was followed by the Cubs' Bill Lee and Boston's Lou Fette. (All six pitchers in the game were righthanders.)

McCarthy's Yankee-studded lineup was a crowd pleaser in view of the fact that the July 11 game was played at New York's Yankee Stadium, before a hefty turnout of 62,892. The city had been awarded the game to help celebrate the New York World's Fair, itself doing a booming business.

The Nationals broke the seal on the game in the top of the third on singles by Pittsburgh's Arky Vaughan and the Cubs' Stan Hack and a two-bagger (the Nationals' only extra-base hit) by Cincinnati's Lonny Frey.

After Derringer worked three shutout innings, the Americans welcomed Lee back to Yankee Stadium, where he had lost the fourth and final game of the 1938 World Series. With one out in the fourth inning, Lee walked Dickey and yielded a single to Greenberg. Selkirk singled Dickey across and Greenberg scored when Vaughan fumbled Gordon's grounder.

DiMaggio closed out the scoring an inning later when, batting against Lee, he filled the mammoth hometown crowd with pride by belting a long home run (the Americans' only extra-base hit) into the left-field stands, making it 3-1, American League.

The Nationals made a run in the sixth when they loaded the bases against Bridges with one out. At this point, McCarthy brought in young Mr. Feller. Bobby turned on the stuff and got the sharp-hitting Vaughan to rap into a first-pitch double play. Thereafter, Feller gave the National Leaguers a demonstration of how he was shrinking American League batting averages by pitching three innings of one-hit ball.

Years later, in retirement, Feller entertained a writer through a long interview. When asked if he, at the age of 20 (too young to vote in those years), had been nervous facing the cream of the other league in his first All-Star Game, the always-candid Feller replied, "I was never nervous on a pitching mound."

The twitching, one imagines, was 60 feet, 6 inches away.

Bob Feller.

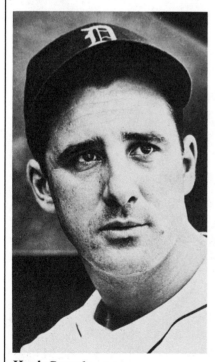

Hank Greenberg.

Mel Ott, in his unorthodox, leg-kicking batting style.

Frank McCormick is out at first with Hank Green-berg taking the throw during action in the 1939 All-Star classic.

Two gentlemen who covered center field as neatly as the grass itself: Joe DiMaggio (left) and Tris Speaker, posing at the 1939 All-Star Game.

Five members of the National League's 1939 All-Star squad (left to right): Frank McCormick, Mel Ott, Morrie Arnovich, Joe Medwick, Ernie Lombardi.

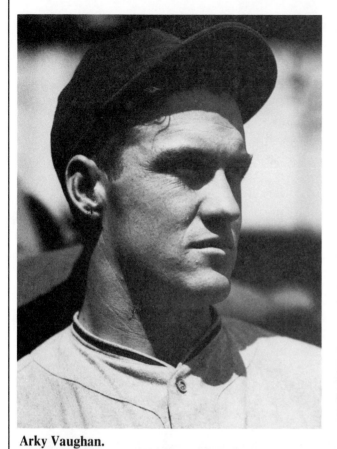

Arky Vaughan.

Tommy Bridges.

Part of the National League's pitching delegation for the 1939 All-Star Game (left to right): Paul Derringer, Bill Lee, Whitlow Wyatt.

1940
TWO T O
1949

The American League At High Tide

The First Shutout

Americans	AB.	R.	H.	RBI.	PO.	A.
Travis (Senators), 3b	3	0	0	0	0	0
Keltner (Indians), 3b	1	0	0	0	2	1
Williams (Red Sox), lf	2	0	0	0	3	0
Finney (Red Sox), rf	0	0	0	0	0	0
Keller (Yankees), rf	2	0	0	0	4	0
Greenberg (Tigers), lf	2	0	0	0	0	0
DiMaggio (Yankees), cf	4	0	0	0	1	0
Foxx (Red Sox), 1b	3	0	0	0	4	2
Appling (White Sox), ss	3	0	2	0	0	0
Boudreau (Indians), ss	0	0	0	0	0	0
Dickey (Yankees), c	1	0	0	0	2	0
Hayes (Athletics), c	1	0	0	0	1	0
Hemsley (Indians), c	1	0	0	0	3	0
Gordon (Yankees), 2b	2	0	0	0	3	1
aMack (Indians), 2b	1	0	0	0	0	0
Ruffing (Yankees), p	1	0	0	0	0	0
Newsom (Tigers), p	1	0	1	0	0	0
Feller (Indians), p	1	0	0	0	1	0
Totals	29	0	3	0	24	4

Nationals	AB.	R.	H.	RBI.	PO.	A.
Vaughan (Pirates), ss	3	1	1	0	0	1
Miller (Braves), ss	1	0	0	0	2	1
Herman (Cubs), 2b	3	1	3	0	0	3
Coscarart (Dodgers), 2b	1	0	0	0	0	2
West (Braves), rf	1	1	1	3	0	0
Nicholson (Cubs), rf	2	0	0	0	1	0
Ott (Giants), rf	0	1	0	0	0	0
Mize (Cardinals), 1b	2	0	0	0	8	0
F. McCormick (Reds), 1b..	1	0	0	0	2	0
Lombardi (Reds), c	2	0	1	0	3	0
Phelps (Dodgers), c	0	0	0	0	1	0
Danning (Giants), c	1	0	1	1	6	0
Medwick (Dodgers), lf	2	0	0	0	1	0
J. Moore (Giants), lf	2	0	0	0	1	0
Lavagetto (Dodgers), 3b ..	2	0	0	0	0	1
May (Phillies), 3b	1	0	0	0	0	0
T. Moore (Cardinals), cf ..	3	0	0	0	2	0
Derringer (Reds), p	1	0	0	0	0	1
Walters (Reds), p	0	0	0	0	0	1
Wyatt (Dodgers), p	1	0	0	0	0	0
French (Cubs), p	0	0	0	0	0	0
Hubbell (Giants), p	0	0	0	0	0	0
Totals	29	4	7	4	27	10

American League	0 0 0	0 0 0	0 0 0—0
National League	3 0 0	0 0 0	0 1 x—4

Americans	IP.	H.	R.	ER.	BB.	SO.
Ruffing (L)	3	5	3	3	0	2
Newsom	3	1	0	0	1	1
Feller	2	1	1	1	2	3

Nationals	IP.	H.	R.	ER.	BB.	SO.
Derringer (W)	2	1	0	0	1	3
Walters	2	0	0	0	0	0
Wyatt	2	1	0	0	0	1
French	2	1	0	0	0	2
Hubbell	1	0	0	0	1	1

aStruck out for Gordon in eighth. E—Hemsley. DP—Nationals 1. LOB—Americans 4, Nationals 7. 2B—Appling. HR—West. SH—F. McCormick, French. HBP—By Feller (May). U—Reardon and Stewart (N.L.), Pipgras and Basil (A.L.). T—1:53. A—32,373.

When you leaf through the pages of World Series history, you find the names of improbable heroes who have risen up to excel for a moment and thereby have achieved enduring fame. Only in the World Series—baseball's premier event—do names like Pepper Martin, Sandy Amoros, Don Larsen and Gene Tenace stand mountaintop high, higher than those of such Valhalla residents as Ty Cobb, Rogers Hornsby and Ted Williams.

To find All-Star Game heroes who are closer to anonymity than to celebrity is, by the game's very definition, most difficult. All-Star Game heroes are almost inevitably named Hubbell, Williams, Musial and Mays, for this was their game. The role of Everyman in All-Star Game play is highly restricted, if indeed there is one at all.

It was in the 1940 game, however, that Everyman had his day. Outfielder Max West of the Boston Bees (as the longtime Braves franchise was then known), who batted .261 with seven home runs that year, etched his name into All-Star history in the first inning of the game played at St. Louis' Sportsman's Park on July 9.

With the Yankees' Red Ruffing on the mound, Arky Vaughan and Billy Herman had led off the bottom of the first with singles. Up stepped West, a third-year major leaguer and a lefthanded hitter with some power (he had hit 19 home runs in 1939). Max caught hold of a Ruffing delivery and sent it on a glorious ride into the stands in right-center, and that—for all intents and purposes—was the ball game. The final score was 4-0, the first shutout in All-Star play.

Ruffing settled down after that, then was followed to the mound in the fourth inning by colorful Detroit righthander Bobo Newsom, who shut down the Nationals on one hit over three innings. Cleveland's Bob Feller finished up for the Americans, allowing a run in his two-inning stint.

There was a unique switch in managers for the American League. With the feeling that Joe McCarthy had guided the select unit often enough, the A.L. squad was handed to Boston's Joe Cronin, whose Red Sox had finished second (17 games back) to the Yankees the year before. Cronin broke with the McCarthy style by employing 18 players, with only Joe DiMaggio and Jimmie Foxx playing the entire game.

The National League manager, Cincinnati's Bill McKechnie, decided to showcase his team and put 22 players into action, with only Cardinals center fielder Terry Moore going the distance.

McKechnie limited his pitchers to two-inning appearances, and his system worked flawlessly. He opened with his own two Cincinnati aces, Paul Derringer (en route to his third straight 20-victory season) and Bucky Walters (on the way to his second consecutive 20-victory year), and followed with Brooklyn's Whitlow Wyatt, an American League castoff coming into years of glory with the Dodgers, and Cubs lefthander Larry French. And McKechnie had Carl Hubbell pitch the ninth. The National League pitchers were in top form, allowing just three hits and two walks in their shutout by committee. (N.L. second baseman Billy Herman, with three singles, matched the Americans' team output.)

For hero Max West, it was a one-time-only All-Star appearance and, ironically, he had just the one at-bat. In the second inning, West was injured while leaping for Luke Appling's smash (which went for a double) and had to leave the game. But for one day at least, Max had been the giant among giants.

Max West—a day in the sun.

Luke Appling.

Bobo Newsom.

Billy Herman.

Whitlow Wyatt.

Bucky Walters.

Paul Derringer.

One year after Max West struck his blow for the common man, the heroics of All-Star Game competition returned to the Olympian athlete for whom the occasion had been designed. It all unfolded as a duly inspired scenarist would have shaped it: The most electrifying belt in All-Star Game history was launched by the most charismatic hitter of his time, a man who was putting together a season that would become enwreathed in legend.

Playing in his second All-Star Game (he had gone 0 for 2 the year before), Ted Williams was on his way to a .406 season batting average, a figure that was to become ever regal and remote as the decades rolled on. At the time of the All-Star Game, played July 8 at Detroit's Briggs Stadium, the slim, young Red Sox marvel was drilling American League pitching at a .405 clip.

The game that was ended by the snap of Williams' bat was the most exciting All-Star Game to that time. There was some good pitching, some lusty hitting and a momentous conclusion. The National League, again guided by Bill McKechnie, used 22 players; the Americans, managed by Detroit's Del Baker, employed 20.

The starting pitchers were Cleveland's Bob Feller and Brooklyn's Whitlow Wyatt, with Feller pitching three shutout innings and Wyatt two. Following a pattern similar to the one he used the year before, McKechnie limited three of his pitchers to two innings apiece, with Paul Derringer coming on in the third.

The American League scored first in the bottom of the fourth on doubles by Washington's Cecil Travis and Boston's Williams. The Nationals tied it in the sixth against White Sox lefthander Thornton Lee when Cincinnati

The Ted Williams Show

Nationals	AB.	R.	H.	RBI.	PO.	A.
Hack (Cubs), 3b	2	0	1	0	3	0
fLavagetto (Dodgers), 3b..	1	0	0	0	0	0
T. Moore (Cardinals), lf	5	0	0	1	0	0
Reiser (Dodgers), cf	4	0	0	0	6	0
Mize (Cardinals), 1b	4	1	1	0	5	0
F. McCormick (Reds), 1b..	0	0	0	0	0	0
Nicholson (Cubs), rf	1	0	0	0	1	0
Elliott (Pirates), rf	1	0	0	0	0	0
Slaughter (Cardinals), rf..	2	1	1	0	0	0
Vaughan (Pirates), ss	4	2	3	4	1	2
Miller (Braves), ss	0	0	0	0	0	1
Frey (Reds), 2b	1	0	1	0	1	3
cHerman (Dodgers), 2b..	3	0	2	0	3	0
Owen (Dodgers), c	1	0	0	0	0	0
Lopez (Pirates), c	1	0	0	0	3	0
Danning (Giants), c	1	0	0	0	3	0
Wyatt (Dodgers), p	1	0	0	0	0	0
aOtt (Giants)	1	0	0	0	0	0
Derringer (Reds), p	0	0	0	0	0	1
Walters (Reds), p	1	1	1	0	0	0
dMedwick (Dodgers)	1	0	0	0	0	0
Passeau (Cubs), p	1	0	0	0	0	0
Totals	35	5	10	5	26	7

Americans	AB.	R.	H.	RBI.	PO.	A.
Doerr (Red Sox), 2b	3	0	0	0	0	0
Gordon (Yankees), 2b	2	1	1	0	2	0
Travis (Senators), 3b	4	1	1	0	1	2
J. DiMaggio (Yanks), cf	4	3	1	1	1	0
Williams (Red Sox), lf	4	1	2	4	3	0
Heath (Indians), rf	2	0	0	0	1	0
D. DiMaggio (Red Sox), rf	1	0	1	1	1	0
Cronin (Red Sox), ss	2	0	0	0	3	0
Boudreau (Indians), ss	2	0	2	1	0	1
York (Tigers), 1b	3	0	1	0	6	0
Foxx (Red Sox), 1b	1	0	0	0	2	2
Dickey (Yankees), c	3	0	1	0	4	2
Hayes (Athletics), c	1	0	0	0	2	0
Feller (Indians), p	0	0	0	0	0	1
bCullenbine (Browns)	1	0	0	0	0	0
Lee (White Sox), p	1	0	0	0	0	1
eKeller (Yankees)	1	0	0	0	0	0
Hudson (Senators), p	0	0	0	0	0	0
Smith (White Sox), p	0	0	0	0	1	0
gKeltner, (Indians)	1	1	1	0	0	0
Totals	36	7	11	7	27	11

National League .... 0 0 0 0 0 1 2 2 0—5
American League .... 0 0 0 1 0 1 0 1 4—7
Two out when winning run scored.

Nationals	IP.	H.	R.	ER.	BB.	SO.
Wyatt	2	0	0	0	1	0
Derringer	2	2	1	1	0	1
Walters	2	3	1	1	2	2
Passeau (L)	2⅔	6	5	5	1	3

Americans	IP.	H.	R.	ER.	BB.	SO.
Feller	3	1	0	0	0	4
Lee	3	4	1	1	0	0
Hudson	1	3	2	2	1	1
Smith (W)	2	2	2	2	0	2

aStruck out for Wyatt in third. bGrounded out for Feller in third. cSingled for Frey in fifth. dGrounded out for Walters in seventh. eStruck out for Hudson in seventh. fGrounded out for Hack in ninth. gSingled for Smith in ninth. E—Reiser 2, Williams, Heath, Smith. DP—Nationals 1, Americans 1. LOB—Nationals 6, Americans 7. 2B—Travis, Williams, Walters, Herman, Mize, J. DiMaggio. HR—Vaughan 2, Williams. SH—Hack, Lopez. U—Summers and Grieve (A.L.), Jorda and Pinelli (N.L.). T—2:23. A—54,674.

pitcher Bucky Walters (who had followed Derringer) doubled and came around on a sacrifice and a fly ball. The Americans untied it against Walters in their half of the sixth on two walks and a single by Indians shortstop Lou Boudreau.

In the seventh inning, things began to accelerate. The Cardinals' Enos Slaughter singled and went to second when Williams misplayed the ball. Arky Vaughan then stepped up and did a most uncharacteristic thing. The Pittsburgh shortstop, who hit only six home runs all season, caught hold of one of Washington

righthander Sid Hudson's pitches and lofted it into the right-field seats, giving the National League a 3-2 lead.

With Cubs righthander Claude Passeau coming on to pitch for the Nationals in the seventh, the game went through the bottom of the inning with the score unchanged. In the top of the eighth, the National League seemed to put a wrap on it. With White Sox lefthander Edgar Smith pitching, the Cardinals' Johnny Mize slugged a one-out double. After Slaughter was called out on strikes, Vaughan came to the plate. Arky, with a home run and a single already tucked away, startled everyone by putting another shot into the right-field stands. That made the score 5-2, gave Vaughan four runs batted in, made him the first player ever to hit two home runs in an All-Star Game and had newspapers all around the country measuring him for the hero's robes.

That American League lineup was packed with dynamite, however, and the package had a dangerously short fuse. In the bottom of the eighth, Joe DiMaggio (48 games into his 56-game hitting streak) doubled. Passeau fanned Williams, but Boston's Dominic DiMaggio singled home big brother for a 5-3 score.

Smith got through the top of the ninth without any noise and the game went into that noted vale of bumps and dips known as the bottom of the ninth.

Passeau began by retiring the first batter, boosting his workload for the day to 2⅓ innings (an All-Star high for a pitcher under McKechnie's tutelage). But then an ambush began. Cleveland's Ken Keltner, whose flashing glove would help put an end to DiMaggio's batting streak nine days later, pinch-hit for Smith and bounced a single off shortstop Eddie Miller's glove. (Eddie had replaced Vaughan.) Yankee Joe Gordon singled and Travis drew a walk, filling the bases. With Joe DiMaggio and Ted Williams the next two batters, Passeau was suddenly in the stormiest region of a pitcher's darkest nightmare.

Passeau, however, appeared home free when he induced DiMaggio to hit sharply to Miller, each bounce of the ball seeming to proclaim double play. Miller fielded it cleanly and fed it to Brooklyn second baseman Billy Herman.

"It should have been a double play, ending the game," Herman said. "Miller played the ball cleanly over to me, but I made a poor throw, pulling the first baseman off the bag (enabling DiMaggio to reach base on a forceout and Keltner to score). Now, a lot of people said that Travis slid in there hard and made me hurry my throw. But that's not true. I simply made a bad throw. So instead of a double play and the game being over, Williams got the chance to hit."

And hit he did. With his eighth-inning strikeout still in mind, young Theodore was a beast of determination. After measuring several of Passeau's pitches, he turned on a belt-high fastball and sent it on a swiftly rising line against the upper parapet of the right-field stands, spinning a 5-4 National League lead around into a 7-5 American League victory.

"I've never been so happy," Williams said. "Halfway down to first, seeing that ball going out, I stopped running and started leaping and jumping and clapping my hands, and I was so happy I laughed out loud."

As more than 54,000 fans stood and roared and cheered, Ted was embraced and pounded by his teammates, and skipper Baker kissed him on the forehead.

Williams' home run remains the single-most resounding shot in All-Star Game competition, a momentously conclusive blow that is to All-Star history what Bobby Thomson's homer is to pennant races and Bill Mazeroski's smash is to World Series play.

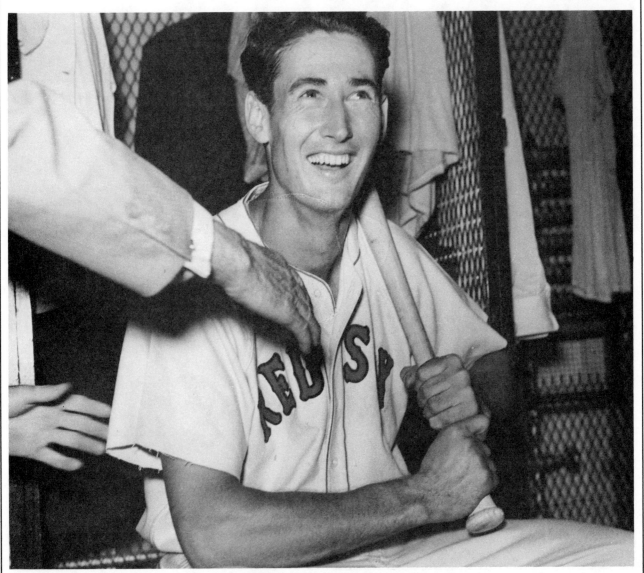

Ted Williams in the clubhouse after the 1941 game: 'I've never been so happy.'

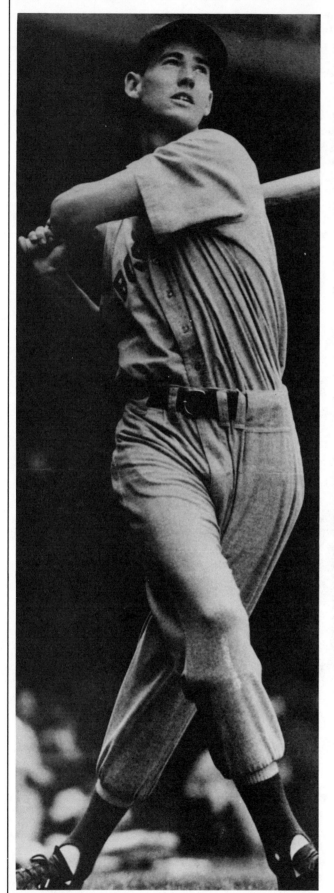

Ted Williams.

Ted Williams arrives home after his game-winning home run.

Cecil Travis.

The starting pitchers for the 1941 All-Star Game: Bob Feller (left) and Whitlow Wyatt.

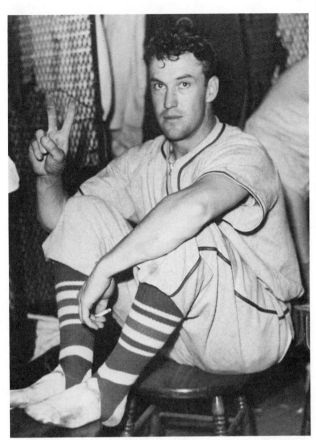

Nearly the hero. Arky Vaughan shows how many home runs he hit in the 1941 game.

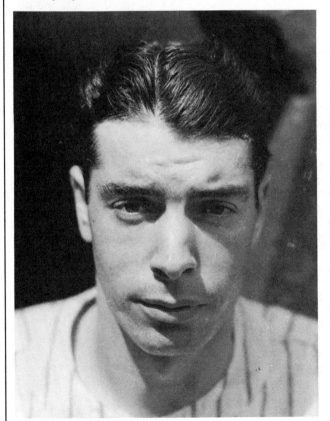

Joe DiMaggio.

Johnny Mize.

A.L. Remains Dominant

Americans	AB.	R.	H.	RBI.	PO.	A.
Boudreau (Indians), ss	4	1	1	1	4	5
Henrich (Yankees), rf	4	1	1	0	2	0
Williams (Red Sox), lf	4	0	1	0	0	0
J. DiMaggio (Yankees), cf	4	0	2	0	2	0
York (Tigers), 1b	4	1	1	2	11	3
Gordon (Yankees), 2b	4	0	0	0	1	4
Keltner (Indians), 3b	4	0	0	0	0	1
Tebbetts (Tigers), c	4	0	0	0	4	1
Chandler (Yankees), p	1	0	0	0	3	1
bJohnson (Athletics)	1	0	1	0	0	0
Benton (Tigers), p	1	0	0	0	0	1
Totals	35	3	7	3	27	16

Nationals	AB.	R.	H.	RBI.	PO.	A.
Brown (Cardinals), 2b	2	0	0	0	1	0
Herman (Dodgers), 2b	1	0	0	0	1	0
Vaughan (Dodgers), 3b	2	0	0	0	1	2
Elliott (Pirates), 3b	1	0	1	0	1	2
Reiser (Dodgers), cf	3	0	1	0	3	0
Moore (Cardinals), cf	1	0	0	0	1	0
Mize (Giants), 1b	2	0	0	0	3	0
F. McCormick (Reds), 1b	2	0	0	0	3	0
Ott (Giants), rf	4	0	0	0	1	0
Medwick (Dodgers), lf	2	0	0	0	1	0
Slaughter (Cardinals), lf	2	0	1	0	1	0
W. Cooper (Cardinals), c	2	0	1	0	7	0
Lombardi (Braves), c	1	0	0	0	2	0
Miller (Braves), ss	2	0	0	0	2	1
Reese (Dodgers), ss	1	0	0	0	0	1
M. Cooper (Cardinals), p	0	0	0	0	0	0
aMarshall (Giants)	1	0	0	0	0	0
Vander Meer (Reds), p	0	0	0	0	0	1
cLitwhiler (Phillies)	1	0	1	0	0	0
Passeau (Cubs), p	0	0	0	0	0	0
dOwen (Dodgers)	1	1	1	1	0	0
Walters (Reds), p	0	0	0	0	0	0
Totals	31	1	6	1	27	7

American League .... 3 0 0   0 0 0   0 0 0—3
National League .... 0 0 0   0 0 0   0 1 0—1

Americans	IP.	H.	R.	ER.	BB.	SO.
Chandler (W)	4	2	0	0	0	2
Benton	5	4	1	1	2	1

Nationals	IP.	H.	R.	ER.	BB.	SO.
M. Cooper (L)	3	4	3	3	0	2
Vander Meer	3	2	0	0	0	4
Passeau	2	1	0	0	0	1
Walters	1	0	0	0	0	1

aForced runner for M. Cooper in third. bSingled for Chandler in fifth. cSingled for Vander Meer in sixth. dHomered for Passeau in eighth. E—Brown. DP—Americans 2. LOB—Americans 5 Nationals 6. 2B—Henrich. HR—Boudreau, York, Owen. HBP—By Chandler (Brown). PB—Tebbetts. U—Ballanfant and Barlick (N.L.), Stewart and McGowan (A.L.). T—2:07. A—34,178.

By the time the 10th All-Star Game was played, at New York's Polo Grounds on July 6, 1942, the country had been at war for seven months. Enlistments and the draft had not yet begun the serious depletion of big-league rosters that would take place over the next several years, but enough major leaguers had entered the service to warrant a game in Cleveland on July 7 between the winning All-Star team and the Service All-Stars, with the proceeds of the latter game going to the Army-Navy Relief Fund.

The 1942 All-Star Game originally had been penciled in for Brooklyn's Ebbets Field, but because proceeds had been earmarked for various war-related charities, the contest was shifted to the Polo Grounds, where the seating capacity was much greater. (A late-afternoon thundershower sent the good intentions awry, however, holding the crowd to just 34,178 for the game, which was billed as a "twilight" contest and had a scheduled starting time of 6:30 p.m.)

The opposing managers, the Yankees' Joe McCarthy and the Dodgers' Leo Durocher, went at the game with different philoso-phies. Leo used virtually his whole squad, employing 22 players; McCarthy played the tightest game in All-Star history, using just 11 men.

Because of the game scheduled in Cleveland the following night, All-Star Game rules, always supple to begin with, were bent to allow pitchers to work as many as five innings. Consequently, McCarthy used only two pitchers—his own Spud Chandler for the first four (no runs and two hits) and Detroit's Al Benton for the last five (one run and four hits).

Durocher kicked in with four pitchers, starting with Mort Cooper, ace righthander of the Cardinals, and following with Johnny Vander Meer of the Reds, Claude Passeau of the Cubs and Cincinnati's Bucky Walters. All but Cooper pitched well, and Mort was rattled only in the first in-ning—but that was enough.

Cleveland's Lou Boudreau led off the game (the start of which was delayed more than 50 minutes because of the rain) with a home run and the Yankees' Tommy Henrich doubled. Cooper then was able to do the hard part, retiring Ted Williams and Joe DiMaggio, but Detroit's Rudy York, a righthanded batter, sliced a low shot down the right-field line into those always-obliging Polo Grounds foul-line bleachers. The two-run homer produced a 3-0 American League lead; that was it for the Americans, and pretty much it for the game.

The National League's only run was delivered by a most unlikely source. Brooklyn catcher Mickey Owen played 133 games that season and stroked exactly zero home runs (and, in fact, he homered only once in the majors from 1940 through 1943). But in the bottom of the eighth, Owen was sent up to pinch-hit for Passeau and he lofted a lazy shot that came down in the left-field stands. That made the score 3-1, but it advanced no further.

The American League had now won seven of the 10 midseason showcases.

Spud Chandler.

Al Benton.

Rudy York.

Walker Cooper is forced at second in the bottom of the third inning of the 1942 All-Star Game. Lou Boudreau's relay to first just missed getting Willard Marshall for the double play.

Some of the National League's pitching strength for the 1942 game (left to right): Whitlow Wyatt, Johnny Vander Meer, Claude Passeau, Mort Cooper.

New York Giants star Mel Ott fouls one back as catcher Birdie Tebbetts and umpire Lee Ballanfant look on.

Pete Reiser.

Mickey Owen.

Lou Boudreau.

Yankeeless Victory

Nationals	AB.	R.	H.	RBI.	PO.	A.
Hack (Cubs), 3b	5	1	3	0	0	2
Herman (Dodgers), 2b	5	0	2	0	3	3
Musial (Cardinals), lf-rf	4	0	1	1	0	0
Nicholson (Cubs), rf	2	0	0	0	0	0
cGalan (Dodgers), lf	1	0	0	0	1	0
Fletcher (Pirates), 1b	2	0	0	0	3	0
dDahlgren (Phillies), 1b	2	0	0	0	3	0
W. Cooper (Cardinals), c	2	0	1	0	7	1
eLombardi (Giants), c	2	0	0	0	3	0
H. Walker (Cardinals), cf	1	0	0	0	1	0
bDiMaggio (Pirates), cf	3	2	3	0	1	0
Marion (Cardinals), ss	2	0	0	0	2	2
gOtt (Giants)	1	0	0	0	0	0
Miller (Reds), ss	1	0	0	0	0	1
M. Cooper (Cardinals), p	1	0	0	0	0	1
Vander Meer (Reds), p	1	0	0	0	0	1
Sewell (Pirates), p	0	0	0	0	0	1
hF. Walker (Dodgers)	1	0	0	1	0	0
Javery (Braves), p	0	0	0	0	0	0
iFrey (Reds)	1	0	0	0	0	0
Totals	37	3	10	2	24	12

Americans	AB.	R.	H.	RBI.	PO.	A.
Case (Senators), rf	2	1	0	0	0	0
Keltner (Indians), 3b	4	1	1	0	2	2
Wakefield (Tigers), lf	4	0	2	1	3	0
R. Johnson (Senators), lf	0	0	0	0	1	0
Stephens (Browns), ss	3	0	1	0	1	3
Siebert (Athletics), 1b	1	0	0	0	3	1
aYork (Tigers), 1b	3	0	1	0	4	0
Laabs (Browns), cf	3	1	0	0	7	0
Early (Senators), c	2	1	0	0	3	0
Doerr (Red Sox), 2b	4	1	2	3	3	3
Leonard (Senators), p	1	0	1	0	0	1
Newhouser (Tigers), p	1	0	0	0	0	0
fHeath (Indians)	1	0	0	0	0	0
Hughson (Red Sox), p	0	0	0	0	0	0
Totals	29	5	8	4	27	10

National League	1	0	0	0	0	0	1	0	1—3
American League	0	3	1	0	1	0	0	0	x—5

Nationals	IP.	H.	R.	ER.	BB.	SO.
M. Cooper (L)	2⅓	4	4	4	2	1
Vander Meer	2⅔	2	1	0	1	6
Sewell	1	0	0	0	0	0
Javery	2	2	0	0	0	3

Americans	IP.	H.	R.	ER.	BB.	SO.
Leonard (W)	3	2	1	1	0	0
Newhouser	3	3	0	0	1	1
Hughson	3	5	2	2	0	2

aStruck out for Siebert in third. bSingled for H. Walker in fourth. cWalked for Nicholson in sixth. dHit into double play for Fletcher in sixth. eFlied out for W. Cooper in sixth. fFlied out for Newhouser in sixth. gStruck out for Marion in seventh. hFlied out for Sewell in seventh. iFlied out for Javery in ninth. E—Hack, Herman 2, Stephens. DP—Nationals 3, Americans 1. LOB—Nationals 8, Americans 6. 2B—Musial, Keltner, Wakefield. 3B—DiMaggio. HR—Doerr, DiMaggio. SH—Stephens, Early. HBP—By M. Cooper (Case). U—Rommel and Rue (A.L.), Conlan and Dunn (N.L.). T—2:07. A—31,938.

"I can beat him with one hand tied behind my back."

A not unfamiliar boastful assertion, and one that Joe McCarthy made in 1943—if not literally, then by implication. Nettled by accusations that he was flagrantly partial to his own Yankee players when it came to selecting his All-Star starters, McCarthy played the entire '43 game without calling on any of the five Yankee players sitting on the bench. Joe's tactic also had a bit of nose-thumbing about it, demonstrating that he could win without the help of some of his best players. (The five spectators in Yankee uniforms were pitchers Ernie Bonham and Spud Chandler, catcher Bill Dickey, outfielder Johnny Lindell and second baseman Joe Gordon.)

The Yankee-less All-Star Game was played on July 13 at Philadelphia's Shibe Park, and it was the first time the game was scheduled to be played at night (with an 8:45 starting time). With the military draft beginning to make deeper inroads upon the major league rosters, the star squads weren't quite as spangled as before. The aura of Joe DiMaggio, Ted Williams, Johnny Mize, Pete Reiser and others was missing. Nevertheless, it was still the All-Star Game, and the men on the field were at the moment the best in the big leagues.

National League Manager Billy Southworth of the Cardinals started his ace, Mort Cooper, and for the second year in a row the big righthander had his problems. After the Nationals had taken a one-run lead in the first inning (the run was driven in by the Cardinals' Stan Musial, playing in the first of his 24 consecutive All-Star Games), the Americans soon began their assault against Cooper.

In the bottom of the second, Cooper walked the Browns' Chet Laabs and the Senators' Jake Early. This is how you spell trouble in capital letters, and the Red Sox's Bobby Doerr drove the point home—along with three runs—when he bashed an All-Star Game souvenir into the left-field stands, giving the Americans a 3-1 lead and probably making Cooper wonder if the honor of being there was worth the aggra-

vation that seemed to accompany it. In the third inning, consecutive doubles by Cleveland's Ken Keltner and Detroit's Dick Wakefield made Southworth sigh and a call for Cincinnati's Johnny Vander Meer was only one batter away.

The Reds' lefthander proceeded to end the inning by striking out Detroit's Rudy York and St. Louis' Laabs on the way to a dynamite performance. In 2⅔ innings, Vander Meer struck out six batters, walked one, allowed two hits and yielded an unearned run in one of the most impressive mound displays in All-Star history. In the fifth inning, when he was nicked for the unearned run, Vander Meer struck out the side.

American League pitching, meanwhile, was highly effective. Washington knuckleballer Dutch Leonard parted with just one run over the first three innings, and Detroit lefthander Hal Newhouser then painted three goose eggs on the scoreboard.

With the score 5-1, Americans, the Nationals began flexing a muscle or two in the top of the seventh—and a man named DiMaggio played a key role. Obviously, it wasn't the Yankees' Joe —but you might have sworn it was. With the American League superstar away in the Army, brother Vince of the Pittsburgh Pirates kept the family torch nicely lit this evening. Vince, who had singled as a pinch-hitter in the fourth inning and stayed in the game, tripled off Boston Red Sox righthander Tex Hughson in the seventh and scored on a fly ball.

In the ninth inning, Vince showed even more muscle when he cracked a long home run off Hughson. It was an impressive showing by the eldest DiMaggio brother, but he had little help (the Cubs' Stan Hack did collect three singles) and Hughson finally wrapped up another American League victory, 5-3.

At this point in All-Star Game history, the veterans were Billy Herman and Mel Ott, playing in their 10th consecutive games. For Billy, it was 10 and out, and the superb Cub and Dodger second baseman left behind a most impressive sheet—13 hits in 30 at-bats for a .433 batting average (all of it, remember, against hand-picked pitching). Ott, the long-time New York Giants outfielder, would appear in his 11th straight —and final—game the following year.

Bobby Doerr.

Stan Musial, as he appeared in 1943, the first of his 24 All-Star Games.

Stan Hack.

Johnny Vander Meer.

Vince DiMaggio.

Tex Hughson.

George Case slides home safely with an American League run in the bottom of the fifth inning of the 1943 game. The catcher is Walker Cooper, the umpire is Tom Dunn and the batter is Rudy York.

The War Takes Its Toll

Americans	AB.	R.	H.	RBI.	PO.	A.
Tucker (White Sox), cf	4	0	0	0	4	0
Spence (Senators), rf	4	0	2	0	2	1
McQuinn (Browns), 1b	4	0	1	0	5	1
Stephens (Browns), ss	4	0	1	0	1	0
Johnson (Red Sox), lf	3	0	0	0	2	1
Keltner (Indians), 3b	4	1	1	0	0	4
Doerr (Red Sox), 2b	3	0	0	0	4	1
Hemsley (Yankees), c	2	0	0	0	2	0
Hayes (Athletics), c	1	0	0	0	3	0
Borowy (Yankees), p	1	0	1	1	0	0
Hughson (Red Sox), p	1	0	0	0	0	0
Muncrief (Browns), p	0	0	0	0	1	0
cHiggins (Tigers)	1	0	0	0	0	0
Newhouser (Tigers), p	0	0	0	0	0	1
Newsom (Athletics), p	0	0	0	0	0	0
Totals	32	1	6	1	24	9

Nationals	AB.	R.	H.	RBI.	PO.	A.
Galan (Dodgers), lf	4	1	1	1	2	0
Cavarretta, (Cubs), 1b	2	1	2	0	12	0
Musial (Cardinals), cf-rf	4	1	1	1	2	1
W. Cooper (Cardinals), c	5	1	2	1	5	2
Mueller (Reds), c	0	0	0	0	0	0
Walker (Dodgers), rf	4	0	2	1	0	0
DiMaggio (Pirates), cf	0	0	0	0	0	0
Elliott (Pirates), 3b	3	0	0	0	0	3
Kurowski (Cardinals), 3b	1	0	1	2	0	1
Ryan (Braves), 2b	4	1	2	0	4	4
Marion (Cardinals), ss	3	1	0	0	2	3
Walters (Reds), p	0	0	0	0	0	1
aOtt (Giants)	1	0	0	0	0	0
Raffensberger (Phil.), p	0	0	0	0	0	0
bNicholson (Cubs)	1	1	1	1	0	0
Sewell (Pirates), p	1	0	0	0	0	0
dMedwick (Giants)	0	0	0	0	0	0
Tobin (Braves), p	0	0	0	0	0	0
Totals	33	7	12	7	27	15

American League ....0 1 0 0 0 0 0 0 0—1
National League ....0 0 0 0 4 0 2 1 x—7

Americans	IP.	H.	R.	ER.	BB.	SO.
Borowy	3	3	0	0	1	0
Hughson (L)	1⅔	5	4	3	1	2
Muncrief	1⅓	1	0	0	0	1
Newhouser	1⅔	3	3	2	2	1
Newsom	⅓	0	0	0	0	0

Nationals	IP.	H.	R.	ER.	BB.	SO.
Walters	3	5	1	1	0	1
Raffensberger (W)	2	1	0	0	0	2
Sewell	3	0	0	0	1	2
Tobin	1	0	0	0	0	0

aFlied out for Walters in third. bDoubled for Raffensberger in fifth. cGrounded out for Muncrief in seventh. dSacrificed for Sewell in eighth. E—McQuinn, Doerr, Hayes, Ryan. DP—Americans 1, Nationals 1. LOB—Americans 5, Nationals 9. 2B—Nicholson. Kurowski. 3B—Cavarretta. SB—Ryan. SH—Marion, Musial, Medwick. WP—Muncrief. U—Barr and Sears (N.L.), Berry and Hubbard (A.L.). T—2:11. A—29,589.

The 12th All-Star Game was played at Pittsburgh's Forbes Field on the night of July 11, 1944. For baseball, it was the darkest of the war years, with most of the game's marquee names scattered around a vibrating globe.

The teams were again managed by Joe McCarthy of the Yankees and Billy Southworth of the Cardinals. The year before, McCarthy had almost superciliously held his Yankees out of the game; this year, with all of his stars in the service and his current New York club a patchwork unit, Joe was hard-pressed to get any of his boys onto the squad. He did wind up with an all-Yankee starting battery, though, with Hank Borowy pitching and Rollie Hemsley catching.

Borowy went three shutout innings, while the American Leaguers pinched a single run off National League starter Bucky Walters (Cincinnati) in the second inning, driven in on Borowy's infield single.

Tex Hughson took the mound for the American League in the bottom of the fourth and the Boston pitcher held the score at 1-0; Ken Raffensberger, cagey lefthander of the Philadelphia Phillies, shut down the Americans in the fourth and fifth.

In the bottom of the fifth, the National Leaguers uncoiled and began sniping at Hughson. Boston Braves second baseman Connie Ryan opened with a single and the door was ajar, not to be shut until Hughson himself had passed through it on his way out.

The Cubs' Bill Nicholson, the National League home run and runs-batted-in leader in 1943 and 1944, pinch-hit for Raffensberger and doubled home Ryan with the tying run. The Dodgers' Augie Galan singled in Nicholson. Hughson dug his pit a bit deeper by walking the Cubs' Phil Cavarretta (who had a fine time in his first All-Star Game with a single, a triple and three walks). Stan Musial grounded to Bobby Doerr, but Browns first baseman George McQuinn dropped the throw and the bases were brimming with National Leaguers. The Cardinals' Walker Cooper singled to left, scoring Galan, but Cavarretta was gunned down at the plate, left fielder Bob Johnson to catcher Frankie Hayes. Brooklyn's Dixie

Walker made it a four-run inning with a single that scored Musial and finished Hughson. Bob Muncrief of the Browns came in and finally closed the door.

Raffensberger was followed to the mound by Pittsburgh's Rip Sewell, a 21-game winner that year. Sewell delighted his hometown fans with a few demonstrations of the pitch for which he had become, and remains, famous —his "ephus" pitch. This curious delivery was a parachute pitch that Sewell lobbed on a high arc and over which he had uncanny control. In the eighth inning (his third and last inning of work), Sewell made the crowd roar when he floated two of these rainbows to McQuinn. McQuinn took the first for a strike, then bunted the other and was thrown out.

By this time, the score was 6-1, the Nationals having scored two runs in the seventh on a double by the Cardinals' Whitey Kurowski against Hal Newhouser. The National League added its final run in the eighth, then watched Braves righthander Jim Tobin follow Sewell's three scoreless innings with a 1-2-3 ninth, sealing the National League's fourth All-Star triumph in 12 tries. The 7-1 outcome produced the widest victory margin yet achieved in the series, and the Nationals' four-run fifth inning was their biggest one-inning outburst to date.

With severe wartime travel restrictions in effect a year later, the 1945 All-Star Game was canceled.

Bucky Walters.

Part of the crowd heads into Pittsburgh's Forbes Field for the 1944 All-Star Game.

National League Manager Billy Southworth (center) embraces two heroes from his 1944 All-Star squad: Rip Sewell (left) and Phil Cavarretta.

Hank Borowy.

Whitey Kurowski.

Walker Cooper.

Ted Shows Off—Again

Nationals	AB.	R.	H.	RBI.	PO.	A.
Schoendienst (Cards), 2b...	2	0	0	0	0	2
cGustine (Pirates), 2b........	1	0	0	0	1	1
Musial (Cardinals), lf.........	2	0	0	0	0	0
dEnnis (Phillies), lf...........	2	0	0	0	0	0
Hopp (Braves), cf.............	2	0	1	0	0	0
eLowrey (Cubs), cf	2	0	1	0	3	0
Walker (Dodgers), rf	3	0	0	0	1	0
Slaughter (Cardinals), rf...	1	0	0	0	0	0
Kurowski (Cardinals), 3b..	3	0	0	0	2	1
iVerban (Phillies)	1	0	0	0	0	0
Mize (Giants), 1b..............	1	0	0	0	7	0
bMcCormick (Phillies), 1b	1	0	0	0	1	1
gCavarretta (Cubs), 1b......	1	0	0	0	1	0
Cooper (Giants), c	1	0	1	0	0	0
Masi (Braves), c...............	2	0	0	0	4	1
Marion (Cardinals), ss	3	0	0	0	4	6
Passeau (Cubs), p............	1	0	0	0	0	1
Higbe (Dodgers), p...........	1	0	0	0	0	0
Blackwell (Reds), p	0	0	0	0	0	0
hLamanno (Reds)	1	0	0	0	0	0
Sewell (Pirates), p	0	0	0	0	0	0
Totals	31	0	3	0	24	13

Americans	AB.	R.	H.	RBI.	PO.	A.
DiMaggio (Red Sox), cf....	2	0	1	0	1	0
Spence (Senators), cf........	0	1	0	0	1	0
Chapman (Athletics), cf....	2	0	0	1	1	0
Pesky (Red Sox), ss..........	2	0	0	0	1	0
Stephens (Browns), ss.......	3	1	2	2	0	4
Williams (Red Sox), lf	4	4	4	5	1	0
Keller (Yankees), rf..........	4	2	1	2	1	0
Doerr (Red Sox), 2b	2	0	0	0	1	1
Gordon (Yankees), 2b........	2	0	1	2	0	1
Vernon (Senators), 1b.......	2	0	0	0	2	1
York (Red Sox), 1b...........	2	0	1	0	5	0
Keltner (Indians), 3b.........	0	0	0	0	0	0
Stirnweiss (Yankees), 3b..	3	1	1	0	0	0
Hayes (Indians), c.............	1	0	0	0	3	0
Rosar (Athletics), c	2	1	1	0	5	0
Wagner (Red Sox), c.........	1	0	0	0	4	0
Feller (Indians), p	0	0	0	0	0	0
aAppling (White Sox)	1	0	0	0	0	0
Newhouser (Tigers), p.......	1	1	1	0	1	0
fDickey (Yankees)	1	0	0	0	0	0
Kramer (Browns), p...........	1	1	1	0	0	0
Totals	36	12	14	12	27	7

National League...........0 0 0 0 0 0 0 0 0— 0
American League...........2 0 0 1 3 0 2 4 x—12

Nationals	IP.	H.	R.	ER.	BB.	SO.
Passeau (L).......................	3	2	2	2	2	0
Higbe...............................	1⅓	5	4	4	1	2
Blackwell........................	2⅔	3	2	2	1	1
Sewell.............................	1	4	4	4	0	0

Americans	IP.	H.	R.	ER.	BB.	SO.
Feller (W)........................	3	2	0	0	0	3
Newhouser.......................	3	1	0	0	0	4
Kramer............................	3	0	0	0	1	3

aGrounded out for Feller in third. bFlied out for Mize in fourth. cStruck out for Schoendienst in sixth. dStruck out for Musial in sixth. eSingled for Hopp in sixth. fStruck out for Newhouser in sixth. gStruck out for McCormick in seventh. hGrounded out for Blackwell in eighth. iFouled out for Kurowski in ninth. E—Pesky. DP—Nationals 2. LOB—Nationals 5, Americans 4. 2B—Stephens, Gordon. HR—Williams 2, Keller. WP—Blackwell. U—Summers and Rommel (A.L.), Boggess and Goetz (N.L.). T—2:19. A—34,906.

"We'd turned a dead turkey of a ball game into a real crowd pleaser."

The speaker was Rip Sewell. The "we" referred to Sewell and Ted Williams; the "dead turkey" was the American League's 12-0 pounding of the Nationals in the 1946 All-Star Game, played July 9 at Williams' own Fenway Park in Boston.

How could anyone have brought to life a slow-death execution? By poking a bit of fun at it, that's how.

The war was over, the stars were back and America's love affair with its national game was never more ardent or enthusiastic. "I don't think I've ever seen a more festive occasion than that '46 All-Star Game," Phillies first baseman Frank McCormick recalled. "Guys who hadn't seen one another in years were crossing back and forth before the game to shake hands and visit. It was great."

American League Manager Steve O'Neill dealt his top card, starting Bob Feller, the Cleveland great who was heading for a 26-victory, 348-strikeout season. National League skipper Charley Grimm of the Cubs started Claude Passeau, his veteran righthander.

With two out in the bottom of the first inning, Passeau walked Williams (who had hit the big bomb off Claude in the ninth inning of the '41 game) and then threw a home run ball to the Yankees' Charlie Keller for a quick 2-0 A.L. lead.

The score held that way into the last of the fourth, with Brooklyn righthander Kirby Higbe now on the mound for the Nationals. Kirby owned a fastball of which he was justly proud, and he liked to challenge hitters with it. Ted Williams, who made his living by accepting such challenges with alacrity and proficiency, parked one of Higbe's swifties beyond reach and the score was 3-0. With Detroit's Hal Newhouser pitching as immaculately as Feller had, the Nationals had a problem reaching base, much less scoring.

In the fifth, the Americans began to turn the game into its turkey status, stuffing it with three more runs. The outburst started when Athletics catcher Buddy Rosar delivered a one-out single and traveled to third on a single by Newhouser, who took second on the throw to third. Washington's Stan Spence was intentionally walked to load the bases. But the Browns' Vern Stephens made hash out of the strategy by doubling in two runs. Williams singled in Spence and ended Higbe's tenure. Ewell Blackwell, Cincinnati's beanpole righthander, came in and applied the brakes to the rally, but by now it was 6-0.

The Americans lathered Blackwell for two runs in the seventh inning, though, raising the ante to 8-0. The turkey was good and dead now, and the Boston fans were enjoying every last feather of it. (Reflecting their pennant runaway of '46—the Red Sox went on to win the American League flag by 12 games—the Sox got six players into the game: center fielder Dom DiMaggio, second baseman Bobby Doerr, first baseman Rudy York, shortstop Johnny Pesky, catcher Hal Wagner and left fielder Williams.)

St. Louis Browns righthander Jack Kramer continued the whitewash through the seventh and eighth, and it was in the bottom of the eighth that the turkey suddenly came to life.

Pittsburgh's Sewell was on the mound now, he of the "ephus" pitch. Rip once explained how the odd delivery received its odd name. A teammate, Maurice Van Robays, was asked by a writer what the pitch was called. "Ephus," Maurice said. "What's an ephus?" the writer asked. And Maurice explained: "An ephus ain't nothing. And that's what that pitch is—nothing."

But in the 1946 All-Star Game it became something.

Rip didn't have much luck throwing his orthodox deliveries to the American Leaguers. Base hits by the Yankees' George Stirnweiss and Kramer and a fly ball brought in one run. Sewell then decided to lighten up the proceedings and began throwing his blooper. After Stephens singled,

Williams strode to the plate and, as usual, he was all business.

"Before the game," Sewell recalled, "Ted said to me, 'Hey, Rip, you wouldn't throw that damned crazy pitch in a game like this, would you?'

"'Sure,' I said. 'I'm gonna throw it to you.'

"'Man,' he said, 'don't throw that ball in a game like this.'

"'I'm gonna throw it to you, Ted,' I said. 'So look out.'"

When Williams stood at the plate in the eighth inning, with the score 9-0 and two men on base, Sewell smiled mischievously at him.

"He must've recalled our conversation," Rip said, "because he shook his head from side to side in quick little movements, telling me not to throw it. I nodded to him: You're gonna get it, buddy. So, I wound up like I was going to throw a fastball, and here comes the blooper. He swung from Port Arthur and just fouled it on the tip of his bat.

"He stepped back in, staring out at me, and I nodded to him again: You're gonna get another one. I threw him another one, but it was outside and he let it go. Now he was looking for it. Well, I threw him a fastball, and he didn't like that. Surprised him. Now I had him one ball, two strikes. I wound up and threw him another blooper, on an arc about 25 feet high. It was a good one. Dropped right down the chute for a strike. He took a couple of steps up on it—which was the right way to attack that pitch, incidentally—and he hit it right out of there. And I mean he *hit* it.

"Well, the fans stood up, and they went crazy. I walked around the base lines with Ted, talking to him. 'Yeah,' I told him, 'the only reason you hit it is because I told you it was coming.' He was laughing all the way around. I got a standing ovation when I walked off the mound after that inning. We'd turned a dead turkey of a ball game into a real crowd pleaser.

"And he was the only man ever to hit a home run off the blooper," Sewell contended. "Ted Williams, in the '46 All-Star Game."

Choosing up sides before the 1946 All-Star Game were (left to right) Mickey Vernon, Ted Williams, Johnny Hopp and Dixie Walker.

Charlie Keller.

The starting pitchers for the 1946 All-Star Game were Bob Feller (left) and Claude Passeau.

Boston's Fenway Park as it looked during the 1946 midseason classic.

Rip Sewell, the inventor and most-notable proponent of the 'ephus ball.'

Ted Williams. 'And I mean he hit it.'

Jack Kramer.

Vern Stephens.

The American Way

Americans	AB.	R.	H.	RBI.	PO.	A.
Kell (Tigers), 3b	4	0	0	0	0	0
Johnson (Yankees), 3b	0	0	0	0	0	0
Lewis (Senators), rf	2	0	0	0	1	0
bAppling (White Sox)	1	1	1	0	0	0
Henrich (Yankees), rf	1	0	0	0	3	0
Williams (Red Sox), lf	4	0	2	0	3	0
DiMaggio (Yankees), cf	3	0	1	0	1	0
Boudreau (Indians), ss	4	0	1	0	4	4
McQuinn (Yankees), 1b	4	0	0	0	9	1
Gordon (Yankees), 2b	2	0	1	0	0	4
Doerr (Red Sox), 2b	2	1	1	0	0	2
Rosar (Athletics), c	4	0	0	0	6	0
Newhouser (Tigers), p	1	0	0	0	0	0
Shea (Yankees), p	1	0	0	0	0	0
cSpence (Senators)	1	0	1	1	0	0
Masterson (Senators), p	0	0	0	0	0	0
Page (Yankees), p	0	0	0	0	0	0
Totals	34	2	8	1	27	11

Nationals	AB.	R.	H.	RBI.	PO.	A.
H. Walker (Phillies), cf	2	0	0	0	1	0
Pafko (Cubs), cf	2	0	1	0	2	0
F. Walker (Dodgers), rf	2	0	0	0	1	0
Marshall (Giants), rf	1	0	0	0	3	0
W. Cooper (Giants), c	3	0	0	0	6	0
Edwards (Dodgers), c	0	0	0	0	2	0
eCavarretta (Cubs), 1b	1	0	0	0	1	0
Mize (Giants), 1b	3	1	2	1	8	0
fMasi (Braves), c	0	0	0	0	0	0
Slaughter (Cardinals), lf	3	0	0	0	1	0
Gustine (Pirates), 3b	2	0	0	0	0	2
Kurowski (Cardinals), 3b..	2	0	0	0	0	1
Marion (Cardinals), ss	2	0	1	0	0	1
Reese (Dodgers), ss	1	0	0	0	0	2
Verban (Phillies), 2b	2	0	0	0	0	1
Stanky (Dodgers), 2b	2	0	0	0	2	2
Blackwell (Reds), p	0	0	0	0	0	0
aHaas (Reds)	1	0	1	0	0	0
Brecheen (Cardinals), p	1	0	0	0	0	0
Sain (Braves), p	0	0	0	0	0	1
dMusial (Cardinals)	1	0	0	0	0	0
Spahn (Braves), p	0	0	0	0	0	0
gRowe (Phillies)	1	0	0	0	0	0
Totals	32	1	5	1	27	9

American League .... 0 0 0 0 0 1 1 0 0—2
National League .... 0 0 0 1 0 0 0 0 0—1

Americans	IP.	H.	R.	ER.	BB.	SO.
Newhouser	3	1	0	0	0	2
Shea (W)	3	3	1	1	2	2
Masterson	1⅔	0	0	0	1	2
Page	1⅓	1	0	0	1	0

Nationals	IP.	H.	R.	ER.	BB.	SO.
Blackwell	3	1	0	0	0	4
Brecheen	3	5	1	1	0	2
Sain (L)	1	2	1	1	0	1
Spahn	2	0	0	0	1	1

aSingled for Blackwell in third. bSingled for Lewis in sixth. cSingled for Shea in seventh. dGrounded out for Sain in seventh. eStruck out for Edwards in eighth. fRan for Mize in eighth. gFlied out for Spahn in ninth. E—Sain. DP—Nationals 1. LOB—Americans 6, Nationals 8. 2B—Williams, Gordon. HR—Mize. SB—Doerr. WP—Blackwell. PB—W. Cooper. U—Boyer and Passarella (A.L.), Conlan and Henline (N.L.). T—2:19. A—41,123.

The 1947 All-Star Game proved a perfect contrast to its immediate predecessor. Whereas the '46 game was a blustering storm of American League hits and runs, capped by the late-game vaudeville show put on by Ted Williams and Rip Sewell, the '47 contest was classic in the trim, precise lines of its structure.

The game was played on July 8 at Chicago's Wrigley Field, a ball park whose overall distances were comparatively neighborly. The coziness of the park, coupled with the always-present possibility of a stiff wind blowing out, led to the expectation of heavy scoring. However, the wind was blowing *in* on this day and the pitchers were at the top of their game.

The Nationals, managed by the Cardinals' Eddie Dyer, threw an extraordinarily strong array of pitchers at the Americans. Dyer started with Cincinnati righthander Ewell Blackwell, who was in the midst of a brilliant season that saw him win 22 games, including 16 in a row. Blackwell was tall and thin, with a blurring sidearm delivery that had earned him the nickname "The Whip" and the memory of which even decades later could pop beads of perspiration upon the brows of long-retired righthanded hitters.

Blackwell went three scintillating innings, fanning four and giving just one hit. Detroit's Hal Newhouser matched his one-hit, shutout pitching.

In the bottom of the fourth, the Nationals broke through against Yankee rookie Frank (Spec) Shea when the Giants' Johnny Mize boomed a home run far into the right-field bleachers.

The Americans tied it in the sixth inning against the Cardinals' canny, screwballing lefthander, Harry Brecheen, whose feline-like craftiness had earned him the nickname "The Cat." Singles by the White Sox's Luke Appling and the Red Sox's Williams and a double-play grounder by Joe DiMaggio brought across the run.

The Americans went up by a run in the seventh, scoring against curveballing righthander Johnny Sain, a 21-game winner for the Braves that year. The run was largely the courtesy of Bobby Doerr, who singled, stole second, went to third on Sain's errant pickoff attempt and scored on a pinch single by Washington's Stan Spence. Sain's Boston teammate, Warren Spahn (also a 21-game winner in 1947), held Joe Cronin's club scoreless over the last two innings.

The Nationals couldn't score in the final three innings against Washington righthander Walt Masterson or Yankee lefthander Joe Page (a bullpen ace that year). Page worked out of the National League's final threat in the bottom of the eighth, getting Enos Slaughter on a fine play by shortstop Lou Boudreau with two on and two out.

The American League's 2-1 victory gave it a 10-4 lead in the series, a margin that irked National League President Ford Frick.

"This is getting painful," Frick muttered after the game. And before it got better, it would get worse.

There was some heavy timber gathering for the 1947 All-Star Game at Chicago's Wrigley Field (left to right): Rudy York, Johnny Mize, Ted Williams and Walker Cooper.

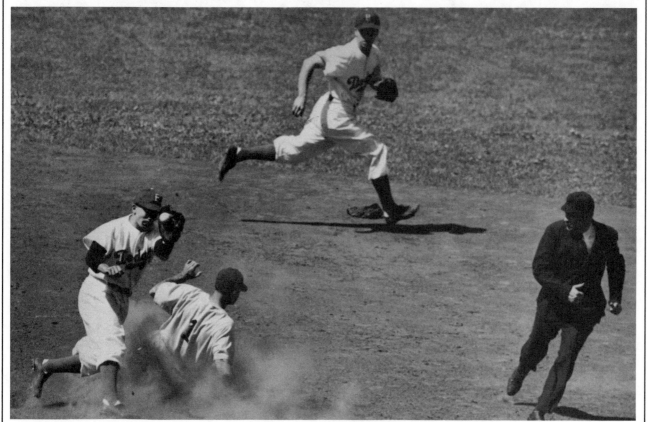

Bobby Doerr steals second base in the seventh inning as Eddie Stanky takes the late throw and Pee Wee Reese backs up the play.

Harry Brecheen.

Ewell Blackwell.

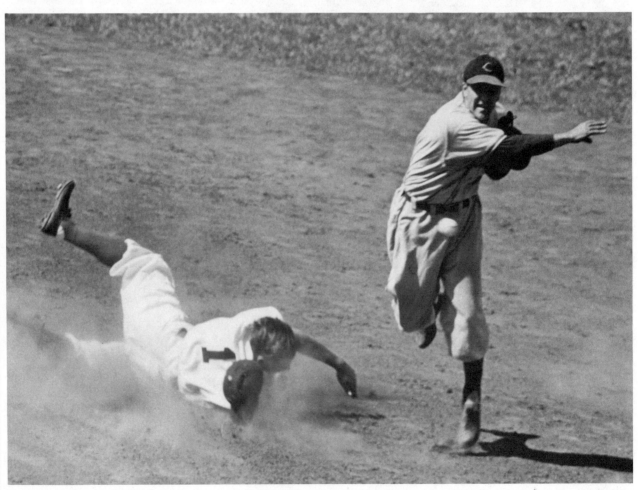

Pee Wee Reese is forced at second base in the bottom of the ninth inning, but Lou Boudreau's relay to first is too late to double Eddie Stanky.

Bobby Doerr.

Joe Page.

American Know-how

Nationals	AB.	R.	H.	RBI.	PO.	A.
Ashburn (Phillies), cf	4	1	2	0	1	0
Kiner (Pirates), lf	1	0	0	0	1	0
Schoendienst (Cards), 2b	4	0	0	0	0	1
Rigney (Giants), 2b	0	0	0	0	2	0
Musial (Cardinals), lf-cf	4	1	2	2	3	0
Mize (Giants), 1b	4	0	1	0	4	1
Slaughter (Cardinals), rf	2	0	1	0	2	0
Holmes (Braves), rf	1	0	0	0	1	0
Pafko (Cubs), 3b	2	0	0	0	0	0
Elliott (Braves), 3b	2	0	1	0	0	0
Cooper (Braves), c	2	0	0	0	3	0
Masi (Braves), c	2	0	1	0	4	0
Reese (Dodgers), ss	2	0	0	0	2	2
Kerr (Giants), ss	2	0	0	0	1	0
Branca (Dodgers), p	1	0	0	0	0	0
bGustine (Pirates)	1	0	0	0	0	0
Schmitz (Cubs), p	0	0	0	0	0	0
Sain (Braves), p	0	0	0	0	0	0
dWaitkus (Cubs)	0	0	0	0	0	0
Blackwell (Reds), p	0	0	0	0	0	0
gThomson (Giants)	1	0	0	0	0	0
Totals	35	2	8	2	24	4

Americans	AB.	R.	H.	RBI.	PO.	A.
Mullin (Tigers), rf	1	0	0	0	0	0
cDiMaggio (Yankees)	1	0	0	1	0	0
Zarilla (Browns), rf	2	0	0	0	2	0
Henrich (Yankees), lf	3	0	0	0	1	0
Boudreau (Indians), ss	2	0	0	1	2	0
Stephens (Red Sox), ss	2	0	1	0	0	0
Gordon (Indians), 2b	2	0	0	0	1	2
Doerr (Red Sox), 2b	2	0	0	0	0	3
Evers (Tigers), cf	4	1	1	1	0	0
Keltner (Indians), 3b	3	1	1	0	1	6
McQuinn (Yankees), 1b	4	1	2	0	14	0
Rosar (Athletics), c	1	0	0	0	1	0
Tebbetts (Red Sox), c	1	1	0	0	5	1
Masterson (Senators), p	0	0	0	0	0	0
aVernon (Senators), p	0	1	0	0	0	0
Raschi (Yankees), p	1	0	1	2	0	1
eWilliams (Red Sox)	0	0	0	0	0	0
fNewhouser (Tigers)	0	0	0	0	0	0
Coleman (Athletics), p	0	0	0	0	0	1
Totals	29	5	6	5	27	14

```
National League .............2 0 0  0 0 0  0 0 0—2
American League.............0 1 1  3 0 0  0 0 x—5
```

Nationals	IP.	H.	R.	ER.	BB.	SO.
Branca	3	1	2	2	3	3
Schmitz (L)	⅓	3	3	3	1	0
Sain	1⅔	0	0	0	0	3
Blackwell	3	2	0	0	3	1

Americans	IP.	H.	R.	ER.	BB.	SO.
Masterson	3	5	2	2	1	4
Raschi (W)	3	3	0	0	1	3
Coleman	3	0	0	0	2	3

aWalked for Masterson in third. bStruck out for Branca in fourth. cFlied out for Mullin in fourth, scoring Tebbetts from third. dWalked for Sain in sixth. eWalked for Raschi in sixth. fRan for Williams in sixth. gStruck out for Blackwell in ninth. LOB—Nationals 10, Americans 8. HR—Musial, Evers. SB—Ashburn, Vernon, Mullin, McQuinn. SH —Coleman. WP—Masterson. U—Berry and Paparella (A.L.), Reardon and Stewart (N.L.). T— 2:27. A—34,009.

The American League went into the 1948 All-Star Game, played at Sportsman's Park, St. Louis, on July 13, under a decided handicap. The league's two noblest fence-busters, Joe DiMaggio and Ted Williams, were hobbled by injuries that limited them to pinch-hitting appearances, and George Kell, the league's premier third baseman, sat out the game because of an ankle injury. Nevertheless, Manager Bucky Harris' team came through with a 5-2 victory, much to the dismay and frustration of National League fans.

Leo Durocher's Nationals certainly started off in the right direction. In the top of the first inning, a single by the Phillies' Richie Ashburn was followed by a home run by hometown hero Stan Musial, against starting pitcher Walt Masterson. Thereafter, the Nationals might just as well have stacked their bats. Masterson settled down and shut them out for the rest of his three-inning stint, and Vic Raschi of the Yankees and Joe Coleman of the A's each worked three scoreless innings.

National League starter Ralph Branca, hard-throwing right-hander of the Brooklyn Dodgers, got through the first inning without damage, but in the second, Detroit's Hoot Evers cut the deficit in half with a home run. In the third, Branca made trouble for himself by walking Washington's Mickey Vernon and Detroit's Pat Mullin. As Branca was striking out Tommy Henrich, Vernon and Mullin executed a double steal. The next batter was Cleveland's shortstop-manager, Lou Boudreau, who was having an inspired year (he finished the season with a .355 batting average and led the Indians to the World Series title). Boudreau flied to right, scoring Vernon with the tying run.

The American League tore into Cubs lefthander Johnny Schmitz in the fourth inning, and the Nationals were never able to put the pieces back together. With one out, Cleveland's Ken Keltner and the Yankees' George McQuinn singled and Red Sox catcher Birdie Tebbetts walked, filling the bases. Harris, manager of the Yankees, let Raschi bat and the pitcher made it a good decision by singling into left field, scoring Keltner and McQuinn and sending Tebbetts to third (and Schmitz to the showers).

The Braves' Johnny Sain was summoned. Joe DiMaggio batted for Mullin and lined to Musial in left, deep enough to score Tebbetts, making it a 5-2 game. And there it stood, as Sain and then Ewell Blackwell tightened the faucets for the National League and Raschi and Coleman gave away nothing for the Americans.

Another American League victory was history, a relatively easy triumph at that. By now, the outcome seemed part of baseball's routine. But turnabout was not far off, and the gradual shift in the balance of power would be accomplished in a most decisive and significant way.

Two of baseball's best hitters, the Cardinals' Stan Musial (left) and Boston's Ted Williams, get together before the 1948 All-Star Game.

The starting pitchers pose for pictures before the 1948 classic: Washington's Walter Masterson (left) and Brooklyn's Ralph Branca.

Vic Raschi, the winning pitcher.

Hoot Evers.

Joe Coleman.

Richie Ashburn.

19 49

The First Blacks

Americans	AB.	R.	H.	RBI.	PO.	A.
D. DiM'gio (R. Sox), rf-cf...	5	2	2	1	2	0
Raschi (Yankees), p...........	1	0	0	0	0	1
Kell (Tigers), 3b...............	3	2	2	0	0	1
dDillinger (Browns), 3b.....	1	2	1	1	0	2
Williams (Red Sox), lf........	2	1	0	0	1	0
Mitchell (Indians), lf..........	1	0	1	1	1	0
J. DiMaggio (Yankees), cf	4	1	2	3	0	0
eDoby (Indians), rf-cf.......	1	0	0	0	2	0
Joost (Athletics), ss	2	1	1	2	2	2
Stephens (Red Sox), ss.......	2	0	0	0	2	0
E. Rob'ns'n (Senators), 1b.	5	1	1	1	8	0
Goodman (Red Sox), 1b	0	0	0	0	1	1
Michaels (White Sox), 2b ..	2	0	0	0	1	3
J. Gordon (Indians), 2b.....	2	1	1	0	3	3
Tebbetts (Red Sox), c	2	0	2	1	2	0
Berra (Yankees), c.............	3	0	0	0	2	1
Parnell (Red Sox), p..........	1	0	0	0	0	1
Trucks (Tigers), p..............	1	0	0	0	0	0
Brissie (Athletics), p	1	0	0	0	0	0
gWertz (Tigers), rf	2	0	0	0	0	0
Totals	41	11	13	10	27	15

Nationals	AB.	R.	H.	RBI.	PO.	A.
Reese (Dodgers), ss...........	5	0	0	0	3	3
J. Robinson (Dodgers), 2b.	4	3	1	0	1	1
Musial (Cardinals), cf-rf...	4	1	3	2	2	0
Kiner (Pirates), lf	5	1	1	2	3	0
Mize (Giants), 1b..............	2	0	1	0	1	0
aHodges (Dodgers), 1b	3	1	1	0	8	2
Marshall (Giants), rf.........	1	1	0	0	1	0
Bickford (Braves), p..........	0	0	0	0	0	0
fThomson (Giants)	1	0	0	0	0	0
Pollet (Cardinals), p.........	0	0	0	0	1	0
Blackwell (Reds), p...........	0	0	0	0	0	0
hSlaughter (Cardinals)	1	0	0	0	0	0
Roe (Dodgers), p...............	0	0	0	0	0	0
Kazak (Cardinals), 3b........	2	0	2	1	0	1
S. Gordon (Giants), 3b......	2	0	1	0	0	4
Seminick (Phillies), c.........	1	0	0	0	3	0
Campanella (Dodgers), c..	2	0	0	0	2	0
Spahn (Braves), p	0	0	0	0	0	0
Newcombe (Dodgers), p ...	1	0	0	1	0	0
bSchoendienst (Cardinals)	1	0	1	0	0	0
Munger (Cardinals), p	0	0	0	0	0	0
cPafko (Cubs), cf...............	2	0	1	0	2	0
Totals	37	7	12	6	27	11

American League....4 0 0 2 0 2 3 0 0—11
National League........2 1 2 0 0 2 0 0 0— 7

Americans	IP.	H.	R.	ER.	BB.	SO.
Parnell.......................	1*	3	3	3	1	1
Trucks (W)	2	3	2	2	2	0
Brissie.......................	3	5	2	2	2	1
Raschi.......................	3	1	0	0	3	1

Nationals	IP.	H.	R.	ER.	BB.	SO.
Spahn.........................	1⅓	4	4	4	2	3
Newcombe (L)............	2⅔	3	2	2	1	0
Munger	1	0	0	0	1	0
Bickford	1	2	2	2	1	0
Pollet	1	4	3	3	0	0
Blackwell	1	0	0	0	0	2
Roe...........................	1	0	0	0	0	0

*Pitched to three batters in second inning.

aRan for Mize in third. bSingled for Newcombe in fourth. cStruck out for Munger in fifth. dRan for Kell in sixth. eRan for J. DiMaggio in sixth. fFlied out for Bickford in sixth. gFlied out for Brissie in seventh. hFlied out for Blackwell in eighth. E—Mitchell, Reese, Mize, Marshall, Seminick, Campanella. DP—Americans 2, Nationals 1. LOB—Americans 8, Nationals 12. 2B—J. Robinson, Tebbetts, S. Gordon, D. DiMaggio, J. DiMaggio, J. Gordon, Mitchell. HR—Musial, Kiner. SB—Kell. HBP—By Parnell (Seminick). U—Barlick, Gore and Ballanfant (N.L.), Hubbard, Summers and Grieve (A.L.). T—3:04. A —32,577.

The National League was soon to become the more powerful of the two major leagues, and though this dominance obviously was achieved by a greater abundance of quality ball players, the story went deeper.

It was in 1947 that the Brooklyn Dodgers brought Jackie Robinson to the big leagues, breaking the majors' modern—and clearly reprehensible—color barrier. A year later, the Dodgers introduced Roy Campanella to the majors and in 1949 they added Don Newcombe to their staff. The New York Giants integrated their lineup in 1949 with Henry Thompson and Monte Irvin and, two years later, 20-year-old Willie Mays joined the team.

Soon, virtually the entire untapped pool of black baseball-playing talent was being courted by Organized Baseball, and the clubs doing the most successful and aggressive courting were mostly in the National League.

Many of baseball's great names of the coming decades—Mays, Bob Gibson, Ernie Banks, Frank Robinson, Henry Aaron, Willie McCovey, Willie Stargell—were black, and they rose to fame in the National League. This one-sided infusion of elite talent was gradually and irresistibly tipping the scales.

The first blacks to participate in an All-Star Game appeared in the 1949 game, played, appropriately enough, at Ebbets Field, Brooklyn, where Robinson had democratized major league baseball two years before. The black players performing in the July 12 game were Robinson, Campanella and Newcombe of the Dodgers, for the National League, and the American League's first black player, Cleveland's Larry Doby.

The game's historical significance was somewhat blurred by a long, high-scoring, rather untidy proceeding. American League pitchers issued eight bases on balls; the National League committed five errors. National League Manager Billy Southworth was criticized for starting lefthander Warren Spahn against an American League lineup stacked with six righthanded hitters.

Neither Spahn nor his infield was very sharp in the top of the first inning. With one out, De- troit's George Kell was safe on a dropped throw by Giants first baseman Johnny Mize. Kell stole second as Spahn was striking out Ted Williams. Joe DiMaggio singled in Kell, A's shortstop Eddie Joost walked and Eddie Robinson of the Senators singled home DiMaggio. An error by Dodgers shortstop Pee Wee Reese let in another run, and still another scored on a base hit by the Red Sox's Birdie Tebbetts. By the time Spahn retired his opposite number, Red Sox lefthander Mel Parnell, the American League had scored four unearned runs.

The National League, however, came right back in its half of the first. Jackie Robinson doubled and Stan Musial, swinging in the park where his lusty hitting had earned him the nickname "Stan the Man," homered over the right-field screen. The senior league scored another run in the second inning, and nearly had more. After loading the bases with none out against Parnell, the Nationals had pitcher Newcombe at the plate as the Americans called in Detroit righthander Virgil Trucks. Newcombe, who had replaced Spahn in the top of the inning, cracked a long drive into the left-field corner, where Williams made a running, one-handed catch. While Newcombe's smash netted a run, Reese then grounded into a double play.

Roughing up Trucks in the third, the Nationals scored two more runs to take a 5-4 lead, with Musial, 3 for 4 in the game, contributing a key single.

The Americans regained the lead with two runs in the fourth when, with men on second and third, Joost hit an erratically spinning grounder that Brooklyn first baseman Gil Hodges—attempting a bare-handed stop—couldn't handle, the ball rolling away for a two-run single.

After Cardinals righthander George (Red) Munger pitched one scoreless inning (something of a feat in this rolling sea of a game), the Americans mounted a DiMaggio-flavored flurry against Boston Braves righthander Vern Bickford in the sixth. Dominic D. doubled, Kell walked and Joseph D. drove in his second and third runs of the game with a line double to left-center, making it 8-5, American League.

With Athletics lefthander Lou Brissie pitching in the last of the sixth (his third inning of work), the Nationals turned it back into a one-run game. Batting with a man on base, Pittsburgh's Ralph Kiner did what he was able to accomplish 54 times during the regular season—hit one where the grass doesn't grow, making it an 8-7 game.

In the seventh, however, the seesaw tipped far over in the direction of the American League. Howie Pollet, the Cardinals' classy lefthander, had no sooner taken the mound than the American Leaguers began a tattoo. Cleveland's Joe Gordon opened with a double and, two outs later, Dom DiMaggio scored him with a single. Dom, who had taken second on a throw home, came around on a single by the Browns' Bob Dillinger, who subsequently scored on a double by Cleveland's Dale Mitchell. Mitchell's hit was the American League's fifth two-bagger of the game, tying a record it had set in 1934. It was now 11-7.

That finished the scoring for the day as the Yankees' Vic Raschi, the game's most effective pitcher, delivered three no-nonsense innings of one-hit, shutout ball. For the Nationals, Ewell Blackwell and Brooklyn lefthander Preacher Roe stopped the Americans over the last two innings.

Joe DiMaggio, with a single and a double and three runs batted in, was the Americans' hitting star. Ironically, American League Manager Lou Boudreau had received a bit of heat for adding the Yankee star to his squad. After all, DiMaggio, suffering with an injured heel, hadn't played his first game of the '49 season until June 28 and, accordingly, was a non-contender in the fans' All-Star balloting. However, Boudreau chose DiMaggio as a reserve and then inserted him into the starting lineup when Yanks outfielder Tommy Henrich, voted to a starting berth, was forced to bow out of the contest because of a knee injury.

Boudreau's explanation for naming DiMaggio to the team was succinct. "Joe DiMaggio," Lou said, "is Joe DiMaggio."

The first black All-Stars gather before the 1949 game (left to right): Roy Campanella, Larry Doby, Don Newcombe and Jackie Robinson.

The starting pitchers for the 1949 classic: Warren Spahn (left) and Mel Parnell.

Ralph Kiner.

Dom DiMaggio.

Joe DiMaggio.

Gil Hodges (left) and Pee Wee Reese.

1950

THREE TO

1959

The Winds Of Change

The Table Turns

Nationals	AB.	R.	H.	RBI.	PO.	A.
Jones (Phillies), 3b	7	0	1	0	2	3
Kiner (Pirates), lf	6	1	2	1	1	0
Musial (Cardinals), 1b	5	0	0	0	11	1
Robinson (Dodgers), 2b	4	1	1	0	3	2
fWyrostek (Reds), rf	2	0	0	0	0	0
Slaughter (Cards), cf-rf	4	1	2	1	3	0
Schoendienst (Cards), 2b	1	1	1	1	1	1
Sauer (Cubs), rf	2	0	0	1	1	0
Pafko (Cubs), cf	4	0	2	0	4	0
Campanella (Dodgers), c.	6	0	0	0	13	2
Marion (Cardinals), ss	2	0	0	0	0	2
Konstanty (Phillies), p	0	0	0	0	0	0
Jansen (Giants), p	2	0	0	0	1	0
gSnider (Dodgers)	1	0	0	0	0	0
Blackwell (Reds), p	1	0	0	0	0	1
Roberts (Phillies), p	1	0	0	0	0	0
Newcombe (Dodgers), p	0	0	0	0	0	1
cSisler (Phillies)	1	0	1	0	0	0
dReese (Dodgers), ss	3	0	0	0	2	4
Totals	52	4	10	4	42	17

Americans	AB.	R.	H.	RBI.	PO.	A.
Rizzuto (Yankees), ss	6	0	2	0	2	2
Doby (Indians), cf	6	1	2	0	9	0
Kell (Tigers), 3b	6	0	2	2	2	4
Williams (Red Sox), lf	4	0	1	1	2	0
D. DiMaggio (Red Sox), lf	2	0	0	0	1	0
Dropo (Red Sox), 1b	3	0	1	0	8	1
eFain (Athletics), 1b	3	0	1	0	2	1
Evers (Tigers), rf	2	0	0	0	1	0
J. DiMaggio (Yankees), rf	3	0	0	0	3	0
Berra (Yankees), c	2	0	0	0	2	0
bHegan (Indians), c	3	0	0	0	7	1
Doerr (Red Sox), 2b	3	0	0	0	1	4
Coleman (Yankees), 2b	2	0	0	0	1	0
Raschi (Yankees), p	0	0	0	0	0	0
aMichaels (Senators)	1	1	1	0	0	0
Lemon (Indians), p	0	1	0	0	1	0
Houtteman (Tigers), p	1	0	0	0	1	0
Reynolds (Yankees), p	1	0	0	0	0	0
hHenrich (Yankees)	1	0	0	0	0	0
Gray (Tigers), p	0	0	0	0	0	0
Feller (Indians), p	0	0	0	0	0	0
Totals	49	3	8	3	42	13

National League	020	000	001	000	01—4
American League	001	020	000	000	00—3

Nationals	IP.	H.	R.	ER.	BB.	SO.
Roberts	3	3	1	1	1	1
Newcombe	2	3	2	2	1	1
Konstanty	1	0	0	0	0	2
Jansen	5	1	0	0	0	6
Blackwell (W)	3	1	0	0	0	2

Americans	IP.	H.	R.	ER.	BB.	SO.
Raschi	3	2	2	2	0	1
Lemon	3	1	0	0	0	2
Houtteman	3	3	1	1	1	0
Reynolds	3	1	0	0	1	2
Gray (L)	1⅓	3	1	1	0	1
Feller	⅔	0	0	0	1	1

aDoubled for Raschi in third. bRan for Berra in fourth. cSingled for Newcombe in sixth. dRan for Sisler in sixth. ePopped out for Dropo in eighth. fFlied out for Robinson in eleventh. gFlied out for Jansen in twelfth. hFlied out for Reynolds in twelfth. E—Coleman. DP—Nationals 1, Americans 1. LOB—Nationals 9, Americans 6. 2B—Michaels, Doby, Kiner. 3B—Slaughter, Dropo. HR—Kiner, Schoendienst. WP—Roberts. PB—Hegan. U—McGowan, Rommel and Stevens (A.L.), Pinelli, Conlan and Robb (N.L.). T—3:19. A—46,127.

"It was annoying," Phillies pitcher Robin Roberts said. "The guys were starting to feel self-conscious about it."

What the guys—the National Leaguers—were annoyed and feeling self-conscious about was their 12-4 deficit in All-Star Game competition. Salting the wound even further was the fact that the American League also had taken the last three World Series.

So it was a highly resolved National League squad, managed by Brooklyn's Burt Shotton, that took the field on July 11 at Chicago's Comiskey Park against Casey Stengel's American Leaguers. (Casey was about to become a fixture of the occasion, managing the American Leaguers 10 times in the 11 All-Star Games played in the 1950s.)

The 1950 affair proved to be one of the most thrilling All-Star Games. It was the first to go into extra innings, featured two dramatic home runs and produced some of the finest pitching ever seen in the midseason matchup.

Shotton started Roberts, a brilliant righthander who that year was to achieve the first of his six straight 20-victory seasons. Opposing him was Stengel's own Vic Raschi, himself in the midst of three consecutive 20-victory seasons.

The Nationals took a 2-0 lead in the top of the second on a single by Jackie Robinson, a triple by Enos Slaughter and a fly ball. In the third inning, Washington's Cass Michaels, batting for Raschi, doubled and went to third when the Yankees' Phil Rizzuto beat out a bunt. A George Kell fly ball scored Michaels and it was 2-1.

In the fifth, the American League took the lead with a pair of runs at the expense of Don Newcombe. The big Dodger fireballer began the inning by walking Cleveland's Bob Lemon (who pitched three scoreless innings). Lemon went to third on a double by Indians teammate Larry Doby, who displayed flashing speed by racing to second base when his sharply hit ground ball caromed off second baseman Jackie Robinson's glove and went into center field. Kell then lofted his second run-scoring fly ball—such efforts were still counted as times at bat and not sacrifice flies—and Ted Williams brought in Doby with a single, giving the American League a 3-2 edge.

Detroit righthander Art Houtteman followed Lemon to the mound in the seventh and allowed no damage for two innings. But Ralph Kiner led off the Nationals' ninth with a long home run to left to tie the score, allowing the National League at least a temporary reprieve from another loss. At that point, the game became a duel between All-Star pitchers.

Phillies relief ace Jim Konstanty had pitched a scoreless sixth inning for the Nationals and then was replaced by Larry Jansen of the New York Giants, a stylish, curveballing righthander. Jansen was dazzling, carrying his club through the 11th inning with five razor-sharp innings of scoreless, one-hit pitching, during which he struck out six.

Matching Jansen's shutout hurling for three innings, through the top of the 12th, was the Yankees' hard-throwing Allie Reynolds. In the last of the 12th, the Reds' Ewell Blackwell brought his intimidating "whip" delivery to the mound for the National League and proceeded to pitch the final three innings, allowing no runs and one hit. Over the last nine innings of the game, Konstanty, Jansen and Blackwell combined to hold the American League to no runs and only two hits.

Detroit lefthander Ted Gray took over for the American League in the 13th and maintained the status quo. In the 14th, however, the National League dropped another leadoff bomb. This time the bombardier was the Cardinals' Red Schoendienst, a switch-hitter batting righthanded against Gray. It had taken Red a long time to get into the game—he had sat by for the first 10 innings as Jackie Robinson played second base. Drawing his first at-bat in the 14th inning after entering the game defensively in the 11th, Schoendienst showed that the time he spent on the bench had aged him to perfection, for he homered into the left-field stands, giving the National League a 4-3 lead. A half inning later, Blackwell sealed the victory for the Nationals when he induced Joe Di-Maggio to bang into a game-ending double play with one out and a man on first. It was the Nationals' first triumph after four straight losses.

In a parallel with the Dean injury in the 1937 game, another star of the first magnitude suffered an injury, the seriousness of which wasn't realized until after the game. In making an excellent running catch of a Kiner drive in the first inning, the Red Sox's Williams had run into the wall and banged his left elbow. Ignoring the increasing pain, Williams remained in the game for eight in-nings, going 1 for 4.

Later, it was determined that Ted had suffered a serious fracture of the left elbow. Forced to undergo surgery, he didn't play regularly again until September 15. And with Williams' Boston club finishing four games behind the pennant-winning Yankees, a strong case could be made that Ted's All-Star Game injury cost his team the American League flag in 1950.

National League Manager Burt Shotton (center) and his home run-hitting 1950 All-Star heroes: Ralph Kiner (left) and Red Schoendienst.

Larry Jansen.

Ewell Blackwell.

Red Schoendienst crosses the plate on his game-winning home run. Giving him the glad hand is Andy Pafko while catcher Jim Hegan watches.

Bob Lemon.

Allie Reynolds.

Enos Slaughter.

Pittsburgh's Ralph Kiner gets a warm greeting from Stan Musial after hitting his game-tying ninth-inning home run.

83

A Power Display

Nationals	AB.	R.	H.	RBI.	PO.	A.
Ashburn (Phillies), cf	4	2	2	0	4	1
Snider (Dodgers), cf	0	0	0	0	0	0
Dark (Giants), ss	5	0	1	0	0	3
Reese (Dodgers), ss	0	0	0	0	0	1
Musial (Cardinals), lf-rf-lf	4	1	2	1	0	0
Westlake (Cardinals), lf	0	0	0	0	0	0
J. Robinson (Dodgers), 2b	4	1	2	1	3	1
Schoendienst (Cards), 2b	0	0	0	0	0	0
Hodges (Dodgers), 1b	5	2	2	2	6	0
Elliott (Braves), 3b	2	1	1	2	1	1
Jones (Phillies), 3b	2	0	0	0	3	0
Ennis (Phillies), rf	2	0	0	0	0	0
Kiner (Pirates), lf	2	1	1	1	1	0
Wyrostek (Reds), rf	1	0	0	0	0	0
Campanella (Dodgers), c	4	0	0	0	9	1
Roberts (Phillies), p	0	0	0	0	0	0
aSlaughter (Cardinals)	1	0	0	0	0	0
Maglie (Giants), p	1	0	0	0	0	0
Newcombe (Dodgers), p	2	0	1	0	0	1
Blackwell (Reds), p	0	0	0	0	0	0
Totals	39	8	12	7	27	9

Americans	AB.	R.	H.	RBI.	PO.	A.
D. DiMaggio (Red Sox), cf	5	0	1	0	1	0
Fox (White Sox), 2b	3	0	1	0	3	1
eDoerr (Red Sox), 2b	1	0	1	0	1	0
Kell (Tigers), 3b	3	1	1	1	4	2
Williams (Red Sox), lf	3	0	1	0	3	0
Busby (White Sox), lf	0	0	0	0	0	0
Berra (Yankees), c	4	1	1	0	4	2
Wertz (Tigers), rf	3	1	1	1	2	0
Rizzuto (Yankees), ss	1	0	0	0	1	2
Fain (Athletics), 1b	3	0	1	1	5	0
fE. Robinson (W. Sox), 1b	1	0	0	0	0	0
Carrasquel (W. Sox), ss	2	0	1	0	0	3
cMinoso (White Sox), rf	2	0	0	0	2	0
Garver (Browns), p	1	0	0	0	0	0
Lopat (Yankees), p	0	0	0	0	0	0
bDoby (Indians)	1	0	0	0	0	0
Hutchinson (Tigers), p	0	0	0	0	0	0
dStephens (Red Sox)	1	0	0	0	0	0
Parnell (Red Sox), p	0	0	0	0	0	0
Lemon (Indians), p	0	0	0	0	1	0
gHegan (Indians)	1	0	1	0	0	0
Totals	35	3	10	3	27	11

National League ...... 1 0 0 3 0 2 1 1 0—8
American League ...... 0 1 0 1 1 0 0 0 0—3

Nationals	IP.	H.	R.	ER.	BB.	SO.
Roberts	2	4	1	1	1	1
Maglie (W)	3	3	2	2	1	1
Newcombe	3	2	0	0	0	3
Blackwell	1	1	0	0	1	2

Americans	IP.	H.	R.	ER.	BB.	SO.
Garver	3	1	1	0	1	1
Lopat (L)	1	3	3	3	0	0
Hutchinson	3	3	3	3	2	0
Parnell	1	3	1	1	0	1
Lemon	1	2	0	0	1	1

aLined out for Roberts in third. bPopped out for Lopat in fourth. cGrounded out for Carrasquel in sixth. dStruck out for Hutchinson in seventh. eSingled for Fox in seventh. fGrounded out for Fain in eighth. gDoubled for Lemon in ninth. E—J. Robinson, Fox, Berra. DP—Americans 1. LOB—Nationals 8, Americans 9. 2B—Ashburn, Hegan. 3B—Fain, Williams. HR—Musial, Elliott, Wertz, Kell, Hodges, Kiner. SH—Kell. PB—Campanella. U—Passarella, Hurley and Honochick (A.L.), Robb, Jorda and Dascoli (N.L.). T—2:41. A—52,075.

In 1951, the National League demonstrated that maybe, just maybe, it was starting to get the hang of this All-Star Game business. Winning for the first time in an American League host park the year before, the Nationals had reason to celebrate again in 1951 after winning two games in a row for the first time.

The game, originally scheduled for Philadelphia but switched to Detroit so it could become part of that city's 250th anniversary celebration, was played at Briggs Stadium on July 10.

The big guns, rolled into place for every All-Star Game, went off with record-making thunder in the 1951 game, the 18th of the series. The National League belted an unprecedented four home runs and the American two, setting a two-club record for the game.

The starting pitcher for Casey Stengel's American League club was one of the miracle men of 1951, St. Louis Browns righthander Ned Garver. Pitching for a last-place club that posted league-low figures in team batting and fielding, Garver won 20 games and lost 12 and, for good measure, batted .305. Ned also excelled in the annual midsummer game of notable names, pitching one-hit ball over three innings and allowing just one unearned run.

The Americans retrieved that run against Robin Roberts in the bottom of the second on a single by Yogi Berra and a triple by the Athletics' Ferris Fain. A few moments later, Fain was thrown out at the plate by Phillies center fielder Richie Ashburn after a short single by the White Sox's Chico Carrasquel, a play on which Fain had briefly held up, thinking the ball would be caught.

After three innings of a 1-1 tie, the National League unloaded on Garver's successor, lefthander Eddie Lopat of the Yankees. Stan Musial started things off by scorching one into the chairs in upper right. One out later, Gil Hodges singled and then Bob Elliott of the Braves homered into the left-field stands for a 4-1 N.L. lead.

With the Giants' Sal Maglie on the mound, Detroit's own Vic Wertz thrilled the hometown fans with a home run in the bottom of the fourth, making it 4-2. Curveballer Maglie, who would become one of the heroes of the Giants' breathtaking drive to a "miracle" pennant that year, coughed up another home run ball in the fifth, and again it was a blow that struck pride through the city of Detroit—Tiger third baseman George Kell rapped it out, cutting the N.L. lead to 4-3.

The home run continued to be the game's most fashionable hit as Brooklyn's Hodges hit one in the sixth with a man aboard to make it 6-3. This blow dampened some of the local ardor, as it was struck against Detroit righthander Fred Hutchinson. The Nationals scored another run off Hutch in the seventh on a squeeze bunt by Jackie Robinson.

With Don Newcombe pitching three innings of scoreless ball and Ewell Blackwell working the final inning, the American League was shut down over the final four. The Nationals closed out the scoring in the eighth inning when Ralph Kiner cleared the wall against Mel Parnell, leaving the score at 8-3. For Kiner, the most prolific home run hitter of the time, it gave him a unique distinction—home runs in three consecutive All-Star Games.

Having now won two straight games and reduced its series deficit to 12-6, the National League was feeling a bit more comfortable about the midsummer classic. Although it was still only an exhibition, Jackie Robinson summed up the general feeling in the athletes' simple but compelling credo: "It's always better when you win."

Part of the American League contingent at the 1951 All-Star Game (left to right): Vic Wertz, Ted Williams, Joe DiMaggio and Minnie Minoso.

National League catcher Roy Campanella tags out American Leaguer Ferris Fain at the plate in the second inning of the 1951 midseason classic.

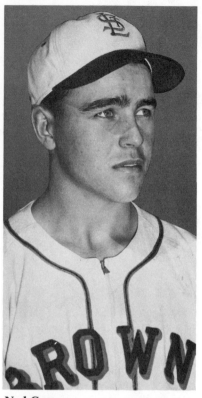

Ned Garver.

Don Newcombe.

Bob Elliott.

The National League's home run-hitting heroes gather for a post-game celebration (left to right standing): Bob Elliott, Gil Hodges, Ralph Kiner and Stan Musial. Seated are N.L. Manager Eddie Sawyer (left) and league President Ford Frick.

Sal Maglie.

George Kell.

Gil Hodges.

It rained on the morning of the 1952 All-Star Game and the rains kept up an intermittent pattern throughout the afternoon. The weather deprived the squads of batting practice and pre-game drills and forced a delay of almost 20 minutes in the start of the game. The game was finally called after five innings, the first and thus far only All-Star affair to be abbreviated because of unco-operative weather.

The game was played on July 8 at Shibe Park in Philadelphia and, appropriately enough, featured some fine work by local artisans, lefthanders Curt Simmons of the Phillies and Bobby Shantz of the Athletics (then still based in the city).

National League Manager Leo Durocher started Simmons; Casey Stengel countered with his own Vic Raschi.

Raschi, working in his fourth All-Star Game in five years, was ruffled early. With one out in the bottom of the first, Jackie Robinson hit one into the upper left-field stands for a 1-0 National League lead.

After Simmons had delivered three innings of one-hit, shutout ball, the American Leaguers went after Chicago Cubs righthander Bob Rush in the fourth inning. Minnie Minoso of the White Sox opened with a double and Cleveland's Al Rosen walked. After an out, the White Sox's Eddie Robinson ripped a single off second baseman Jackie Robinson's glove into right field, scoring Minoso and sending Rosen to third. Cleveland's Bobby Avila then scratched out an infield hit to score Rosen, giving the A.L. a 2-1 edge. Rush averted further damage by getting Phil Rizzuto to ground into a double play.

With Bob Lemon on the mound for the American League, the Nationals retaliated in their half of the fourth and took a 3-2 lead. Stan Musial was nicked with a pitch and the Cubs' Hank Sauer, enjoying a banner year that earned him the Most Valuable

Player award, drove Lemon's first delivery on a booming flight to the left-field roof, sending the Nationals in front.

Rush blanked the Americans in the fifth and then Shantz took over for Lemon. The 5-foot-6 Shantz, a small man having a big year (he boasted a 24-7 record at season's end and captured an MVP plaque), put on a brief but memorable show. Thrilling his hometown fans, he struck out, in order, Whitey Lockman of the Giants, Jackie Robinson and Musial. Whether Bobby could have gone on and tied or broken Carl Hubbell's record-book five consecutive strikeouts not even a computer can tell us.

With Rush pitching to Minoso in the sixth, the rain, falling heavily now, caused the game to be halted. After a 56-minute delay, the game was called, leaving Bobby Shantz on the rim of the record books and sealing a 3-2 National League victory, the senior league's third consecutive triumph.

Short and Sweet

Americans	AB.	R.	H.	RBI.	PO.	A.
DiMaggio (Red Sox), cf	2	0	1	0	1	0
Doby (Indians), cf	0	0	0	0	0	0
Bauer (Yankees), rf	3	0	1	0	2	0
Jensen (Senators), rf	0	0	0	0	0	0
Mitchell (Indians), lf	1	0	0	0	1	0
cMinoso (White Sox), lf	1	1	1	0	0	0
Rosen (Indians), 3b	1	1	0	0	3	1
Berra (Yankees), c	2	0	0	0	6	0
E. Robinson (W. Sox), 1b	2	0	1	1	1	0
Avila (Indians), 2b	2	0	1	1	0	0
Rizzuto (Yankees), ss	2	0	0	0	1	0
Raschi (Yankees), p	0	0	0	0	0	0
aMcDougald (Yankees)	1	0	0	0	0	0
Lemon (Indians), p	1	0	0	0	0	0
Shantz (Athletics), p	0	0	0	0	0	0
Totals	18	2	5	2	15	1

Nationals	AB.	R.	H.	RBI.	PO.	A.
Lockman (Giants), 1b	3	0	0	0	5	0
J. Robinson (Dodgers), 2b.	3	1	1	1	2	2
Musial (Cardinals), cf	2	1	0	0	1	0
Sauer (Cubs), lf	2	1	1	2	0	0
Campanella (Dodgers), c..	1	0	0	0	5	1
Slaughter (Cardinals), rf ..	2	0	1	0	0	0
Thomson (Giants), 3b	2	0	0	0	1	1
Hamner (Phillies), ss	1	0	0	0	1	3
Simmons (Phillies), p	0	0	0	0	0	0
bReese (Dodgers)	1	0	0	0	0	0
Rush (Cubs), p	1	0	0	0	0	0
Totals	18	3	3	3	15	7

American League .... 0 0 0   2 0—2
National League .... 1 0 0   2 0—3
Stopped by rain.

Americans	IP.	H.	R.	ER.	BB.	SO.
Raschi	2	1	1	1	0	3
Lemon (L)	2	2	2	2	2	0
Shantz	1	0	0	0	0	3

Nationals	IP.	H.	R.	ER.	BB.	SO.
Simmons	3	1	0	0	1	3
Rush (W)	2	4	2	2	1	1

aGrounded out for Raschi in third. bFlied out for Simmons in third. cDoubled for Mitchell in fourth. DP—Nationals 1. LOB—Americans 3, Nationals 3. 2B—DiMaggio, Minoso, Slaughter. HR—J. Robinson, Sauer. HBP—By Lemon (Musial). U—Barlick, Boggess and Warneke (N.L.), Berry, Summers and Soar (A.L.). T—1:29. A—32,785.

American League Manager Casey Stengel and young lefthander Bobby Shantz.

Curt Simmons.

Jackie Robinson.

Hank Sauer.

Minnie Minoso.

Ugly in July

Americans	AB.	R.	H.	RBI.	PO.	A.
Goodman (Red Sox), 2b	2	0	0	0	1	1
Fox (White Sox), 2b............	1	0	0	0	1	0
Vernon (Senators), 1b........	3	0	0	0	6	0
Fain (White Sox), 1b	1	1	1	0	1	1
Bauer (Yankees), rf	2	0	0	0	3	0
jMize (Yankees)..................	1	0	1	0	0	0
Mantle (Yankees), cf...........	2	0	0	0	0	0
eHunter (Browns)...............	0	0	0	0	0	0
Doby (Indians), cf..............	1	0	0	0	1	1
Rosen (Indians), 3b...........	4	0	0	0	2	4
Zernial (Athletics), lf.........	2	0	1	0	1	0
Minoso (White Sox), lf	2	0	2	1	0	0
Berra (Yankees), c.............	4	0	0	0	4	0
Carrasquel (W. Sox), ss......	2	0	0	0	2	1
gKell (Red Sox).................	1	0	0	0	0	0
Rizzuto (Yankees), ss.........	0	0	0	0	1	0
Pierce (White Sox), p..........	1	0	0	0	0	0
Reynolds (Yankees), p........	0	0	0	0	0	0
cKuenn (Tigers)..................	1	0	0	0	0	0
Garcia (Indians), p.............	0	0	0	0	1	0
hE. Robinson (Athletics)...	1	0	0	0	0	0
Paige (Browns), p..............	0	0	0	0	0	0
Totals	31	1	5	1	24	8

Nationals	AB.	R.	H.	RBI.	PO.	A.
Reese (Dodgers), ss............	4	0	2	2	1	1
Hamner (Phillies), ss..........	0	0	0	0	0	0
Schoendienst (Cards), 2b..	3	0	0	0	0	3
Williams (Giants), 2b.........	0	0	0	0	2	0
Musial (Cardinals), lf.........	4	0	2	0	3	0
Kluszewski (Reds), 1b........	3	1	0	5	0	0
dHodges (Dodgers), 1b.......	1	0	0	0	1	0
Campanella (Dodgers), c...	4	1	1	0	6	2
Mathews (Braves), 3b........	3	1	0	0	0	0
Bell (Reds), cf...................	3	0	0	0	4	0
iSnider (Dodgers), cf..........	0	1	0	0	1	0
Slaughter (Cardinals), rf ...	3	2	2	1	4	0
Roberts (Phillies), p...........	0	0	0	0	0	1
aKiner (Cubs)....................	1	0	0	0	0	0
Spahn (Braves), p..............	0	0	0	0	0	0
bAshburn (Phillies)............	1	0	1	1	0	0
Simmons (Phillies), p.........	0	0	0	0	0	0
fJ. Robinson (Dodgers)......	1	0	0	0	0	0
Dickson (Pirates), p...........	1	0	1	1	0	0
Totals..........................	32	5	10	5	27	7

```
American League .................. 0 0 0  0 0 0  0 0 1—1
National League ..................0 0 0  0 2 0  1 2 x—5
```

Americans	IP.	H.	R.	ER.	BB.	SO.
Pierce.............................	3	1	0	0	0	1
Reynolds (L).....................	2	2	2	2	1	0
Garcia..............................	2	4	1	1	1	2
Paige	1	3	2	2	1	0

Nationals	IP.	H.	R.	ER.	BB.	SO.
Roberts.............................	3	1	0	0	1	2
Spahn (W)	2	0	0	0	1	2
Simmons...........................	2	1	0	0	1	1
Dickson............................	2	3	1	1	0	0

aStruck out for Roberts in third. bSingled for Spahn in fifth. cLined out for Reynolds in sixth. dRan for Kluszewski in sixth. eRan for Mantle in seventh. fPopped out for Simmons in seventh. gFlied out for Carrasquel in eighth. hLined out for Garcia in eighth. iWalked for Bell in eighth. jSingled for Bauer in ninth. DP—Americans 1. LOB—Americans 6, Nationals 7. 2B—Reese. SB—Slaughter. HBP—By Reynolds (Mathews). U—Conlan, Donatelli and Engeln (N.L.), Stevens, McKinley and Napp (A.L.). T—2:19. A—30,846.

"I can't understand it," Casey Stengel said. "I'm beautiful in October and ugly in July."

Stengel was referring to the fact that he had directed World Series victories in 1949, 1950, 1951 and 1952 as manager of the Yankees but had suffered All-Star Game losses in 1950, 1951, 1952 and 1953 while guiding the American League squad. The Nationals' fourth straight triumph in the '53 game, in fact, equaled the hammerlock that the Americans had held on the N.L. from 1946 through 1949.

All-Star Game No. 20 was played on July 14 at Cincinnati's Crosley Field. Crosley was a comparatively small park; indeed, 185 home runs were hit there in 1953. Oddly, despite the accommodating fences, no homers were struck in the 1953 All-Star Game, the first time since 1944 that one of these games went without a big bang.

National League Manager Charlie Dressen of the Brooklyn Dodgers started things off with the right man, the Phillies' Robin Roberts, a 28-game winner the year before and on his way to 23 victories this season. Opposing him was White Sox lefthander Billy Pierce. The two starters worked with similar efficiency, each delivering three innings of one-hit, shutout ball. The batons were then handed to Warren Spahn of the Braves and the Yankees' Allie Reynolds, each of whom continued painting circles on the scoreboard.

In the bottom of the fifth, the Nationals began roiling the waters. With one out, young slugger Eddie Mathews of the Braves was hit on the foot by a Reynolds pitch. After another out, the Cardinals' 37-year-old Enos Slaughter walked. Richie Ashburn batted for Spahn and singled to center, scoring Mathews with the icebreaker. Up came Brooklyn's Pee Wee Reese, laboring under a 0-for-15 All-Star Game history, dating to 1942. But Pee Wee ended his 11-year slump with a single that scored Slaughter.

In the sixth inning, with Curt

Simmons now on the mound for the Nationals, Slaughter ran down a drive hit by Detroit's Harvey Kuenn, making a diving, tumbling grab along the right-field line that was hailed as one of the greatest defensive plays ever seen in the midsummer pageant.

The score held at 2-0 until the seventh. Then, against Cleveland's fastballing righthander, Mike Garcia, who had survived a first-and-third, no-out scare in the sixth, the Nationals scored again. With one out, Slaughter singled and stole second. A moment later, Enos checked in on Reese's double, the game's lone extra-base hit.

In the eighth inning, Stengel brought in Satchel Paige to pitch. The 47-year-old Paige, the oldest man ever to play in an All-Star Game and an employee of the St. Louis Browns, was one of the game's bona fide legends. Denied an opportunity in Organized Baseball because of the color barrier, Paige had not reached the major leagues until 1948, with the Cleveland Indians. With ace pitcher Bob Lemon still available to him, Stengel opted for Paige, a decision that probably had an element of theater to it. But Casey was never averse to crowd-pleasing.

The Nationals, however, showed the venerable Paige no courtesies. With one out, Brooklyn's Roy Campanella singled. After another out, the Dodgers' Duke Snider walked. Up came the veteran Slaughter, a mere stripling compared with Paige. Enos, who already had stolen the show with his bat, legs and glove, stayed hot with a single to center that scored Campanella. Pittsburgh's 36-year-old Murry Dickson, who had come in to pitch in the top of the eighth, popped a single into short left-center to score Snider, making it a 5-0 game. Murry, however, got frisky on the base paths and was thrown out at second trying to make two bases out of what clearly had been designed as one.

Held to just two singles for eight innings, the American League staged a minor flurry in the ninth and escaped the embarrassment of a shutout. Singles by Ferris Fain, Johnny Mize and Minnie Minoso were worth a run, but Dickson allowed nothing further. The final score was 5-1.

The American League advantage in games, which once stood at 12-4, now had been trimmed to 12-8.

Billy Pierce.

Members of the American League's 1953 All-Star team (left to right): Billy Goodman, Al Rosen, Yogi Berra, Mickey Mantle and George Kell.

National League President Warren Giles (right) congratulates Pee Wee Reese after the N.L.'s 1953 victory. Manager Charlie Dressen (back left) and Enos Slaughter enjoy the celebration.

Satchel Paige, in his Kansas City Monarchs Negro League uniform before reaching the major leagues.

Robin Roberts.

Warren Spahn.

Bombs Away

Nationals	AB.	R.	H.	RBI.	PO.	A.
Hamner (Phillies), 2b	3	0	0	0	0	0
Schoendienst (Cards), 2b	2	0	0	0	1	0
Dark (Giants), ss	5	0	1	0	1	2
Snider (Dodgers), cf-rf	4	2	3	0	2	0
Musial (Cardinals), rf-lf	5	1	2	0	2	1
Kluszewski (Reds), 1b	4	2	2	3	5	0
Hodges, (Dodgers), 1b	1	0	0	0	1	0
Jablonski (Cardinals), 3b	3	1	1	1	0	1
Jackson (Cubs), 3b	2	0	0	0	1	1
Robinson (Dodgers), lf	2	1	1	2	0	0
Mays (Giants), cf	2	1	1	0	1	0
Campanella (Dodgers), c	3	0	1	0	9	0
Burgess (Phillies), c	0	0	0	0	1	0
Roberts (Phillies), p	1	0	0	0	0	0
aMueller (Giants)	1	0	1	1	0	0
Antonelli (Giants), p	0	0	0	0	0	0
cThomas (Pirates)	1	0	0	0	0	0
Spahn (Braves), p	0	0	0	0	0	0
Grissom (Giants), p	0	0	0	0	0	0
eBell (Reds)	1	1	1	2	0	0
Conley (Braves), p	0	0	0	0	0	0
Erskine (Dodgers), p	0	0	0	0	0	0
Totals	40	9	14	9	24	5

Americans	AB.	R.	H.	RBI.	PO.	A.
Minoso (White Sox), lf-rf	4	1	2	0	1	0
Piersall (Red Sox), rf	0	0	0	0	0	0
Avila (Indians), 2b	3	1	3	2	1	1
Keegan (White Sox), p	0	0	0	0	0	0
Stone (Senators), p	0	0	0	0	0	0
fDoby (Indians), cf	1	1	1	1	0	0
Mantle (Yankees), cf	5	1	2	0	2	0
Trucks (White Sox), p	0	0	0	0	0	0
Berra (Yankees), c	4	2	2	0	5	0
Rosen (Indians), 1b-3b	4	2	3	5	7	0
Boone (Tigers), 3b	4	1	1	1	1	3
gVernon (Senators), 1b	1	0	0	0	1	0
Bauer (Yankees), rf	2	0	0	1	0	0
Porterfield (Senators), p	1	0	0	0	0	0
dFox (White Sox), 2b	2	0	1	2	1	0
Carrasquel (W. Sox), ss	5	1	1	0	5	4
Ford (Yankees), p	1	0	0	0	0	0
Consuegra (White Sox), p	0	0	0	0	0	0
Lemon (Indians), p	0	0	0	0	0	0
bWilliams (Red Sox), lf	2	1	0	0	2	0
Noren (Yankees), lf	0	0	0	0	0	0
Totals	39	11	17	11	27	8

National League ...... 0 0 0 5 2 0 0 2 0—9
American League ...... 0 0 4 1 2 1 0 3 x—11

Nationals	IP.	H.	R.	ER.	BB.	SO.
Roberts	3	5	4	4	2	5
Antonelli	2	4	3	3	0	2
Spahn	⅔	4	1	1	1	0
Grissom	1⅓	0	0	0	0	2
Conley (L)	⅓	3	3	3	1	0
Erskine	⅔	1	0	0	0	1

Americans	IP.	H.	R.	ER.	BB.	SO.
Ford	3	1	0	0	1	0
Consuegra	⅓	5	5	5	0	0
Lemon	⅔	1	0	0	0	0
Porterfield	3	4	2	2	0	1
Keegan	⅔	3	2	2	0	1
Stone (W)	⅓	0	0	0	0	0
Trucks	1	0	0	0	1	0

aDoubled for Roberts in fourth. bStruck out for Lemon in fourth. cStruck out for Antonelli in sixth. dStruck out for Porterfield in seventh. eHomered for Grissom in eighth. fHomered for Stone in eighth. gStruck out for Boone in eighth. E—Minoso. DP—Americans 1. LOB—Nationals 6, Americans 9. 2B—Robinson, Mueller, Snider. HR—Rosen 2, Boone, Kluszewski, Bell, Doby. SF—Avila. U—Rommel, Honochick and Paparella (A.L.), Ballanfant, Stewart and Gorman (N.L.). T—3:10. A—68,751.

The greatest baseball players in the world got together in the 1954 All-Star Game and put on a real barn-burner, a rip-snortin' bomb-dropper that had all the subtlety of a barroom brawl. Perhaps inspired by the almost 70,000 whoopers and hollerers who came to bear witness at capacious Cleveland Stadium on July 13, the big guns boomed and roared with a vigor that for a time threatened to make an endangered species of the pitching fraternity.

The game tied or established some robust records—most home runs by both teams (6), most homers by one team (4, American League), most runs by both teams (20), most hits by both teams (31), most hits by one team (17, American League) and on and on, including most crushed pitching egos (many). For pure excitement, few, if any, All-Star Games have ever topped this bruiser.

For Casey Stengel, it was a long-awaited first All-Star victory. The losing skipper was a freshman manager in the majors, but one who would endure the good and the bad of it for 23 years and eventually become the dean of big-league managers, Walter Alston. Alston had replaced Charlie Dressen in Brooklyn after Dressen left the club in a contract dispute; Walter also inherited the job of masterminding the National League All-Stars.

It was not uncommon for home-team players to put on smashing performances in All-Star Games (Carl Hubbell at the Polo Grounds in 1934, Ted Williams at Fenway Park in 1946 and Bobby Shantz at Shibe Park in 1952, for example). This sense of theater was never more vividly demonstrated than in the 1954 swing-out at Cleveland's lakefront ball park. Three Indians players

—Al Rosen, Bobby Avila and Larry Doby—delivered gaudy performances that delighted the locals, combining for seven hits in eight at-bats and driving in eight runs.

One of the few pitchers to survive the afternoon with his dignity intact was American League starter Whitey Ford. The classy Yankee lefthander delivered three innings of one-hit, shutout ball which, in the war-zone context, made him a marvel of efficiency.

The National League's Robin Roberts, making his fourth All-Star start in five years, matched Ford for the first two innings, but in the bottom of the third saw his vaunted fastball dispatched on long-distance journeys. Roberts began the inning by walking Minnie Minoso, the popular emissary from the Chicago White Sox. Avila, who went 3 for 3 in the game, hit his second single. Roberts retired the next two batters, then faced Rosen.

Aside from his hitting in the game, Al also provided an intriguing sidebar story. The gritty player was suffering pain from a slow-healing right index finger, which had been fractured a few weeks before; in fact, he had come close to asking to be removed from the game after striking out in the first inning, but his pride forbade it. Swinging through the pain in the third inning, Rosen rode a Roberts pitch over the fence in left-center for a three-run homer. The blow sent the Cleveland fans into loud demonstrations of approval, the echoes of which were still tossing the waters of nearby Lake Erie when Detroit's Ray Boone (a former Indian) followed with another home run belt, making it 4-0.

In the fourth inning, the Nationals greeted White Sox righthander Sandy Consuegra with a fusillade of hits. With one out, Duke Snider and Stan Musial singled. Snider scored when Ted Kluszewski, Cincinnati's Museum of Muscles, singled. The Cardinals' Ray Jablonski kept it going with another single, scoring Musial. Jackie Robinson then drove a double into right-center, knocking in Kluszewski and Jablonski and making it 4-4.

Much to the dismay of the Nationals, Consuegra was given the hook and Cleveland's Bob Lemon took the mound. Bob got an out, but the Giants' Don Mueller hit for Roberts and doubled home Robinson, giving the Nationals a 5-4 lead. Lemon then retired the side.

In the Americans' fourth, ace Giants lefthander Johnny Antonelli was nicked for the tying run on singles by Chico Carrasquel and Minoso and Avila's sacrifice fly.

The Nationals put on another charge in the fifth, against Washington's Bob Porterfield. A single by Snider was followed by a Kluszewski homer and it suddenly was 7-5. The Americans matched that with uncanny precision in their half of the fifth on a single by Yogi Berra and another home run, aching finger or not, by Rosen.

The relentless American League, scoring for the fourth consecutive inning, seized an 8-7 lead in the sixth against Warren Spahn. Ted Williams walked and came around on singles by Minoso and the ever-present Avila. When Avila's hit was boxed around by Musial in left, Minoso tried to go to third but Musial gunned him down. This became an important play because Mickey Mantle and Rosen filled the bases with infield singles. Giants righthander Marv Grissom then replaced Spahn and got Boone to hit an inning-ending fly ball.

After being quieted in the sixth and seventh innings by Porterfield, the Nationals broke loose again in the eighth, roughing up White Sox righthander Bob Keegan. With one out, Willie Mays (yes, there he was, in the first of his 24 All-Star Games) singled. After another out, Cincinnati's Gus Bell, hitting for Grissom, blasted a one-way ticket over the fence in right-center, sending the Nationals bobbing to the top again with a 9-8 edge.

No further N.L. runs followed Bell's blast, but a lot of huffing and puffing ensued in the Nationals' eighth. The Cardinals' Red Schoendienst reached second when Minoso dropped his fly ball after a long run. Alvin Dark of the Giants sent Schoendienst to third with an infield single. At that point, Senators lefthander Dean Stone took over for Keegan. As Stone was pitching to Snider, Schoendienst tried to steal home. Red was out, retiring the side, but National League coaches Charley Grimm and Leo Durocher charged home to claim that Stone, in hurrying his motion, had balked. The protest was given a vigorous airing, but plate umpire Bill Stewart, to no one's surprise, remained unconvinced.

The American Leaguers reared up one more time, scoring three runs in the last of the eighth off 6-foot-8 righthander Gene Conley of the Milwaukee Braves. With one out, Doby sent the hometown folk into fresh extremes of ecstasy when he pinch-hit a game-tying home run. The Yankee connection then took over as Mantle and Berra followed with singles. Conley walked Rosen, loading the bases.

Brooklyn's Carl Erskine replaced Conley and struck out pinch-hitter Mickey Vernon of the Senators for the second out. What happened next was one of those things that keeps the phrase "that's baseball" ever bright and blooming. After all the long-distance belting, it was a bleeding, blooping, dying Texas League tap into short center by the White Sox's Nelson Fox that scored the game's final and winning runs. Fox had struck a telling blow for "the little man."

The Nationals almost made it back in the ninth. With White Sox righthander Virgil Trucks on the mound in place of Stone (who now was the A.L.'s pitcher of record), Snider opened with a walk. Musial then ripped two shots just foul into the right-field stands. Stan then grounded out and Trucks herded the final two batters back into the corral, ending the carnage.

The most pulsating game in All-Star history was over, the Americans winning it by an 11-9 score. And Stone, in a one-for-the-book occurrence, wound up with the pitching victory despite not retiring a single batter.

Al Rosen.

Gus Bell.

Ray Boone.

Duke Snider.

Nelson Fox.

Ted Kluszewski.

Whitey Ford.

Bobby Avila.

Larry Doby.

Stan's the Man

Americans	AB.	R.	H.	RBI.	PO.	A.
Kuenn (Tigers), ss	3	1	1	0	1	0
Carrasquel (W. Sox), ss	3	0	2	0	1	3
Fox (White Sox), 2b	3	1	1	0	2	0
Avila (Indians), 2b	1	0	0	0	1	2
Williams (Red Sox), lf	3	1	1	0	1	0
Smith (Indians), lf	1	0	0	0	0	0
Mantle (Yankees), cf	6	1	2	3	3	0
Berra (Yankees), c	6	1	1	0	8	2
Kaline (Tigers), rf	4	0	1	0	6	0
Vernon (Senators), 1b	5	0	1	1	8	0
Finigan (Athletics), 3b	3	0	0	0	2	0
Rosen (Indians), 3b	2	0	0	0	0	0
Pierce (White Sox), p	0	0	0	0	0	0
bJensen (Red Sox)	1	0	0	0	0	0
Wynn (Indians), p	0	0	0	0	0	1
gPower (Athletics)	1	0	0	0	0	0
Ford (Yankees), p	1	0	0	0	0	1
Sullivan (Red Sox), p	1	0	0	0	0	0
Totals	44	5	10	4	33	9

Nationals	AB.	R.	H.	RBI.	PO.	A.
Schoendienst (Cards), 2b	6	0	2	0	3	2
Ennis (Phillies), lf	1	0	0	0	1	0
cMusial (Cardinals), lf	4	1	1	1	0	0
Snider (Dodgers), cf	2	0	0	0	3	0
Mays (Giants), cf	3	2	2	0	3	0
Kluszewski (Reds), 1b	5	1	2	0	9	1
Mathews (Braves), 3b	2	0	0	0	0	3
Jackson (Cubs), 3b	3	1	1	1	0	0
Mueller (Giants), rf	2	0	1	0	0	0
dAaron (Braves), rf	2	1	2	1	0	0
Banks (Cubs), ss	2	0	0	0	2	1
Logan (Braves), ss	3	0	1	1	1	1
Crandall (Braves), c	1	0	0	0	1	0
eBurgess (Reds), c	1	0	0	0	2	0
hLopata (Phillies), c	3	0	0	0	10	0
Roberts (Phillies), p	0	0	0	0	1	1
aThomas (Pirates)	1	0	0	0	0	0
Haddix (Cardinals), p	0	0	0	0	0	2
fHodges (Dodgers)	1	0	1	0	0	0
Newcombe (Dodgers), p	0	0	0	0	0	0
iBaker (Cubs)	1	0	0	0	0	0
Jones (Cubs), p	0	0	0	0	0	0
Nuxhall (Reds), p	2	0	0	0	0	1
Conley (Braves), p	0	0	0	0	0	0
Totals	45	6	13	4	36	12

American League...4 0 0 0 0 1 0 0 0 0 0 0—5
National League......0 0 0 0 0 0 2 3 0 0 0 1—6
None out when winning run scored.

Americans	IP.	H.	R.	ER.	BB.	SO.
Pierce	3	1	0	0	0	3
Wynn	3	3	0	0	0	1
Ford	1⅔	5	5	3	1	0
Sullivan (L)	3⅓*	4	1	1	1	4

Nationals	IP.	H.	R.	ER.	BB.	SO.
Roberts	3	4	4	4	1	0
Haddix	3	3	1	1	0	2
Newcombe	1	1	0	0	0	1
Jones	⅔	0	0	0	2	1
Nuxhall	3⅓	2	0	0	3	5
Conley (W)	1	0	0	0	0	3

*Pitched to one batter in twelfth.

aPopped out for Roberts in third. bPopped out for Pierce in fourth. cStruck out for Ennis in fourth. dRan for Mueller in fifth. eHit into force play for Crandall in fifth. fSingled for Haddix in sixth. gPopped out for Wynn in seventh. hSafe on error for Burgess in seventh. iFlied out for Newcombe in seventh. E—Carrasquel, Rosen, Mathews. DP—Americans 1, Nationals 1. LOB—Americans 12, Nationals 8. 2B—Kluszewski, Kaline. HR—Mantle, Musial. SH—Pierce, Avila. HBP—By Jones (Kaline). WP—Roberts. PB—Crandall. U—Barlick, Boggess and Secory (N.L.), Soar, Summers and Runge (A.L.). T—3:17. A—45,643.

Milwaukee celebrated its third year of possessing the transplanted Braves by hosting the 1955 All-Star Game at County Stadium. What the 45,000-plus spectators saw was a game symbolic in its implications, for it reflected what was happening in the larger scheme of All-Star competition: The American League got off to an early and substantial lead, only to watch the Nationals begin a late, highly resolved and, finally, triumphant comeback.

The '55 game was played on July 12, the day on which funeral services were held in Chicago for Arch Ward, the Chicago Tribune sports editor who had founded the midsummer classic. Ward had died on July 9.

The opposing managers for the 22nd edition of Ward's "dream game" were Cleveland's Al Lopez and the Giants' Leo Durocher. Lopez started the White Sox's Billy Pierce, and the high-caliber lefthander pitched brilliantly while continuing a curious pattern. For the third straight time, a lefthander starting for the American League pitched three innings of one-hit, scoreless ball—Pierce in 1953, Whitey Ford in 1954 and now Pierce again. Billy was followed by Cleveland's tough, brawny Early Wynn, who also fired three scoreless innings. At the end of six, it was 5-0, American League, and with Ford next out of the chute, the victory seemed waiting only to be gift-wrapped and delivered.

What brought the Nationals to this gloomy circumstance was another rocky outing for Robin Roberts. Starting his fifth All-Star Game in six years, the Phillies' ace again suffered the embarrassment of a four-run inning. A year before, it had been the third inning; this time, the hailstones came from a practically clear sky.

Detroit's Harvey Kuenn opened the game with a single, and a Nelson Fox single sent Kuenn to third. Roberts then gave clear indication that he had sprung a leak by wild-pitching Kuenn home and Fox to second. Working carefully to Ted Williams (there was, one supposes, no other way), Roberts walked him. Mickey Mantle then put one out of sight beyond the center-field fence and it was 4-0. Four men up, four men in.

Roberts held off the Americans

after that and was succeeded in the fourth inning by Cardinals lefthander Harvey Haddix, who held firm until the sixth when a single by Yogi Berra, a double by Detroit's Al Kaline (20 years old and on the way to a batting championship) and a ground ball made it 5-0.

In the Americans' seventh, Willie Mays made the play of the game. Williams slammed a Don Newcombe pitch high and deep to right-center. It looked like another notch in the Williams bat, but Mays made a leaping grab to deprive Ted of a home run. From that moment on, it was all National League.

Ford came on in the bottom of the seventh and the Nationals pounced. Mays led off with a single and, after two outs, the Braves' Henry Aaron (playing in the first of his 23 All-Star Games) walked. Johnny Logan, another delegate from the Milwaukee club, singled Mays home. Phillies catcher Stan Lopata grounded to Chico Carrasquel, but the White Sox's shortstop booted the ball, allowing Aaron to score, making it 5-2. Ford then got the third out.

In the American League's eighth-inning at-bat, Chicago Cubs righthander Sam Jones loaded the bases with two out on a hit batsman and two walks, but Cincinnati lefthander Joe Nuxhall came in and retired the side.

With two out in the Nationals' half of the eighth, singles by Mays, Ted Kluszewski and the Cubs' Randy Jackson scored one run and sent Ford out of the game. Red Sox righthander Frank Sullivan took over and was greeted by Aaron's run-scoring single. As Jackson headed for third, Kaline's throw to the bag got away from Al Rosen and Randy kept on going, scoring the tying run.

After that, Sullivan and Nuxhall matched goose eggs as an All-Star Game went into extra innings for the second time. Nuxhall survived a scare in the 11th. With men on first and second and two out, Berra bounced one over the middle that seemed ticketed for a run-scoring single. Red Schoendienst, however, flashed to his right and made what one writer described as "a miraculous stop," and then completed an off-balance throw that just nipped Berra at first.

After Nuxhall had pitched 3⅓ scoreless innings, Milwaukee's Gene Conley took over in the 12th, much to the delight of the crowd. Gene delighted the fans even more when he fanned Kaline, Mickey Vernon and Rosen, one, two, three.

The leadoff man for the National League in the bottom of the 12th was Stan Musial. As he stood to one side watching Sullivan take his warmups, Musial said to Berra, "I'm getting tired."

"Me too," said the always-agreeable Yogi, catching the entire game for the fifth consecutive year.

The late-afternoon shadows were crossing the infield like a water line as Musial stepped in and eased into his slight, cork-screw crouch. He was tired. He wanted to get out of there. There was one sure way.

Sullivan's first pitch was a fastball; to Musial's unerring eye, it looked ripe. Stan uncoiled.

"I never even looked back," Sullivan said. "As soon as he hit it, I knew that was that."

For Musial, the home run that gave the National League a 6-5, 12-inning victory over the American Leaguers was his record-setting fourth in All-Star competition, breaking a tie with Williams and Ralph Kiner. As he had been on so many other occasions, Stan was The Man that day.

The American and National League contingents line up for the National Anthem before the start of the 1955 All-Star Game at Milwaukee's County Stadium.

Willie Mays.

Stan Musial and Robin Roberts at the 1955 game.

Billy Pierce.

Early Wynn.

Mickey Mantle.

A happy National League squad greets Stan Musial after the St. Louisan's game-winning home run in the 12th inning.

Winning pitcher Gene Conley (left), Joe Nuxhall and Stan Musial examine the bat Musial used to end the 1955 classic.

Stars Shine Bright

Nationals	AB.	R.	H.	RBI.	PO.	A.
Temple (Reds), 2b	4	1	2	1	2	3
Robinson (Reds), lf	2	0	0	0	1	0
dSnider (Dodgers), cf	3	0	0	0	1	0
Musial (Cardinals), rf-lf	4	1	1	1	2	0
Aaron (Braves), lf	1	0	0	0	0	0
Boyer (Cardinals), 3b	5	1	3	1	3	1
Bell (Reds), cf	1	0	0	0	2	0
bMays (Giants), cf-rf	3	2	1	2	2	0
Long (Pirates), 1b	2	0	0	0	6	0
fKluszewski (Reds), 1b	2	1	2	1	2	0
Bailey (Reds), c	3	0	0	0	3	1
Campanella (Dodgers), c..	0	0	0	0	1	0
McMillan (Reds), ss	3	1	2	0	1	5
Friend (Pirates), p	0	0	0	0	0	0
cRepulski (Cardinals)	1	0	0	0	0	0
Spahn (Braves), p	1	0	0	0	0	0
Antonelli (Giants), p	1	0	0	0	1	0
Totals	36	7	11	6	27	10

Americans	AB.	R.	H.	RBI.	PO.	A.
Kuenn (Tigers), ss	5	0	1	0	2	3
Fox (White Sox), 2b	4	1	2	0	1	0
Williams (Red Sox), lf	4	1	1	2	2	0
Mantle (Yankees), cf	4	1	1	1	0	0
Berra (Yankees), c	2	0	2	0	10	1
gLollar (White Sox), c..	2	0	1	0	4	0
Kaline (Tigers), rf	3	0	1	0	0	0
Piersall (Red Sox), rf	1	0	0	0	1	0
Vernon (Red Sox), 1b	2	0	0	0	4	0
hPower (Athletics), 1b	2	0	1	0	3	0
Kell (Orioles), 3b	4	0	1	0	0	1
Pierce (White Sox), p..	0	0	0	0	0	1
aSimpson (Athletics)	1	0	0	0	0	0
Ford (Yankees), p	0	0	0	0	0	0
Wilson (White Sox), p	0	0	0	0	0	0
eMartin (Yankees)	1	0	0	0	0	0
Brewer (Red Sox), p	0	0	0	0	0	0
iBoone (Tigers)	1	0	0	0	0	0
Score (Indians), p	0	0	0	0	0	0
Wynn (Indians), p	0	0	0	0	0	0
jSievers (Senators)	1	0	0	0	0	0
Totals	37	3	11	3	27	7

National League .... 0 0 1 2 1 1 2 0 0—7
American League .... 0 0 0 0 0 3 0 0 0—3

Nationals	IP.	H.	R.	ER.	BB.	SO.
Friend (W)	3	3	0	0	0	3
Spahn	2*	4	3	3	0	1
Antonelli	4	4	0	0	0	1

Americans	IP.	H.	R.	ER.	BB.	SO.
Pierce (L)	3	2	1	1	1	5
Ford	1	3	2	2	1	2
Wilson	1	2	1	1	0	1
Brewer	2	4	3	3	1	2
Score	1	0	0	0	1	1
Wynn	1	0	0	0	0	1

*Pitched to three batters in sixth.

aStruck out for Pierce in third. bHomered for Bell in fourth. cFouled out for Friend in fourth. dFlied out for Robinson in fifth. eGrounded out for Wilson in fifth. fDoubled for Long in sixth. gSingled for Berra in sixth. hFlied out for Vernon in sixth. iLined out for Brewer in seventh. jPopped out for Wynn in ninth. DP—Nationals 1. LOB—Nationals 7, Americans 7. 2B—Kluszewski 2. HR—Mays, Williams, Mantle, Musial. SB—Temple. SH—Friend. WP—Brewer 2. U—Berry, Hurley and Flaherty (A.L.), Pinelli, Gore and Jackowski (N.L.). T—2:45. A—28,843.

It was what you went to an All-Star Game expecting to see—magnificent performances by the sport's greatest players. After all, these contests were advertised as games matching the best versus the best. And if the best couldn't always satisfy the demands of the moment, well, that was the way the eagle flew.

In the 1956 All-Star Game, played at Washington's Griffith Stadium on July 10, the stars of the stars were a promoter's dream. Four home runs were hit and each originated just about where you'd expect: Willie Mays and Stan Musial connected for the National League, and Mickey Mantle (on the way to a Triple Crown season) and Ted Williams for the American. The big boomers notwithstanding, the star of the game—with three singles and three dazzling plays in the field—was St. Louis Cardinals third baseman Ken Boyer.

For the National League, managed by Walter Alston, it was a 7-3 victory, making it six out of the last seven for the Nationals, closing the gap in games to 13-10. The Americans, under Casey Stengel (now 1-5 in the competition), were simply finding it more and more difficult to match the National League firepower.

Alston started Pittsburgh righthander Bob Friend, while Stengel sent out a pitcher he always greatly admired, Billy Pierce. For the White Sox standout, it was his third All-Star start in four years.

The National League's starting lineup featured five Cincinnati Reds—Johnny Temple at second base, Frank Robinson in left field, Gus Bell in center, Ed Bailey catching and Roy McMillan at shortstop. While these were five fine ball players, the votes that put them into the starting lineup were generated, in part, by a Cincinnati radio station's aggressive electoral campaign appealing to civic pride.

Boyer set the tone of the game in the first inning. The American League's first batter, Harvey Kuenn of the Tigers, ripped a low line drive to the left of Boyer, who made a diving, one-handed grab.

Friend sailed through three innings without giving up a run; Pierce was scratched for one in the third on a walk to McMillan, a sacrifice by Friend and a single by Temple.

The American League used three pitchers over the next four innings, and the Nationals scored in each inning. Whitey Ford was first for the Americans. Ford, who never had the success against the National League in All-Star Games that he did in World Series play, struck out Musial to open the fourth but then gave up a single to Boyer and a home run to Mays, batting for Bell.

In the fifth, with White Sox righthander Jim Wilson on the mound, the Nationals' Temple laid down a bunt that rolled mischievously along the third-base line for a single. Johnny went to second on an infield out and scored on another Boyer single, making it 4-0, N.L.

Boyer gave still another demonstration of his versatility in the last of the fifth, and once more the victim was Kuenn. Still determined to hit one past third, Harvey ripped a shot just inside the line, but Boyer flashed to his right, speared the ball and nailed his man at first base.

Stengel's fourth pitcher in six innings was Red Sox righthander Tom Brewer. The Nationals initiated him with a run fashioned out of a Ted Kluszewski double, a

McMillan single and a wild pitch, and now it was 5-0. They did a bit better in the seventh, scoring twice against Brewer on Musial's homer, a Mays walk and another Kluszewski double.

The Americans, meanwhile, had come out of their cocoon in the bottom of the sixth against Warren Spahn. After Nelson Fox singled, Williams and Mantle slugged successive home runs. The Giants' Johnny Antonelli replaced Spahn (who had entered the game in the fourth inning) and pitched shutout ball the rest of the game, allowing four hits. Cleveland pitchers Herb Score and Early Wynn shut down the Nationals in the eighth and ninth.

Boyer made his third superb defensive play in the seventh inning. After earlier going to both his left and right to rob Kuenn, Ken this time victimized Detroit's Ray Boone with a leaping stab of a line drive. The only way to get one past Boyer this afternoon, it seemed, was to hit it underground.

Mickey Mantle and Ted Kluszewski at the 1956 All-Star Game.

The Ted Williams swing.

Stan Musial.

The camera's eye is on Willie Mays.

Ken Boyer.

Nelson Fox (left) and Harvey Kuenn compare gloves before the 1956 classic.

The pitching stalwarts of the National League's 1956 victory were (left to right) Warren Spahn, Johnny Antonelli and Bob Friend.

A.L. Holds On

Americans	AB.	R.	H.	RBI.	PO.	A.
Kuenn (Tigers), ss	2	0	0	1	0	1
McDougald (Yankees), ss.	2	1	0	0	1	0
Fox (White Sox), 2b	4	0	0	0	2	4
Kaline (Tigers), rf	5	1	2	2	1	1
Mantle (Yankees), cf	4	1	1	0	4	0
Williams (Red Sox), lf	3	1	0	0	2	0
Minoso (White Sox), lf	1	0	1	1	1	1
Wertz (Indians), 1b	2	0	1	1	3	0
Skowron (Yankees), 1b	3	1	2	0	5	1
Berra (Yankees), c	3	0	1	1	6	0
Kell (Orioles), 3b	2	0	0	0	0	1
Malzone (Red Sox), 3b	2	0	0	0	1	1
Bunning (Tigers), p	1	0	0	0	0	0
aMaxwell (Tigers)	1	0	1	0	0	0
Loes (Orioles), p	1	0	0	0	0	1
Wynn (Indians), p	0	0	0	0	0	0
Pierce (White Sox), p	1	1	1	0	1	0
Mossi (Indians), p	0	0	0	0	0	0
Grim (Yankees), p	0	0	0	0	0	0
Totals	37	6	10	6	27	11

Nationals	AB.	R.	H.	RBI.	PO.	A.
Temple (Reds), 2b	2	0	0	0	3	0
eSch'nd'nst (Braves), 2b.	2	0	0	0	0	0
Aaron (Braves), rf	4	0	1	0	2	0
Musial (Cardinals), 1b	3	1	1	0	9	0
Mays (Giants), cf	4	2	2	1	2	0
Bailey (Reds), c	3	1	1	0	2	0
hFoiles (Pirates)	1	1	1	0	0	0
Robinson (Reds), lf	2	0	1	0	5	0
fBell (Reds), lf	1	0	1	2	0	0
Hoak (Reds), 3b	1	0	0	0	1	0
bMathews (Braves), 3b.	3	0	0	0	0	1
McMillan (Reds), ss	1	0	0	0	2	0
cBanks (Cubs), ss	3	0	1	1	0	3
Simmons (Phillies), p	0	0	0	0	0	0
Burdette (Braves), p	1	0	0	0	0	0
Sanford (Phillies), p	0	0	0	0	0	0
dMoon (Cardinals)	1	0	0	0	0	0
Jackson (Cardinals), p	0	0	0	0	0	1
gCimoli (Dodgers)	1	0	0	0	0	0
Labine (Dodgers), p	0	0	0	0	0	1
iHodges (Dodgers)	1	0	0	0	0	0
Totals	34	5	9	4	27	5

American League ....0 2 0 0 0 1 0 0 3—6
National League ....0 0 0 0 0 0 2 0 3—5

Americans	IP.	H.	R.	ER.	BB.	SO.
Bunning (W)	3	0	0	0	0	1
Loes	3	3	0	0	0	1
Wynn	⅓	3	2	2	0	0
Pierce	1⅔†	2	3	3	2	3
Mossi	⅔	1	0	0	0	0
Grim	⅓	0	0	0	0	1

Nationals	IP.	H.	R.	ER.	BB.	SO.
Simmons (L)	1*	2	2	2	2	0
Burdette	4	2	2	0	1	0
Sanford	1	2	1	1	0	0
Jackson	2	1	0	0	1	0
Labine	1	3	3	1	0	1

*Pitched to four batters in second.
†Pitched to four batters in ninth.

aSingled for Bunning in fourth. bHit into force play for Hoak in fifth. cHit into double play for McMillan in fifth. dGrounded out for Sanford in sixth. eFlied out for Temple in sixth. fDoubled for Robinson in seventh. gStruck out for Jackson in eighth. hSingled for Bailey in ninth. iFlied out for Labine in ninth. E—Schoendienst. DP—Americans 1. LOB—Americans 9, Nationals 4. 2B—Musial, Skowron, Bell, Minoso. 3B—Mays. SF—Fox. WP—Sanford, Pierce. U—Dascoli, Dixon and Landes (N.L.), Napp, Stevens and Chylak (A.L.). T—2:43. A—30,693.

Those fervent Cincinnati voters were up to their old tricks again in 1957, this time voting their whole team with the exception of first baseman George Crowe and the batboy onto the National League's starting lineup for the All-Star Game. Reacting like an old-time ward heeler, an exasperated Commissioner Ford Frick ignored some of the votes by removing Reds outfielders Gus Bell and Wally Post from the starting nine. To prevent such well-meant, but wrong-headed electoral landslides of this nature in the future, Frick, with the acquiescence of the owners, delivered the All-Star voting responsibility into the hands of the players, managers, and coaches the following year. (In 1970, Commissioner Bowie Kuhn returned the vote to the fans.)

The 1957 game was played at Busch Stadium, St. Louis, and it was overseen by the same managers of a year earlier, Casey Stengel and Walter Alston. For the second time in four years (but for only the second time in eight seasons overall), the American League came up a winner, 6-5, in a contest that with just a bit of license might be called a "one-inning" game. The inning was the ninth.

The game went into the final inning with the visiting American Leaguers holding a 3-2 advantage. Stengel's men had scored twice in the second inning—both runs were charged to Nationals starter Curt Simmons—on an infield hit by Mickey Mantle, a walk to Ted Williams (who batted a skyscraping .388 that year), a single by Cleveland's Vic Wertz and walks to Yogi Berra and Harvey Kuenn. The latter free ticket—which forced in a run—was issued by the Braves' Lew Burdette, who had replaced Simmons after the walk to Berra and recorded two quick outs. Burdette wound up pitching shutout ball in his four-inning stint, yielding only two hits.

The Americans raised the score to 3-0 against Phillies rookie righthander Jack Sanford in the sixth on a Yankee entry—a double by Bill Skowron and a single by Berra.

American League pitching was airtight for six innings. Jim Bunning, Detroit's fine sidewheeling righthander, started and gulped the National lineup like an unfed wolf—nine up, nine down. He was followed by Baltimore Orioles righthander Billy Loes, who spun three more scoreless innings.

The only thing the predominantly National League crowd had to cheer about in the early going was a superb running catch by Willie Mays to rob Al Kaline in the first inning. (The New York Giants' star made another spectacular grab in the eighth, against Williams.)

The Nationals broke into daylight in the seventh against Cleveland veteran Early Wynn, who had just entered the game. Wynn was scuffed by singles by Mays and Cincinnati's Ed Bailey. Alston then sent up Bell, scrubbed from the starting lineup by Frick but installed here as a pinch-hitter. Batting for Reds teammate Frank Robinson, Gus doubled in two runs, making it a one-run A.L. lead. Billy Pierce replaced Wynn and held things in place.

Pierce and Cardinals righthander Larry Jackson (pitching his second straight scoreless inning) kept the score at 3-2 through the eighth inning, then the pot boiled over.

With sinkerballing relief ace Clem Labine of Brooklyn on the mound, Pierce led off the Americans' ninth with an infield single. The Yankees' Gil McDougald was safe when Milwaukee second baseman Red Schoendienst fumbled his grounder. Nelson Fox sacrificed the runners up one station each and then Kaline delivered them with a ringing single. Minnie Minoso, who had entered the game defensively in the eighth inning, brought Kaline around with a double, making it 6-2, Americans.

The Nationals, however, had some kick left. Pierce began the bottom of the ninth by handing out the American League pitching staff's first walk of the game, to Musial. Mays then sliced a triple to right, scoring Musial, and Willie himself came in a moment later on a wild pitch. When Pittsburgh's Hank Foiles singled and Bell walked, things really got sticky.

Cleveland lefthander Don Mossi replaced Pierce and fanned Eddie Mathews for the first out. The Cubs' Ernie Banks singled to left, scoring Foiles and making it 6-5; however, when Bell tried to go to third on the play, the game's key moment occurred. Minoso fielded the ball and fired accurately to Red Sox third baseman Frank Malzone, getting Bell for the second out. Banks, the potential tying run, went to second on the throw.

With the game on the line, the managers relied on familiar faces. Brooklyn's Alston sent up Dodgers veteran Gil Hodges to bat for Labine, and the Yankees' Stengel countered with New York's Bob Grim, a righthander who possessed one of the game's nastier sliders.

Hodges caught hold of one of Grim's pitches and sent a shot to left-center that looked like a BB leaving an air rifle. But a racing Minoso—who in a brief appearance had thus far contributed an RBI double and a crucial outfield assist—brought it all to a dramatic conclusion with a fine running catch.

Willie Mays.

Jim Bunning.

Al Kaline.

Minnie Minoso.

Billy Loes.

Another All-Star appearance for Dizzy Dean, this time behind the microphone.

At bat, Gus Bell.

Yogi Berra.

A Singular Sensation

Nationals	AB.	R.	H.	RBI.	PO.	A.
Mays (Giants), cf	4	2	1	0	1	0
Skinner (Pirates), lf	3	0	1	1	2	0
gWalls (Cubs), lf	1	0	0	0	0	0
Musial (Cardinals), 1b	4	1	1	0	7	0
Aaron (Braves), rf	2	0	0	1	2	0
Banks, (Cubs), ss	3	0	0	0	2	3
Thomas (Pirates), 3b	3	0	1	0	1	3
Mazeroski (Pirates), 2b	4	0	0	0	4	5
Crandall (Braves), c	4	0	0	0	5	0
Spahn (Braves), p	0	0	0	0	0	1
aBlasingame (Cardinals)	1	0	0	0	0	0
Friend (Pirates), p	0	0	0	0	0	0
Jackson (Cardinals), p	0	0	0	0	0	0
fLogan (Braves)	1	0	0	0	0	0
Farrell (Phillies) p	0	0	0	0	0	0
Totals	30	3	4	2	24	12

Americans	AB.	R.	H.	RBI.	PO.	A.
Fox (White Sox), 2b	4	1	2	1	5	3
Mantle (Yankees), cf	2	0	1	0	3	0
Jensen (Red Sox), rf	4	0	0	1	1	0
Cerv (Athletics), lf	2	0	1	0	4	0
O'Dell (Orioles), p	0	0	0	0	0	0
Skowron (Yankees), 1b	4	0	0	0	8	0
Malzone (Red Sox), 3b	4	1	1	0	0	2
Triandos (Orioles), c	2	0	1	0	1	0
cBerra (Yankees), c	2	0	0	0	3	0
Aparicio (White Sox), ss	2	1	0	0	1	1
dWilliams (Red Sox), lf	2	0	0	0	1	0
Kaline (Tigers), lf	0	0	0	0	0	0
Turley (Yankees), p	0	0	0	0	0	0
Narleski (Indians), p	1	0	1	0	0	0
bVernon (Indians)	1	1	1	0	0	0
Wynn (White Sox), p	0	0	0	0	0	0
eMcDougald (Yanks), ss	1	0	1	1	0	3
Totals	31	4	9	3	27	9

National League	2	1	0	0	0	0	0	0	0—3	
American League	1	1	0	0	1	1	0	0	x—4	

Nationals	IP.	H.	R.	ER.	BB.	SO.
Spahn	3	5	2	1	0	0
Friend (L)	2⅓	4	2	1	2	0
Jackson	⅔	0	0	0	0	0
Farrell	2	0	0	0	1	4

Americans	IP.	H.	R.	ER.	BB.	SO.
Turley	1⅔	3	3	3	2	0
Narleski	3⅓	1	0	0	1	0
Wynn (W)	1	0	0	0	0	0
O'Dell	3	0	0	0	0	2

aFlied out for Spahn in fourth. bSingled for Narleski in fifth. cPopped out for Triandos in sixth. dSafe on error for Aparicio in sixth. eSingled for Wynn in sixth. fFlied out for Jackson in seventh. gGrounded out for Skinner in seventh. E—Banks, Thomas, Fox, Triandos. DP—Nationals 3, Americans 1. LOB—Nationals 5, Americans 7. SB—Mays. SH—O'Dell. SF—Aaron. HBP—By Turley (Banks). WP—Turley. U—Rommel, McKinley and Umont (A.L.), Gorman, Conlan and Secory (N.L.). T—2:13. A—48,829.

The noise of one-base hits dropping is only slightly louder than the sound of one hand clapping. Accordingly, you have an idea of the decibel count at the 1958 All-Star Game—the first contest in All-Star history to pass without an extra-base hit.

This undemonstrative game—the 25th in the series—was played at Baltimore's Memorial Stadium on July 8. The managers were Casey Stengel (for the eighth time in nine years) and Milwaukee's Fred Haney.

There were 13 hits in the game, nine singles by the American League, four by the National (and all of the latter coming in the first three innings). The Nationals went down in order in five of the last six innings, the only man reaching base doing so on an error. It was no way for an All-Star team to comport itself.

Credit, of course, must be given the American League pitchers—except, that is, for starter Bob Turley. The Yankees' fastballing ace took the brunt of the Nationals' "attack," allowing three runs and three hits in 1⅔ innings. In the top of the first, Willie Mays (now of the *San Francisco* Giants) led off with a single, went to third on Stan Musial's single and scored on Henry Aaron's sacrifice fly. Another run was edged across on a hit batsman, a walk and a wild pitch.

The American League also scored in the first inning, getting a tainted run. Nelson Fox was safe on an error by shortstop Ernie Banks, went to third on Mickey Mantle's single and scored as Jackie Jensen of the Red Sox was banging into a double play. This was against National League starter Warren Spahn.

In the second, the Nationals scored their final run of the day. Spahn walked and was forced by Mays, who stole second, continued to third on an errant throw by Baltimore catcher Gus Triandos and then scored on a single by Pittsburgh's Bob Skinner. At that point, Stengel yanked Turley and replaced him with Cleveland's Ray Narleski, a righthander who threw hard.

Narleski was on the money for 3⅓ innings, and he was followed by Early Wynn for one inning and then Baltimore's own Billy O'Dell, a talented lefthander who warmed the hearts of the locals by pitching three perfect innings.

The American League had scored in the second on an RBI single by Fox, making it 3-2, Nationals. The Americans then got single runs off Bob Friend in the fifth and sixth, scoring in the fifth on two singles, a walk and a groundout and netting the winning run in the sixth on Frank Malzone's single, an error by Pirates third baseman Frank Thomas and a single by Gil McDougald.

While righthanders Larry Jackson of the Cardinals and Dick Farrell of the Phillies held the Americans after that (Farrell struck out four batters in two innings), the damage—as underwhelming as it was—had been done. National League bats remained to the end as gentle as palm fronds and the final score was 4-3, American League.

Henry Aaron.

Baltimore's Memorial Stadium, site of the 1958 All-Star Game.

Larry Jackson.

Ray Narleski.

Gil McDougald.

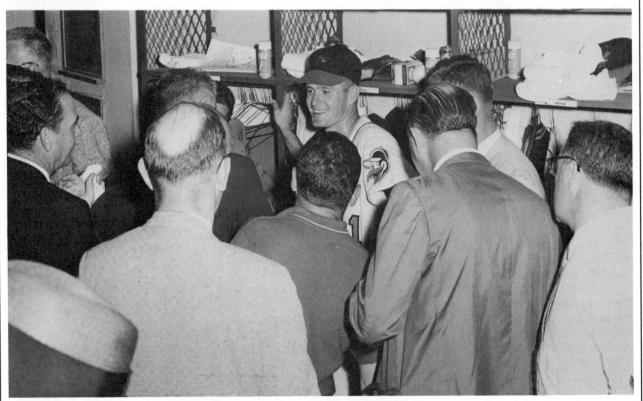

Billy O'Dell meets the press after his shutout pitching in the 1958 game.

The first game of the first All-Star "doubleheader" was played at Forbes Field, Pittsburgh, on July 7, 1959, in conjunction with the city's bicentennial celebration. The game featured some dazzling work by Los Angeles' Don Drysdale, making the first of eight All-Star appearances that would stamp the Dodger righthander as one of the most effective pitchers in the classic's history.

The 26th midseason game started out as a blazing pitching duel. After Drysdale had pitched three perfect innings, striking out four, National League Manager Fred Haney of the Braves brought in one of his own aces, Lew Burdette. Burdette, who was frequently accused of throwing wet baseballs (the accusations grew so noisy through the years that one might have expected Lew to be pitching with a tarpaulin on the mound), yielded one run in his three-inning stint, a home run by Al Kaline in the fourth inning.

Kaline's homer matched a shot launched by the Nationals' Eddie Mathews off Early Wynn in the first inning. Wynn allowed only one other hit in his three innings. He was followed by Yankees reliever Ryne Duren, whom skipper Casey Stengel turned loose for three innings. Duren, whose fastball arrived with eye-blink suddenness, smothered the Nationals through the sixth, at which point the game was a 1-1 tie.

Pittsburgh reliever Roy Face then took over for the National League, much to the delight of the hometown fans, and he retired the Americans in order in the seventh inning.

In the Nationals' seventh, the bats began coming out of the rack with some smoke on them. With Detroit's Jim Bunning on the mound, the National Leaguers broke the tie with two runs. The

A Double Dose

Americans	AB.	R.	H.	RBI.	PO.	A.
Minoso (Indians), lf	5	0	0	0	0	1
Fox (White Sox), 2b	5	1	2	0	2	0
Kaline (Tigers), cf	3	1	1	1	1	0
Kuenn (Tigers), cf	1	1	0	0	0	0
Skowron (Yankees), 1b	3	0	2	0	3	0
Power (Indians), 1b	1	1	1	1	3	0
Colavito (Indians), rf	3	0	1	0	1	0
bWilliams (Red Sox)	0	0	0	0	0	0
cMcDougald (Yanks), ss	0	0	0	0	0	0
Triandos (Orioles), c	4	0	1	2	8	0
fMantle (Yankees), rf	0	0	0	0	0	0
Killebrew (Senators), 3b	3	0	0	0	0	1
Bunning (Tigers), p	0	0	0	0	0	0
dRunnels (Red Sox)	0	0	0	0	0	0
eSievers (Senators)	0	0	0	0	0	0
Ford (Yankees), p	0	0	0	0	0	1
Daley (Athletics), p	0	0	0	0	0	0
Aparicio (White Sox), ss	3	0	0	0	4	2
gLollar (White Sox), c	1	0	0	0	1	0
Wynn (White Sox), p	1	0	0	0	1	0
Duren (Yankees), p	1	0	0	0	0	0
Malzone (Red Sox), 3b	2	0	0	0	0	0
Totals	36	4	8	4	24	5

Nationals	AB.	R.	H.	RBI.	PO.	A.
Temple (Reds), 2b	2	0	0	0	1	3
aMusial (Cardinals)	1	0	0	0	0	0
Face (Pirates), p	0	0	0	0	0	0
Antonelli (Giants), p	0	0	0	0	0	0
hBoyer (Cardinals), 3b	1	1	1	0	1	0
Mathews (Braves), 3b	3	1	1	1	2	1
iGroat (Pirates)	0	0	0	0	0	0
Elston (Cubs), p	0	0	0	0	0	0
Aaron (Braves), rf	4	1	2	1	2	0
Mays (Giants), cf	4	0	1	1	2	0
Banks (Cubs), ss	3	1	2	0	1	2
Cepeda (Giants), 1b	4	0	0	0	6	0
Moon (Dodgers), lf	2	0	0	0	1	0
Crandall (Braves), c	3	1	1	1	10	0
Drysdale (Dodgers), p	1	0	0	0	0	0
Burdette (Braves), p	1	0	0	0	0	0
Mazeroski (Pirates), 2b	1	0	1	1	1	0
Totals	30	5	9	5	27	6

American League	0 0 0	1 0 0	0 3 0—4			
National League	1 0 0	0 0 0	2 2 x—5			

Americans	IP.	H.	R.	ER.	BB.	SO.
Wynn	3	2	1	1	1	3
Duren	3	1	0	0	1	4
Bunning	1	3	2	2	0	1
Ford (L)	1/3	3	2	2	0	0
Daley	2/3	0	0	0	0	1

Nationals	IP.	H.	R.	ER.	BB.	SO.
Drysdale	3	0	0	0	0	4
Burdette	3	4	1	1	0	2
Face	1 2/3	3	3	3	2	2
Antonelli (W)	1/3	0	0	0	1	0
Elston	1	1	0	0	0	1

aPopped out for Temple in sixth. bWalked for Colavito in eighth. cRan for Williams in eighth. dAnnounced as batter for Bunning in eighth. eWalked for Runnels in eighth. fRan for Triandos in eighth. gHit into force play for Aparicio in eighth. hSingled for Antonelli in eighth. iSacrificed for Mathews in eighth. E—Mathews. DP—Americans 1. LOB—Americans 8, Nationals 4. 2B—Banks 2, Triandos. 3B—Mays. HR—Mathews, Kaline. SH —Groat. WP—Elston. U—Barlick, Donatelli and Crawford (N.L.), Runge, Paparella and Rice (A.L.). T—2:33. A—35,277.

Cubs' Ernie Banks started the breakout with a double. After Bunning put away the next two batters, Milwaukee's Del Crandall singled Banks home. Crandall went to second on the throw to the plate and scored a moment later when Pirates second baseman Bill Mazeroski brought the crowd to its feet with a base hit that gave the National League a 3-1 lead.

Inspired by this flurry, the American League responded with one of its own against Face in the eighth inning. The forkballing Face, a Pittsburgh hero all summer (the righthander had a 12-0 record at the break and finished 18-1), retired the first two hitters before Nelson Fox singled and Harvey Kuenn walked. The Indians' Vic Power laced a single that scored Fox and put Kuenn on second. Face then walked a most formidable pinch-hitter, Ted Williams, filling the bases. Baltimore's Gus Triandos met the challenge with a two-run double inside the third-base bag, giving the Americans a 4-3 lead. The Giants' Johnny Antonelli relieved Face and got the side out.

Whitey Ford came on for the American League in the bottom half of the inning. Ken Boyer welcomed the Yankees' star with a single and advanced a notch on a sacrifice. Henry Aaron then singled to center, scoring Boyer and tying the game.

Up next was Willie Mays. Ford no doubt was aware of his history vis-a-vis Willie in these games. They had faced each other three times in All-Star competition—twice in 1955, when Mays reached Ford for two singles, and once in 1956, when the Giants' star lathered Whitey for a home run.

Willie quickly made it 4 for 4, and with emphasis, driving the ball to deep right-center for a triple, scoring Aaron. Ford departed and, with one out and Mays on third, Athletics lefthander Bud Daley retired the side without further scoring.

Chicago Cubs righthander Don Elston put the American Leaguers away in the ninth and the game went into the books as a 5-4 National League victory.

Taking a leaf from Joe McCarthy's old book, Haney let six of his starters go the full nine innings—Aaron, Mays, Banks, Crandall, the Dodgers' Wally Moon and the Giants' Orlando Cepeda.

Don Drysdale.

Willie Mays.

Frank Robinson (left) and Orlando Cepeda check out the All-Star program.

Ryne Duren.

Gus Triandos.

Ernie Banks.

Lew Burdette.

Bill Mazeroski displays the skill that made him one of the best second basemen ever.

Eddie Mathews.

Al Kaline.

1959

The second All-Star Game of 1959 was contested in a grand monstrosity of a ball park, the Los Angeles Memorial Coliseum (the makeshift home of the Dodgers, who were two years removed from their Brooklyn origins and awaiting construction of a new stadium).

From home plate to the left-field foul pole at the Coliseum, it was 251 feet. In an attempt to compensate for this unusually cozy distance, a 40-foot screen had been installed at the left-field wall. Conversely, fences were distant in center field and right-center. No matter, baseball's best players were ready to square off on August 3.

Personnel was to differ little from the July game, except for injury-related substitutions (which, it turned out, forced numerous alterations in the Americans' roster) and pitching changes.

For this game, the managers were not bound to a voted-in starting lineup; instead, they could start whichever players they wanted from the All-Star rosters. Casey Stengel took advantage of this to stack his lineup with lefthanded hitters against righthander Don Drysdale, again opening for the Nationals. Stengel's first six batters all hit from the left side: Pete Runnels of the Red Sox, Nelson Fox, Ted Williams, Yogi Berra, Mickey Mantle (a switch-hitter) and the Athletics' Roger Maris (who would be traded to the Yankees in December).

A.L. Wins, but . . .

Americans	AB.	R.	H.	RBI.	PO.	A.
Runnels (Red Sox), 1b	3	0	0	0	9	0
Power (Indians), 1b	1	0	0	0	4	0
Fox (White Sox), 2b	4	1	2	1	3	1
Williams (Red Sox), lf	3	0	0	0	0	0
Kaline (Tigers), lf-cf	2	0	0	0	0	0
Berra (Yankees), c	3	1	1	2	2	0
Lollar (White Sox), c	0	0	0	0	2	0
Mantle (Yankees), cf	3	0	1	0	3	0
O'Dell (Orioles), p	0	0	0	0	0	0
McLish (Indians), p	0	0	0	0	0	0
Maris (Athletics), rf	2	0	0	0	1	0
Colavito (Indians), rf	2	1	1	1	0	0
Malzone (Red Sox), 3b	4	1	1	1	1	6
Aparicio (White Sox), ss	3	0	0	0	1	2
Walker (Orioles), p	1	0	0	0	0	0
bWoodling (Orioles)	1	0	0	0	0	0
Wynn (White Sox), p	0	0	0	0	1	0
Wilhelm (Orioles), p	0	0	0	0	0	0
fKubek (Yankees), lf	1	1	0	0	0	0
Totals	33	5	6	5	27	9

Nationals	AB.	R.	H.	RBI.	PO.	A.
Temple (Reds), 2b	2	1	1	0	1	1
dGilliam (Dodgers), 3b	2	1	1	1	0	0
Boyer (Cardinals), 3b	2	0	0	0	0	1
Neal (Dodgers), 2b	1	0	0	0	0	2
Aaron (Braves), rf	3	0	1	1	2	0
Mays (Giants), cf	4	0	0	0	3	0
Banks (Cubs), ss	4	0	0	0	2	0
Musial (Cardinals), 1b	0	0	0	0	3	1
Robinson (Reds), 1b	3	1	3	1	3	0
Moon (Dodgers), lf	2	0	0	0	1	0
Crandall (Braves), c	2	0	1	0	7	1
Smith (Cardinals), c	2	0	0	0	5	0
Drysdale (Dodgers), p	0	0	0	0	0	0
aMathews (Braves)	1	0	0	0	0	0
Conley (Phillies), p	0	0	0	0	0	1
cCunningham (Cards)	1	0	0	0	0	0
ePinson (Reds)	0	0	0	0	0	0
Jones (Giants), p	0	0	0	0	0	1
gGroat (Pirates)	1	0	0	0	0	0
Face (Pirates), p	0	0	0	0	0	0
hBurgess (Pirates)	1	0	0	0	0	0
Totals	31	3	6	3	27	7

American League ....0 1 2 0 0 0 1 1 0—5
National League ....1 0 0 0 1 0 1 0 0—3

Americans	IP.	H.	R.	ER.	BB.	SO.
Walker (W)	3	2	1	1	1	1
Wynn	2	1	1	1	3	1
Wilhelm	1	1	0	0	0	0
O'Dell	1	1	1	1	0	0
McLish	2	1	0	0	1	2

Nationals	IP.	H.	R.	ER.	BB.	SO.
Drysdale (L)	3	4	3	3	3	5
Conley	2	0	0	0	1	2
Jones	2	1	1	0	2	3
Face	2	1	1	1	0	2

aStruck out for Drysdale in third. bGrounded out for Walker in fourth. cHit into force play for Conley in fifth. dWalked for Temple in fifth. eRan for Cunningham in fifth. fWalked for Wilhelm in seventh. gGrounded out for Jones in seventh. hGrounded out for Face in ninth. E—Banks, Robinson, Jones. DP—Americans 1. LOB—Americans 7, Nationals 7. 2B—Temple. HR—Malzone, Berra, Robinson, Gilliam, Colavito. SB—Aparicio. SF—Aaron. U—Jackowski, Venzon and Burkhart (N.L.), Berry, Summers and Soar (A.L.). T—2:42. A—55,105.

The Baltimore Orioles' Jerry Walker, a 20-year-old righthander, started for the American League and was touched for a run in the first inning. The Reds' Johnny Temple opened with a double on a ball that bounced past Williams in left, and he came around on a groundout and Henry Aaron's sacrifice fly.

Drysdale, who maneuvered through the first inning without any trouble, encountered a rough spot in the second caused, ironically, by a righthanded hitter. After Mantle had been caught attempting to steal (after bunting for a hit) and Maris struck out, the Red Sox's Frank Malzone popped one just over the sociable screen in left to tie the score.

In the third inning, Drysdale, in one of his few ineffective All-Star outings, gave up a single to Fox and then a home run to Berra, making it 3-1, Americans.

The Nationals made it 3-2 in the fifth when Cincinnati's Frank Robinson hit a long home run into the left-center bleachers against Early Wynn.

With Drysdale's departure, National League pitching buzzed through three hitless innings, two by the Phillies' Gene Conley and one by the Giants' Sam Jones.

Then, in the seventh, the Americans scored an untidy run against Jones. The Yankees' Tony Kubek opened with a walk and advanced to second on Jones' errant pickoff attempt. Kubek reached third and Runnels first when Ernie Banks fumbled Pete's grounder. Fox, seemingly ubiquitous in American League scoring sessions, then singled Kubek home, making it 4-2, American League.

The Nationals tightened it up in the bottom of the inning when the Dodgers' Jim Gilliam drew the afternoon's loudest cheer with a home run belt over the screen, the shot served up by Baltimore lefthander Billy O'Dell, who had tormented the National Leaguers a year before.

The Americans quickly got the run back when Cleveland's Rocky

Colavito rapped a Roy Face delivery over the screen in the eighth.

With Cleveland righthander Cal McLish trying to protect his team's 5-3 lead in the last of the ninth, the Nationals put on a push. Robinson opened with a single and Wally Moon walked. Cardinals catcher Hal Smith, after two unsuccessful sacrifice attempts, fanned. Pirate Smoky Burgess, pinch-hitting for Face, rolled out, moving the tying runs to second and third.

With Gilliam at bat, the more than 55,000 fans were roaring for the game-tying hit. McLish's full name was Calvin Coolidge Julius Caesar Tuskahoma McLish, and before anyone could say it, Cal had induced Gilliam to ground out to first baseman Vic Power, ending the game.

The American League now held a 16-11 advantage in games. It was a lead that would dissipate quick-ly, as year by year the National League—benefiting more and more from the influx of black talent—asserted its dominance. The makeup of the two squads in the Los Angeles game in 1959 perhaps told a revealing story: One black player, Power, got into the game for the American League; the Nationals showed eight—Gilliam, Aaron, Banks, Robinson, Jones, Willie Mays, the Dodgers' Charlie Neal and the Reds' Vada Pinson.

Frank Robinson.

Nelson Fox.

Frank Malzone.

Relief ace Roy Face (left) of the Pirates and knuckleballer Hoyt Wilhelm of the Orioles.

Yogi Berra.

Rocky Colavito.

Jim Gilliam is greeted by Charlie Neal after his seventh-inning home run in the second 1959 All-Star Game.

1960

FOUR TO

1969

The
Turning
Of
The Tide

1960

The Rampage Begins

Nationals	AB.	R.	H.	RBI.	PO.	A.
Mays (Giants), cf	4	1	3	0	4	0
Pinson (Reds), cf	1	0	0	0	1	0
Skinner (Pirates), lf	4	1	1	1	1	0
Cepeda (Giants), lf	1	0	0	0	0	0
Mathews (Braves), 3b	4	0	0	0	1	0
Boyer (Cardinals), 3b	0	0	0	0	0	2
Aaron (Braves), rf	4	0	0	0	0	1
Clemente (Pirates), rf	1	0	0	0	2	0
Banks (Cubs), ss	4	2	2	2	2	2
Groat (Pirates), ss	0	0	0	0	0	1
Adcock (Braves), 1b	3	0	2	0	3	0
bWhite (Cardinals), 1b	1	0	0	0	4	0
Mazeroski (Pirates), 2b	2	0	1	1	2	2
eMusial (Cardinals)	1	0	1	0	0	0
fTaylor (Phillies)	0	0	0	0	0	0
Neal (Dodgers), 2b	0	0	0	0	0	0
Crandall (Braves), c	3	1	2	1	4	0
Burgess (Pirates), c	1	0	0	0	3	0
Friend (Pirates), p	2	0	0	0	0	0
McCormick (Giants), p	1	0	0	0	0	0
Face (Pirates), p	0	0	0	0	0	0
gLarker (Dodgers)	1	0	0	0	0	0
Buhl (Braves), p	0	0	0	0	0	0
Law (Pirates), p	0	0	0	0	0	0
Totals	38	5	12	5	27	8

Americans	AB.	R.	H.	RBI.	PO.	A.
Minoso (White Sox), lf	3	0	0	0	0	0
Lemon (Senators), lf	1	0	0	0	1	0
Malzone (Red Sox), 3b	3	0	0	1	1	1
Robinson (Orioles), 3b	2	0	0	0	1	0
Maris (Yankees), rf	2	0	0	0	1	0
Kuenn (Indians), rf	3	1	1	0	1	0
Mantle (Yankees), cf	0	0	0	0	2	0
Kaline (Tigers), cf	2	1	2	1	2	0
Skowron (Yankees), 1b	3	0	1	0	9	0
Lary (Tigers), p	0	0	0	0	0	0
hLollar (White Sox)	1	0	0	0	0	0
B. Daley (Athletics), p	0	0	0	0	0	0
Berra (Yankees), c	2	0	0	0	5	0
Howard (Yankees), c	1	0	0	0	4	0
Runnels (Red Sox), 2b	1	0	0	0	0	0
Fox (White Sox), 2b	2	0	1	1	1	3
Hansen (Orioles), ss	2	0	1	0	0	0
Aparicio (White Sox), ss	2	0	0	0	1	1
Monbouquette (R. Sox), p	0	0	0	0	0	0
aWilliams (Red Sox)	1	0	0	0	0	0
Estrada (Orioles), p	0	0	0	0	0	0
Coates (Yankees), p	0	0	0	0	0	1
cSmith (White Sox)	1	0	0	0	0	0
Bell (Indians), p	0	0	0	0	0	1
dGentile (Orioles), 1b	2	0	1	0	0	0
Totals	34	3	6	3	27	8

National League	3 1 1	0 0 0	0 0 0	—5
American League	0 0 0	0 0 1	0 2 0	—3

Nationals	IP.	H.	R.	ER.	BB.	SO.
Friend (W)	3	1	0	0	1	2
McCormick	2⅓	3	1	0	3	2
Face	1⅔	0	0	0	0	2
Buhl	1½	2	2	1	1	1
Law	⅔	0	0	0	0	0

Americans	IP.	H.	R.	ER.	BB.	SO.
Monbouquette (L)	2	5	4	4	0	2
Estrada	1	4	1	1	0	1
Coates	2	2	0	0	0	0
Bell	2	0	0	0	0	0
Lary	1	1	0	0	0	1
B. Daley	1	0	0	0	1	2

aGrounded out for Monbouquette in second. bRan for Adcock in fifth. cFlied out for Coates in fifth. dStruck out for Bell in seventh. eSingled for Mazeroski in eighth. fRan for Musial in eighth. gGrounded into force play for. Face in eighth. hGrounded out for Lary in eighth. E—Mathews 2, Neal, Burgess, B. Daley. DP—Nationals 1, Americans 1. LOB—Nationals 8, Americans 9. 2B—Banks, Mays, Adcock. 3B—Mays. HR—Banks, Crandall, Kaline. SB—Skinner. HBP—by Coates (Mazeroski). WP—Friend. Balk—Friend. U—Honochick, Chylak and Stevens (A.L.), Gorman, Boggess and Smith (N.L.). T—2:39. A—30,619.

The two All-Star Games of 1960 were played nearly back-to-back, on July 11 at Kansas City's Municipal Stadium and July 13 at New York's Yankee Stadium, with the Dodgers' Walter Alston and the White Sox's Al Lopez in charge of the rival teams.

The Kansas City game was played on a blazing-hot afternoon during which the temperature reached an unforgiving 101 degrees. In deference to the extreme heat, neither manager allowed anyone to play a full game; it was the first time in All-Star competition that at least one player didn't go all the way.

It also was the first time an All-Star Game had been played in Kansas City, home of the Athletics since only 1955.

The partisan Kansas City crowd, prepared to cheer *and* perspire, did mostly the latter as the Nationals jumped to a 5-0 lead after three innings. Willie Mays, whom neither rain nor snow nor gloom of night nor the heat of Kansas City could keep from his appointed rounds, opened the game by tripling off Red Sox righthander Bill Monbouquette. Willie came home on a single by the Pirates' Bob Skinner and, after two National Leaguers had been retired, Ernie Banks sent one winging and it was 3-0.

In the second, Milwaukee's Del Crandall hit a home run and it was 4-0, Nationals. A combination of broiling sun and steaming bats helped force Monbouquette from the game after two innings. In the third, against Baltimore righthander Chuck Estrada, the National League scored its fifth and final run of the game. This was styled on a double by Banks and singles by Milwaukee's Joe Adcock and the Pirates' Bill Mazeroski. Thereafter, the Nationals' offense was laid low by right-handers Jim Coates of the Yankees, Gary Bell of the Indians and Frank Lary of the Tigers and lefthander Bud Daley of the Athletics.

Pittsburgh's Bob Friend started for the National League and whipped through three scoreless innings. Giants lefthander Mike McCormick gave up an unearned run in the sixth, an inning in which he had to be bailed out of a bases-loaded jam by Roy Face, who fed a double-play pitch to Luis Aparicio.

Milwaukee's Bob Buhl yielded two runs in the eighth—one earned and one unearned. A boot by Dodgers second baseman Charlie Neal put Harvey Kuenn on base and then Al Kaline (a solid All-Star performer in his career, with a .324 batting average for 16 games) hit one out. That made it 5-3, Nationals.

In the bottom of the ninth, the Americans tried to stir something up, but in that melting heat it wasn't easy. They did get two on with one out, but Pittsburgh's Vernon Law took over for Buhl and retired Brooks Robinson and Kuenn to end it, allowing the bone-weary players to come in out of the sun.

The hitting stars for the National League were Banks with his homer and double and Mays with a single, a double and a triple. The trip east to play in New York two days later wasn't going to cool Willie down one bit, either.

The opposing managers, Al Lopez (left) and Walter Alston, get a grip on things before the first All-Star Game of 1960.

The men from Baltimore (left to right): First baseman Jim Gentile, third baseman Brooks Robinson, shortstop Ron Hansen and pitcher Chuck Estrada.

Frank Lary.

Del Crandall.

Bob Friend.

Ernie Banks.

Willie Mays.

Willie Mays slides safely into second base in the first 1960 classic as Ron Hansen makes the play.

Willie Returns

Nationals	AB.	R.	H.	RBI.	PO.	A.
Mays (Giants), cf	4	1	3	1	5	0
Pinson (Reds), cf	0	0	0	0	0	0
Skinner (Pirates), lf	3	0	1	0	2	0
Cepeda (Giants), lf	2	0	0	0	0	0
Aaron (Braves), rf	3	0	0	0	1	0
hClemente (Pirates), rf	0	0	0	0	0	0
Banks (Cubs), ss	3	0	1	0	2	3
iGroat (Pirates), ss	1	0	0	0	0	1
Adcock (Braves), 1b	2	1	1	0	3	0
White (Cardinals), 1b	1	0	0	0	2	0
kLarker (Dodgers), 1b	0	1	0	0	3	0
Mathews (Braves), 3b	3	1	1	2	0	1
Boyer (Cardinals), 3b	1	1	1	2	1	0
Mazeroski (Pirates), 2b	2	0	0	0	0	0
Neal (Dodgers), 2b	1	0	0	0	1	2
Taylor (Phillies), 2b	1	0	1	0	2	1
Crandall (Braves), c	2	0	0	0	3	0
S. Williams (Dodgers), p	0	0	0	0	0	0
dMusial (Cardinals)	1	1	1	1	0	0
Jackson (Cardinals), p	0	0	0	0	0	0
Bailey (Reds), c	1	0	0	0	0	0
Law (Pirates), p	1	0	0	0	0	0
Podres (Dodgers), p	0	0	0	0	0	1
bBurgess (Pirates), c	2	0	0	0	2	0
Henry (Reds), p	0	0	0	0	0	0
McDaniel (Cardinals), p	0	0	0	0	0	0
Totals	34	6	10	6	27	10

Americans	AB.	R.	H.	RBI.	PO.	A.
Minoso (White Sox), lf	2	0	0	0	1	0
eT. Williams (Red Sox)	1	0	1	0	0	0
fRobinson (Orioles), 3b	1	0	0	0	0	0
Runnels (Red Sox), 2b	2	0	0	0	0	1
Staley (White Sox), p	0	0	0	0	1	0
gKaline (Tigers), lf	1	0	1	0	3	0
Maris (Yankees), rf	4	0	0	0	0	0
Mantle (Yankees), cf	4	0	1	0	3	0
Skowron (Yankees), 1b	1	0	1	0	6	0
Power (Indians), 1b	2	0	0	0	5	1
Berra (Yankees), c	2	0	0	0	4	1
Lollar (White Sox), c	2	0	1	0	0	0
Malzone (Red Sox), 3b	2	0	0	0	2	2
Lary (Tigers), p	0	0	0	0	0	0
jSmith (White Sox)	1	0	0	0	0	0
Bell (Indians), p	0	0	0	0	0	1
Hansen (Orioles), ss	4	0	2	0	2	4
Ford (Yankees), p	0	0	0	0	0	0
aKuenn (Indians)	1	0	0	0	0	0
Wynn (White Sox), p	0	0	0	0	0	0
cFox (White Sox), 2b	3	0	1	0	0	1
Totals	33	0	8	0	27	12

National League .... 0 2 1 0 0 0 1 0 2—6
American League .... 0 0 0 0 0 0 0 0 0—0

Nationals	IP.	H.	R.	ER.	BB.	SO.
Law (W)	2	1	0	0	0	1
Podres	2	1	0	0	3	1
S. Williams	2	2	0	0	1	2
Jackson	1	1	0	0	2	0
Henry	1	2	0	0	0	0
McDaniel	1	1	0	0	0	0

Americans	IP.	H.	R.	ER.	BB.	SO.
Ford (L)	3	5	3	3	0	1
Wynn	2	0	0	0	0	2
Staley	2	2	1	1	0	0
Lary	1	1	0	0	1	0
Bell	1	2	2	2	2	0

aFlied out for Ford in third. bStruck out for Podres in fifth. cSingled for Wynn in fifth. dHomered for S. Williams in seventh. eSingled for Minoso in seventh. fRan for T. Williams in seventh. gWalked for Staley in seventh. hWalked for Aaron in eighth. iHit into double play for Banks in eighth. jPopped out for Lary in eighth. kWalked for White in ninth. DP—Nationals 2, Americans 1. LOB—Nationals 5, Americans 12. 2B—Lollar. HR—Mathews, Mays, Musial, Boyer. SB—Mays. SH—Henry. U—Chylak, Honochick and Stevens (A.L.), Boggess, Gorman and Smith (N.L.). T—2:42. A—38,362.

For many New York fans, the second All-Star Game of 1960 was a special occasion, for it marked the return—if only for a day—of Willie Mays. Gone from the city of his big-league birth since the departure of the Giants and Dodgers three years earlier (the National League would not return to New York for another two years, when the New York Mets were hatched), the 29-year-old center fielder with the alien "San Francisco" lettering across his uniform blouse put on a rousing show for his enthusiastic fans.

Against his favorite All-Star pitcher, Whitey Ford, Mays singled leading off the first inning of the game at Yankee Stadium and then made his followers proud and wistful with a home run in the third, also off Ford. This made him 6 for 6 in All-Star play against one of the great pitchers of all time.

Willie, who added a single later on (giving him his second 3-for-4 All-Star performance in three days), was only part of a booming show that was all National League. In the second inning, Eddie Mathews rocked Ford for a two-run homer, while in the seventh pinch-hitter Stan Musial belted his sixth All-Star homer, connecting against White Sox righthander Gerry Staley for a long, high beauty that sailed into the stadium's third deck. In the ninth, more National League

power erupted as Ken Boyer shot one out with a man on against Cleveland's Gary Bell, making it 6-0, the final score. It was the third shutout in All-Star Game history.

Walter Alston achieved his nine goose eggs with a string of six pitchers (the Dodger skipper employed a record 26 players in all). Vernon Law, who finished up the game in Kansas City, started this

one and worked two innings. The Pirates' standout was followed by the Dodgers' Johnny Podres and Stan Williams (two innings apiece), St. Louis' Larry Jackson (one), Cincinnati's Bill Henry (one) and the Cardinals' Lindy McDaniel (one). The collective shutout was an eight-hitter, with the Americans collecting just one extra-base hit, a double by the White Sox's Sherm Lollar.

American League Manager Al Lopez used five pitchers. The luckless Ford was trailed to the mound by Early Wynn (who pitched two shutout innings), Staley, Frank Lary (unscathed in one) and Bell.

The game saw the 18th and final All-Star appearance of Ted Williams, who retired as the 1960 season drew to a close. Ted marked it well, with a pinch single in the seventh. The incomparable Boston slugger left the competition with a .304 batting average, four home runs, 12 runs batted in (still an All-Star Game record) and 10 runs scored.

Wynn's stint also ended his All-Star participation. A 300-game winner in a big-league career that would end in 1963, Wynn posted a 1-0 record in seven All-Star Game appearances.

The Nationals' double triumph in '60 narrowed their deficit in the series to 16-13, and they were closing fast.

Early Wynn.

Vern Law.

Ken Boyer.

Willie Mays.

Stan Musial watches the flight of his sixth All-Star home run.

Eddie Mathews.

Sherm Lollar.

Blowing in the Wind

Americans	AB.	R.	H.	RBI.	PO.	A.
Temple (Indians), 2b	3	0	0	0	1	2
fGentile (Orioles), 1b	2	0	0	0	2	0
Cash (Tigers), 1b	4	0	1	0	6	1
gFox (White Sox), 2b	0	2	0	0	1	0
Mantle (Yankees), cf	3	0	0	0	3	0
Kaline (Tigers), cf	2	1	1	1	1	0
Maris (Yankees), rf	4	0	1	0	3	0
Colavito (Tigers), lf	4	0	0	1	1	0
Kubek (Yankees), ss	4	0	0	0	1	2
Romano (Indians), c	3	0	0	0	7	0
hBerra (Yankees), c	1	0	0	0	0	0
Howard (Yankees), c	0	0	0	0	0	0
B. Robinson (Orioles), 3b	2	0	0	0	0	2
Bunning (Tigers), p	0	0	0	0	1	0
dBrandt (Orioles)	1	0	0	0	0	0
Fornieles (Red Sox), p	0	0	0	0	0	0
Wilhelm (Orioles), p	1	0	0	0	0	0
Ford (Yankees), p	1	0	0	0	0	0
Lary (Tigers), p	0	0	0	0	0	0
Donovan (Senators), p	0	0	0	0	0	0
cKillebrew (Twins), 3b	2	1	1	1	0	0
Howser (Athletics), 3b	1	0	0	0	0	1
Totals	38	4	4	3	27	8

Nationals	AB.	R.	H.	RBI.	PO.	A.
Wills (Dodgers), ss	5	0	1	0	0	2
Mathews (Braves), 3b	2	0	0	0	0	0
Purkey (Reds), p	0	0	0	0	1	0
bMusial (Cardinals)	1	0	0	0	0	0
McCormick (Giants), p	0	0	0	0	0	0
eAltman (Cubs)	1	1	1	1	0	0
Face (Pirates), p	0	0	0	0	0	0
Koufax (Dodgers), p	0	0	0	0	0	0
Miller (Giants), p	0	0	0	0	0	0
iAaron (Braves)	1	1	1	0	0	0
Mays (Giants), cf	5	2	2	1	3	0
Cepeda (Giants), lf	3	0	0	0	1	0
F. Robinson (Reds), lf	1	0	1	0	2	0
Clemente (Pirates), rf	4	1	2	2	2	0
White (Cardinals), 1b	3	0	1	1	7	1
Bolling (Braves), 2b	3	0	0	0	1	3
Zimmer (Cubs), 2b	1	0	0	0	0	0
Burgess (Pirates), c	4	0	1	0	13	0
Spahn (Braves), p	0	0	0	0	0	1
aStuart (Pirates)	1	0	1	0	0	0
Boyer (Cardinals), 3b	2	0	0	0	0	1
Totals	37	5	11	5	30	8

American League...........0 0 0 0 0 1 0 0 2 1—4
National League............0 1 0 1 0 0 0 1 0 2—5
None out when winning run scored.

Americans	IP.	H.	R.	ER.	BB.	SO.
Ford	3	2	1	1	0	2
Lary	0*	0	1	0	0	0
Donovan	2	4	0	0	0	1
Bunning	2	0	0	0	0	2
Fornieles	⅓	2	1	1	0	0
Wilhelm (L)	1⅔‡	3	2	2	1	1

Nationals	IP.	H.	R.	ER.	BB.	SO.
Spahn	3	0	0	0	0	3
Purkey	2	0	0	0	0	1
McCormick	3	1	1	1	1	3
Face	⅓	2	2	2	0	1
Koufax	0†	1	0	0	0	0
Miller (W)	1⅔	0	1	0	1	4

*Pitched to one batter in fourth.
†Pitched to one batter in ninth.
‡Pitched to four batters in tenth.

aDoubled for Spahn in third. bFlied out for Purkey in fifth. cHomered for Donovan in sixth. dStruck out for Bunning in eighth. eHomered for McCormick in eighth. fStruck out for Temple in ninth. gRan for Cash in ninth. hSafe on error for Romano in ninth. iSingled for Miller in tenth. E—Gentile, Kubek, Cepeda, Zimmer, Burgess, Boyer 2. LOB—Americans 6, Nationals 9. 2B—Stuart, Cash, Mays. 3B—Clemente. HR—Killebrew, Altman. SB—F. Robinson. SF—Clemente, White. HBP —By Wilhelm (F. Robinson). PB—Howard. Balk—Miller. U—Landes, Crawford and Vargo (N.L.), Umont, Runge and Drummond (A.L.). T—2:53. A—44,115.

Baseball immortality comes in various degrees and through various agencies. It comes with the thunderbolt drama of a long home run, the blazing excitement of a crucial strikeout, the fury of a mad dash around the bases, the thrilling elegance of a great running catch. For San Francisco Giants pitcher Stu Miller, it came in a gust of wind.

This famous gust—actually, it was part of a wall of invisible turbulence moving with near gale-force strength—whipped its way into baseball lore during the first All-Star Game of 1961, played in San Francisco on July 11.

Candlestick Park, new home of the Giants, had gained a dubious reputation in its season and a half of use as a place that generated more wind than a political campaign. These winds, though, were more like Tower of Babel winds in that they swept and curved and gyrated and crisscrossed and danced and spun with mischievous abruptness from all points of the compass, often making hearty contributions to a game's shape.

The opposing managers were Pittsburgh's Danny Murtaugh for the National League and Baltimore's Paul Richards. With Casey Stengel having been given the boot as the Yankees' manager after winning the pennant the year before, the American League's All-Star managerial responsibilities were delegated to Richards, whose Orioles had finished second in 1960.

Much of the game—the first eight innings, in fact—was played under normal conditions, San Francisco affording the proceedings a hot, almost windless afternoon. The Nationals had crafted a 3-1 lead through the eighth, built on some well-placed hitting and masterful one-hit pitching by the threesome of 40-year-old Warren Spahn (the first three innings), Cincinnati righthander Bob Purkey (the next two) and Giants left-hander Mike McCormick (the next three). McCormick had surrendered the only hit, a pinch home run by the Twins' Harmon Killebrew in the sixth.

The Nationals had clipped starter Whitey Ford for a run in the second on a triple by Roberto Clemente and a sacrifice fly by the Cardinals' Bill White. Otherwise, Ford pitched effectively and, at last, even retired Willie Mays. He struck out the Giants' star in the first inning.

In the fourth, batting against Detroit's Frank Lary, Mays reached second when Yankees shortstop Tony Kubek committed a two-base error on Willie's grounder. Lary, who faced just the one batter, left the game because of a sore shoulder and was replaced by Washington right-hander Dick Donovan. Donovan pitched well but couldn't prevent Mays from coming around on a ground ball and a sacrifice fly by Clemente, who loomed large in this game.

Donovan delivered two scoreless innings, as did his successor, Jim Bunning. The Nationals made it 3-1 in the eighth against the Red Sox's Mike Fornieles, the run being a one-man product—a pinch home run by the Cubs' George Altman.

By this time the prevailing calm was gone as the late-afternoon winds began blowing in off San Francisco Bay, and what had been a rather staid and conventional game of baseball turned into a wind-blown circus.

With the wind increasing in velocity, Roy Face took the mound for the Nationals in the ninth and tried to put a lock on the two-run lead. With one out, Detroit's Norm Cash drilled a double, only the second hit for the American League. The third one followed immediately when Al Kaline, Cash's Tiger teammate, singled home pinch-runner Nelson Fox. Face left in favor of the Dodgers' Sandy Koufax, just beginning to emerge as the game's most overpowering pitcher. Koufax, however, was nicked for a single by Roger Maris (who was in the midst of his 61-homer season). The hit put men on first and second. With righthanded-hitting Rocky Colavito coming up, Murtaugh took out Koufax and brought in Miller.

Miller was a slightly built righthander whose well-documented pitching repertoire featured three speeds: slow, slower and slowest, each pitch tempting and tantalizing and not all that easy to put a bat on.

A hellacious wind was blowing now, whipping into the air whatever would rise, from dirt and dust to hot-dog wrappers and bits of paper and, almost, Stu Miller. As Miller prepared to pitch to Colavito, a particularly lusty gust buffeted the reliever and caused him to balk. The umpires were sympathetic, but they had to call it, advancing the runners to second and third. These were the tying and lead runs, and there was just one out.

Colavito then hit a grounder to third, where normally slick-hand-ed Ken Boyer fumbled the ball. The error sent in Kaline with the tying run.

With the local weather vanes now spinning like tops, the wind played impishly with Kubek's ensuing pop foul and catcher Smoky Burgess dropped the ball for another error. This one proved harmless, however, as Kubek fanned. Then Cubs second baseman Don Zimmer fielded Yogi Berra's grounder cleanly, only to see his throw sail in the wind and pull first baseman White off the bag. This error loaded the bases, but Miller pitched his way clear by getting Athletics infielder Dick Howser to fly out.

Knuckleballing righthander Hoyt Wilhelm of Baltimore held the Nationals scoreless in the ninth, sending the game into extra innings. Wilhelm's knuckler, eccentric in flight to begin with, must have been a sight to see under those conditions.

In the 10th, with the wind still blowing relentlessly and colliding with itself all over the ball park, the Americans were blown into a 4-3 lead. With two out, Fox walked. Kaline grounded to Boyer and what began as a perfect throw to first was suddenly levitated by the currents and sailed into right field, scoring Fox.

In the last of the 10th, the Nationals came back against Wilhelm with a businesslike rally. Henry Aaron opened with a single, went to second on a passed ball and scored the tying run on Mays' double. The wind then ran a Wilhelm knuckler into Frank Robinson and there were men on first and second. Clemente hammered a single to right, scoring Mays easily with the winning run, and everyone came in out of the wind.

It was a dramatic comeback, giving the Nationals a 5-4 triumph in what always will be remembered in All-Star annals as the "Stu Miller Game." It gave the National Leaguers four victories in the last five games and 10 in the last 14.

There was a wind blowing, to be sure.

San Francisco's windy Candlestick Park as viewed from the right-field stands during the first All-Star Game of the 1961 season.

Dick Donovan.

George Altman.

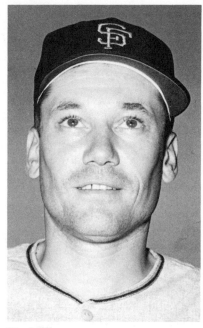

Stu Miller.

Warren Spahn delivers the first pitch of the first 1961 classic to Johnny Temple. The catcher is Smoky Burgess and the umpire is Stan Landes.

Harmon Killebrew.

Mike McCormick.

The three National League heroes who delivered key 10th-inning hits that resulted in another victory over the American Leaguers (left to right): Pittsburgh's Roberto Clemente, San Francisco's Willie Mays and Milwaukee's Henry Aaron.

Nobody Wins

Nationals	AB.	R.	H.	RBI.	PO.	A.
Wills (Dodgers), ss	2	0	1	0	1	1
Aaron (Braves), rf	2	0	0	0	1	0
Miller (Giants), p	0	0	0	0	0	0
Mathews (Braves), 3b	3	1	0	0	0	2
Mays (Giants), cf	3	0	1	0	1	0
Cepeda (Giants), lf	3	0	0	0	0	0
Clemente (Pirates), rf	2	0	0	0	0	0
Kasko (Reds), ss	1	0	1	0	2	4
eBanks (Cubs), ss	1	0	0	0	0	0
White (Cardinals), 1b	4	0	2	1	11	1
Bolling (Braves), 2b	4	0	0	0	3	2
Burgess (Pirates), c	1	0	0	0	2	0
Roseboro (Dodgers), c	3	0	0	0	6	0
Purkey (Reds), p	0	0	0	0	0	1
aStuart (Pirates)	1	0	0	0	0	0
Mahaffey (Phillies), p	0	0	0	0	0	0
cMusial (Cardinals)	1	0	0	0	0	0
Koufax (Dodgers), p	0	0	0	0	0	0
dAltman (Cubs), rf	1	0	0	0	0	0
Totals	32	1	5	1	27	11

Americans	AB.	R.	H.	RBI.	PO.	A.
Cash (Tigers), 1b	4	0	0	0	11	0
Colavito (Tigers), lf	4	1	1	1	3	0
Kaline (Tigers), rf	4	0	2	0	1	0
Mantle (Yankees), cf	3	0	0	0	2	0
Romano (Indians), c	1	0	0	0	1	0
bMaris (Yankees)	1	0	0	0	0	0
Howard (Yankees), c	2	0	0	0	6	0
Aparicio (White Sox), ss	2	0	0	0	1	3
fSievers (White Sox)	1	0	0	0	0	0
Temple (Indians), 2b	2	0	0	0	2	3
B. Robinson (Orioles), 3b	3	0	1	0	0	3
Bunning (Tigers), p	1	0	0	0	0	0
Schwall (Red Sox), p	1	0	0	0	0	0
Pascual (Twins), p	1	0	0	0	0	0
Totals	30	1	4	1	27	9

National League	0	0	0	0	0	1	0	0	0—1
American League	1	0	0	0	0	0	0	0	0—1

Called because of rain.

Nationals	IP.	H.	R.	ER.	BB.	SO.
Purkey	2	1	1	1	2	2
Mahaffey	2	0	0	0	1	0
Koufax	2	1	0	0	0	1
Miller	3	1	0	0	0	5

Americans	IP.	H.	R.	ER.	BB.	SO.
Bunning	3	0	0	0	0	1
Schwall	3	5	1	1	1	2
Pascual	3	0	0	0	1	4

aGrounded out for Purkey in third. bPopped out for Romano in fourth. cStruck out for Mahaffey in fifth. dFlied out for Koufax in seventh. eStruck out for Kasko in eighth. fStruck out for Aparicio in ninth. E—Bolling. DP—Nationals 2. LOB—Nationals 7, Americans 5. 2B—White. HR—Colavito. SB—Kaline. HBP—By Schwall (Cepeda). PB—Burgess. U—Napp, Flaherty and Smith (A.L.), Secory, Sudol and Pelekoudas (N.L.). T—2:27. A—31,851.

The American League didn't lose the second All-Star Game in 1961, but the Americans didn't win it either, coming away with the doubtful consolation of a tie. The game, played at Boston's Fenway Park on July 31, was called after nine innings because of a heavy downpour, ending in a 1-1 deadlock.

Because the game was played at Fenway, with the lure of the park's beckoning left-field wall, some muscular hitting was expected. But baseball proved it was a game of surprises, with the affair being dominated by the pitchers. The Nationals managed just five hits, while for the second consecutive game the Americans were held to four. (The American League's composite batting average for the two 1961 games was a feeble .118.)

Expectations for some lusty hitting were heightened when Detroit's Rocky Colavito belted one over the wall in the first inning off Cincinnati's Bob Purkey for the American League run. After a two-inning stint by Purkey, hard-throwing righthander Art Mahaffey of the Phillies came in and pitched two shutout innings. Sandy Koufax delivered two more, but the man who stood out for the National League with three scoreless innings—he allowed only one hit and struck out five batters—was none other than Stu Miller.

At Candlestick Park, Stu had been battered by the wind; in Fenway, he was drenched by the rain. The Giants' pitcher proved himself an all-weather man, though, by performing splendidly on both occasions, giving no earned runs and fanning nine in 4⅔ innings overall.

The American League pitching was handled `deftly by Jim Bunning, who opened with three hitless and scoreless innings, followed by Red Sox righthander Don Schwall, and then the Twins' Camilo Pascual, who also turned in three innings of no-hit, no-run ball (and struck out four).

The lone National League run, scored against Schwall in the sixth, was slightly tarnished. With one out, Eddie Mathews walked. After another out, Schwall hit the Giants' Orlando Cepeda with a pitch. The game's key play followed. The Reds' Eddie Kasko grounded slowly to Luis Aparicio. Instead of charging the ball, Luis let it come to him. This tentativeness was costly as Kasko beat the throw for an infield single, loading the bases.

A moment later, Aparicio, who made the Hall of Fame primarily through the wizardry of his glove, displayed the real Aparicio. The Cardinals' Bill White hit one through the middle, the ball slightly deflected by Schwall. Aparicio raced behind second and made a dazzling stop to prevent the ball from going through for a two-run single. White's infield hit nevertheless scored Mathews with the tying run.

Miller was heroic under ever-darkening and wet skies in the bottom of the ninth. After Al Kaline singled, putting the winning run on base with no one out, Miller then slow-balled the opposition to death. In succession, he struck out Mickey Mantle, Elston Howard (Kaline stole second during the Yankee catcher's at-bat) and the Chicago White Sox's Roy Sievers.

The skies really opened up just as the ninth inning concluded. After a half-hour, the umpires, hearing unpromising weather reports, called the contest, creating the first tie in All-Star Game history. A 1-1 game, one of the most brilliantly pitched battles of the now 31-game series, had taken place in the long-ball paradise of Fenway Park.

Recently retired Red Sox slugger Ted Williams throws out the ceremonial first ball for the second 1961 All-Star Game. American League President Joe Cronin watches.

Jim Bunning.

Camilo Pascual.

Detroit stars Al Kaline (left) and Rocky Colavito (center) meet with former teammate Frank Bolling before the second 1961 classic.

Sandy Koufax.

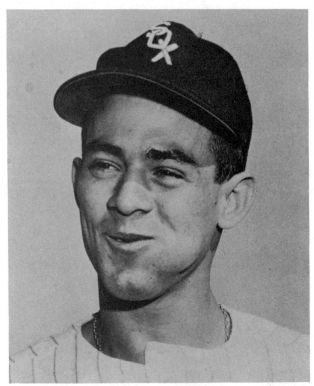

Luis Aparicio.

American Leaguers (left to right) John Romano, Norm Cash and Elston Howard.

Wills Runs Wild

Nationals	AB.	R.	H.	RBI.	PO.	A.
Groat (Pirates), ss	3	1	1	1	3	3
Davenport (Giants), 3b	1	0	1	0	0	1
Clemente (Pirates), rf	3	0	3	0	2	0
F. Alou (Giants), rf	0	0	0	1	0	0
Mays (Giants), cf	3	0	0	0	3	0
Cepeda (Giants), 1b	3	0	0	1	2	2
Purkey (Reds), p	0	0	0	0	0	1
eCallison (Phillies)	1	0	1	0	0	0
Shaw (Braves), p	0	0	0	0	1	0
T. Davis (Dodgers), lf	4	0	0	0	2	0
Boyer (Cardinals), 3b	2	0	0	0	1	0
Banks (Cubs), 1b	2	0	0	0	4	1
Crandall (Braves), c	4	0	0	0	5	0
Mazeroski (Pirates), 2b	2	0	0	0	1	0
Bolling (Braves), 2b	2	0	0	0	1	3
Drysdale (Dodgers), p	1	0	0	0	1	0
Marichal (Giants), p	0	0	0	0	0	0
cMusial (Cardinals)	1	0	1	0	0	0
dWills (Dodgers), ss	1	2	1	0	1	1
Totals	33	3	8	3	27	12

Americans	AB.	R.	H.	RBI.	PO.	A.
Rollins (Twins), 3b	2	1	1	0	1	3
Robinson (Orioles), 3b	0	0	0	0	0	1
Moran (Angels), 2b	3	0	1	0	0	0
Richardson (Yanks), 2b	1	0	0	0	1	0
Maris (Yankees), cf	2	0	0	1	2	0
Landis (White Sox), cf	1	0	0	0	2	0
Mantle (Yankees), rf	1	0	0	0	0	0
bColavito (Tigers), lf	1	0	0	0	1	0
Gentile (Orioles), 1b	3	0	0	0	8	0
Wagner (Angels), lf-rf	4	0	0	0	4	0
Battey (Twins), c	2	0	0	0	4	1
Romano (Indians), c	2	0	1	0	1	0
Aparicio (White Sox), ss	4	0	1	0	3	2
Bunning (Tigers), p	0	0	0	0	0	0
aL. Thomas (Angels)	1	0	0	0	0	0
Pascual (Twins), p	1	0	0	0	0	1
Donovan (Indians), p	0	0	0	0	0	0
fSiebern (Athletics)	1	0	0	0	0	0
Pappas (Orioles), p	0	0	0	0	0	0
Totals	29	1	4	1	27	8

National League	0 0 0	0 0 2	0 1 0	—3
American League	0 0 0	0 0 1	0 0 0	—1

Nationals	IP.	H.	R.	ER.	BB.	SO.
Drysdale	3	1	0	0	1	3
Marichal (W)	2	0	0	0	1	0
Purkey	2	2	1	1	0	1
Shaw	2	1	0	0	1	1

Americans	IP.	H.	R.	ER.	BB.	SO.
Bunning	3	1	0	0	0	2
Pascual (L)	3	4	2	2	1	1
Donovan	2	3	1	1	0	0
Pappas	1	0	0	0	0	0

aPopped out for Bunning in third. bRan for Mantle in fourth. cSingled for Marichal in sixth. dRan for Musial in sixth. eSingled for Purkey in eighth. fGrounded out for Donovan in eighth. DP—Nationals 1, Americans 1. LOB—Nationals 5, Americans 7. 2B—Clemente. 3B—Aparicio. SB—Mays, Wills. SF—Maris. F. Alou. HBP—By Drysdale (Rollins), by Shaw (Robinson). U—Hurley, Stewart and Schwarts (A.L.), Donatelli, Venzon and Steiner (N.L.). T—2:33. A—45,480.

It was a watershed year for baseball, as Maury Wills ran the game into the era of the stolen base. The Dodger shortstop's startling total of 104 stolen bases in 1962 was to baseball's running game what the breaking of the sound barrier was to flight and the first sub-4-minute mile was to track.

By breaking Ty Cobb's 47-year-old major league record of 96 steals in one year and at the same time proving the effectiveness of a running game (the Dodgers finished the 1962 season in a first-place tie with the Giants before losing in a playoff), Wills unleashed baseball's rabbits for the coming decades. And in the first All-Star Game of '62, played on July 10 at Washington's newly opened District of Columbia Stadium (later renamed in honor of Robert F. Kennedy), Wills gave a demonstration of his craft.

In the top of the sixth inning of a scoreless game, the Nationals' Stan Musial pinch-hit a single. For the 41-year-old Musial, limited now to what amounted to honorary appearances, it was his 22nd All-Star Game and his 20th and final All-Star hit. Wills went in to pinch-run. Maury, who already had stolen 46 bases for the Dodgers in '62, took off for second immediately—thanks to a jump so big that Twins catcher Earl Battey never bothered to throw. Pittsburgh's Dick Groat then singled in Wills with the game's first run. Groat went to

second on Roberto Clemente's third hit of the game and came around on a pair of outs.

The Americans drew within 2-1 in the bottom of the inning. The Twins' Rich Rollins singled off Cincinnati's Bob Purkey (who had just entered the game), went to third on a single by the Angels' Billy Moran and scored when Roger Maris flied deep to Willie Mays in center, Willie leaping at the fence to deprive Maris of what looked to be a three-run homer.

The Nationals seized a two-run advantage in the eighth, and again it was the lightning moves of Wills that made it possible. Maury opened the inning with a pop-fly single to left. When the

Giants' Jim Davenport followed with another hit to left, Wills challenged left fielder Rocky Colavito, possessor of a powerful arm, by racing around second base. Colavito, apparently thinking Wills would try to return to second, fired to that base, but Wills sped on to third. From there, Maury daringly scored on a foul fly to short right.

Pitching again was the dominant factor in the All-Star Game. Don Drysdale started for Manager Fred Hutchinson's Nationals and worked three innings of one-hit, shutout ball. The Giants' high-kicking Juan Marichal then added two more scoreless innings. Purkey and the Braves' Bob Shaw finished up the 3-1 victory.

Ralph Houk's Americans wasted some good pitching by Jim Bunning. Starter Bunning matched Drysdale with one-hit pitching over three scoreless innings, giving the A.L. ace eight consecutive shutout innings in his last three All-Star appearances. The Tiger righthander was followed by Minnesota's Camilo Pascual, who surrendered two runs in three innings, and Cleveland's Dick Donovan and Baltimore's Milt Pappas.

In narrowing the American League's lead in the series to just one game (16-15-1), National League pitchers held the Americans to four hits for the third straight game. Over those three games, the once-mighty American League lineup batted .124.

President John F. Kennedy delivers the ceremonial first pitch of the first 1962 All-Star Game.

Dick Groat.

Don Drysdale.

The high-kicking Juan Marichal.

Roger Maris.

Maury Wills scores the National Leaguers' final run in the eighth inning. The catcher is John Romano and the umpire is Ed Hurley.

Roberto Clemente.

Temporary Relief

Americans	AB.	R.	H.	RBI.	PO.	A.
Rollins (Twins), 3b	3	0	1	0	0	1
B. Robinson (Orioles), 3b	1	1	0	0	0	1
Moran (Angels), 2b	4	0	1	0	1	4
fBerra (Yankees)	1	0	0	0	0	0
gRichardson (Yanks), 2b	0	1	0	0	2	0
Maris (Yankees), cf	4	2	1	1	4	0
Colavito (Tigers), rf	4	1	1	4	2	0
Gentile (Orioles), 1b	4	0	1	0	10	0
Battey (Twins), c	2	1	0	0	2	0
dKaline (Tigers)	0	1	0	0	0	0
Howard (Yankees), c	2	0	0	0	2	0
Wagner (Angels), lf	4	1	3	2	1	0
L. Thomas (Angels), lf	0	0	0	0	1	0
Aparicio (White Sox), ss	2	0	0	0	2	3
Tresh (Yankees), ss	2	0	1	1	0	4
Stenhouse (Senators), p	0	0	0	0	0	0
aRunnels (Red Sox)	1	1	1	1	0	0
Herbert (White Sox), p	1	0	0	0	0	0
Aguirre (Tigers), p	2	0	0	0	0	0
Pappas (Orioles), p	0	0	0	0	0	0
Totals	37	9	10	9	27	13

Nationals	AB.	R.	H.	RBI.	PO.	A.
Groat (Pirates), ss	3	0	2	2	3	3
Wills (Dodgers), ss	1	0	0	0	0	1
Clemente (Pirates), rf	2	0	0	0	2	0
F. Robinson (Reds), rf	3	0	0	0	1	0
Mays (Giants), cf	2	0	2	0	2	0
H. Aaron (Braves), cf	2	0	0	0	1	0
Cepeda (Giants), 1b	1	0	0	0	2	0
Banks (Cubs), 1b	2	1	1	0	1	0
T. Davis (Dodgers), lf	1	0	0	0	0	1
bMusial (Cardinals), lf	2	0	0	0	0	0
Williams (Cubs), lf	1	0	0	1	2	0
Boyer (Cardinals), 3b	3	0	1	0	1	2
Mathews (Braves), 3b	1	0	0	0	0	0
Crandall (Braves), c	1	0	0	0	3	0
Roseboro (Dodgers), c	3	1	1	1	6	0
Mazeroski (Pirates), 2b	1	0	0	0	0	0
cAltman (Cubs)	1	0	0	0	0	0
Gibson (Cardinals), p	0	0	0	0	0	0
Farrell (Colts), p	0	0	0	0	0	0
eAshburn (Mets)	1	1	1	0	0	0
Marichal (Giants), p	0	0	0	0	0	0
hCallison (Phillies)	0	0	0	0	0	0
Podres (Dodgers), p	1	1	1	0	0	0
Mahaffey (Phillies), p	0	0	0	0	0	0
Bolling (Braves), 2b	3	0	1	0	3	1
Totals	35	4	10	4	27	10

American League .... 0 0 1 2 0 1 3 0 2—9
National League .... 0 1 0 0 0 0 1 1 1—4

Americans	IP.	H.	R.	ER.	BB.	SO.
Stenhouse	2	3	1	1	1	1
Herbert (W)	3	3	0	0	0	0
Aguirre	3	3	2	2	0	2
Pappas	1	1	1	1	1	0

Nationals	IP.	H.	R.	ER.	BB.	SO.
Podres	2	2	0	0	0	2
Mahaffey (L)	2	2	3	3	1	1
Gibson	2	1	1	1	2	1
Farrell	1	3	3	3	1	2
Marichal	2	2	2	1	0	2

aHomered for Stenhouse in third. bGrounded out for T. Davis in third. cFlied out for Mazeroski in fourth. dRan for Battey in sixth. eSingled for Farrell in seventh. fSafe on error for Moran in ninth. gRan for Berra in ninth. hWalked for Marichal in ninth. E—Groat, T. Davis, Mathews 2. DP —Americans 2. LOB—Americans 6, Nationals 7. 2B—Podres, Tresh, Bolling, Maris. 3B—Banks. HR —Runnels, Wagner, Colavito, Roseboro. SF—Colavito. HBP—By Stenhouse (Groat). WP—Marichal 2, Stenhouse. U—Conlan, Burkhart and Forman (N.L.), McKinley, Rice and Kinnamon (A.L.). T— 2:28. A—38,359.

The American League stars had a good feeling when they won the second All-Star Game of 1962 (the last of the two-game years). For one thing, they finally ended their batting slump; the Americans scored nine runs, equaling their total for the previous five games, and collected 10 hits. For another thing, their victory prevented the Nationals from tying the series at 16-all.

All of the satisfaction would have been tempered, however, if the American Leaguers had known that nearly a decade would pass before they won again.

Chicago's Wrigley Field was the scene of the July 30 game, with Fred Hutchinson and Ralph Houk again supplying the brain power. Wrigley was one of those snugly built big-league parks— one where the batter could see the whites of the outfielders' eyes— and some big hitting was expected (just as it had been anticipated 15 years earlier at the Cubs' park, when a 2-1 All-Star Game unfold- ed).

Houk's starter was something of a surprise—Washington rookie righthander Dave Stenhouse (10-4 at the time, but 11-12 by season's end), while Hutchinson began with Dodger lefthander Johnny Podres. In addition to pitching two scoreless innings, Podres dou- bled in the second inning and

scored the game's first run on Dick Groat's single.

The starters departed after two innings. White Sox righthander Ray Herbert took over for the Americans and worked three shutout innings. The Phillies' Art Mahaffey, who pitched the third and fourth for the Nationals, had less success. In the third, the Red Sox's Pete Runnels, not noted for his power (he singled and doubled his way to a .326 batting title that year), struck a pinch-hit home

run, tying the game. An inning later, the Americans began pull- ing away when the Angels' Leon Wagner pickled a Mahaffey serv- ing after Earl Battey had walked, making it 3-1, Americans.

The Americans added another run in the sixth off the Cardinals' Bob Gibson (making his All-Star Game debut), the run driven in by Yankee Tom Tresh's double. Then, in the seventh, Detroit's Rocky Colavito made it a con- vincing 7-1 lead when he jolted Houston's Dick Farrell for a three-run homer.

The Nationals scored single runs in each of the last three in- nings (the first two against De- troit's Hank Aguirre, the third off Baltimore's Milt Pappas), the final run coming on a homer by the Dodgers' John Roseboro. The Americans, meanwhile, scored twice more in the top of the ninth against Juan Marichal, one of the runs crossing on Colavito's sacri- fice fly.

Colavito with four RBIs and Wagner with three hits paced the American League's 9-4 victory. For the Nationals, Willie Mays was 2 for 2, boosting his batting record for 13 All-Star Games to 19 for 45. That worked out to a .422 average, making most under- standable Willie's comment on his affection for the midsummer special: "I always enjoy playing in All-Star Games."

Ray Herbert.

Rocky Colavito.

John Roseboro.

Leon Wagner.

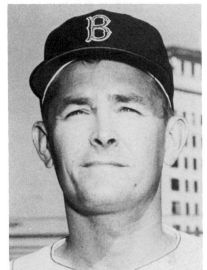

Pete Runnels.

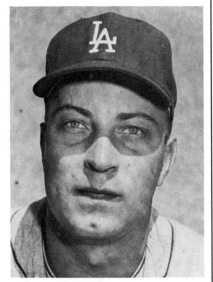

Johnny Podres.

Domination Begins

Nationals	AB	R	H	RBI	PO	A
T. Davis (Dodgers), lf	3	1	1	0	2	1
eSnider (Mets), lf	1	0	0	0	0	0
H. Aaron (Braves), rf	4	1	0	0	3	0
White (Cardinals), 1b	4	1	1	0	5	3
Mays (Giants), cf	3	2	1	2	1	0
Clemente (Pirates), cf	0	0	0	0	0	0
Bailey (Giants), c	1	0	1	1	4	1
aMusial (Cardinals)	1	0	0	0	0	0
Culp (Phillies), p	0	0	0	0	0	1
Santo (Cubs), 3b	1	0	1	1	0	0
Boyer (Cardinals), 3b	3	0	0	0	0	0
Woodeshick (Colts), p	0	0	0	0	0	1
dMcCovey (Giants)	1	0	0	0	0	0
Drysdale (Dodgers), p	0	0	0	0	0	0
Groat (Cardinals), ss	4	0	1	1	2	2
Javier (Cardinals), 2b	4	0	0	0	4	1
O'Toole (Reds), p	1	0	0	0	1	0
Jackson (Cubs), p	1	0	0	0	1	0
Edwards (Reds), c	2	0	0	0	5	0
Totals	34	5	6	5	27	10

Americans	AB	R	H	RBI	PO	A
Fox (White Sox), 2b	3	0	1	0	3	1
Richardson (Yankees), 2b	2	0	0	0	0	1
Pearson (Angels), cf	4	1	2	0	4	0
Tresh (Yankees), cf	0	0	0	0	0	0
Kaline (Tigers), rf	3	0	0	0	2	0
Allison (Twins), rf	1	0	0	0	0	0
Malzone (Red Sox), 3b	3	1	1	1	1	3
Bouton (Yankees), p	0	0	0	0	0	0
Pizarro (White Sox), p	0	0	0	0	0	0
cKillebrew (Twins)	1	0	0	0	0	0
Radatz (Red Sox), p	0	0	0	0	0	0
Wagner (Angels), lf	3	1	2	0	1	0
Howard (Yankees), c	1	0	0	0	5	0
Battey (Twins), c	2	0	1	1	1	0
bYastrzemski (R. Sox), lf	2	0	0	0	1	0
Pepitone (Yankees), 1b	4	0	0	0	8	0
Versalles (Twins), ss	1	0	1	0	0	2
Aparicio (Orioles), ss	1	0	0	0	0	0
McBride (Angels), p	1	0	1	1	0	0
Bunning (Tigers), p	0	0	0	0	0	0
Robinson (Orioles), 3b	2	0	2	0	1	1
Totals	34	3	11	3	27	8

National League	0	1	2	0	1	0	0	1	0	—5
American League	0	1	2	0	0	0	0	0	0	—3

Nationals	IP	H	R	ER	BB	SO
O'Toole	2	4	1	1	0	1
Jackson (W)	2	4	2	2	0	3
Culp	1	1	0	0	0	0
Woodeshick	2	1	0	0	1	3
Drysdale	2	1	0	0	0	2

Americans	IP	H	R	ER	BB	SO
McBride	3	4	3	3	2	1
Bunning (L)	2	0	1	0	1	0
Bouton	1	0	0	0	0	0
Pizarro	1	0	0	0	0	0
Radatz	2	2	1	1	0	5

aLined out for Bailey in fifth. bFouled out for Battey in fifth. cStruck out for Pizarro in seventh. dStruck out for Woodeshick in eighth. eStruck out for T. Davis in ninth. E—Richardson. DP—Nationals 3. LOB—Nationals 5, Americans 7. 2B—Pearson. SB—Mays 2, White. SH—Bunning. HBP —By O'Toole (Versalles). U—Soar, Smith and Haller (A.L.), Jackowski, Pryor and Harvey (N.L.). T—2:20. A—44,160.

The National League began its onslaught upon the laws of probability (baseball style) in 1963, as the All-Star Game reverted to its original one serving per year. With the game played at Cleveland Stadium on July 9, the National League began a logic-defying dominance of the American that would see the older league win eight straight games, drop one and then score 11 consecutive victories, leaving in a shambles the supremacy that once upon a time had been established by Ruth, Gehrig, Foxx and Simmons and later was perpetuated by DiMaggio, Williams, Feller and others.

Whatever the nature of the particular contest—tightly pitched, high-scoring, extra-inning—the Nationals would find a way to win in 19 of 20 games. When National League victories got to the point where they seemed almost inevitable, Pete Rose said, "Winning is contagious." From the steady losers, there was no explanation.

The American League had the consolation in 1963 of outhitting its rival, 11 to 6, but the statistic was made irrelevant by the National League's not-so-secret weapon, Willie Mays, for whom these games seemed to have been designed. Willie got only one hit (a single in three tries), but drove in two runs and scored two in his team's 5-3 triumph. Additionally, he stole two bases and made the defensive play of the game, a running catch to deprive the Yankees' Joe Pepitone of extra bases in the eighth inning.

The early scoring followed a curious pattern, each team getting one run in the second and two in the third. Willie started it off with a walk, a steal of second and then a journey home courtesy of a single by the Cardinals' Dick Groat. The Americans responded with a base hit, a hit batsman and a run-scoring single by pitcher Ken McBride in their half of the second, but the Nationals rebounded in the third, with Mays again the pivot. After the Dodgers' Tommy Davis singled and was forced by Henry Aaron, Aaron moved to second on an infield out and scored on Willie's single. The Giants' five-ply threat (hit, run, throw, field, inspire) stole second again and came around on a single by Giants teammate Ed Bailey.

The Americans tied it in their half of the third on a double (the game's only extra-base hit) by the Angels' Albie Pearson, a single by Boston's Frank Malzone, an infield out and a single by Earl Battey.

The Nationals' first three runs came off Angels righthander McBride, whom A.L. skipper Ralph Houk had started. Giants Manager Alvin Dark had begun with Reds lefthander Jim O'Toole for the N.L. and followed him with the Cubs' Larry Jackson, who gave up the two runs in the third and worked a scoreless fourth inning. Thereafter, three National League pitchers—Ray Culp, Hal Woodeshick and Don Drysdale—gave up just three hits and no runs over the last five innings. The Phillies' Culp worked one inning, while Woodeshick (Houston) and Drysdale pitched two each.

McBride was followed to the mound by Jim Bunning, the Yankees' Jim Bouton, Juan Pizarro of the White Sox and Boston's intimidating Dick Radatz, a hard-throwing righthander who struck out five batters in two innings.

The Nationals went ahead to stay with an unearned run in the fifth. The run, a pretty thin bit of gruel, came around on Bunning's walk to Davis, an error by second baseman Bobby Richardson and an infield out by Mays.

The Nationals had one thing left to prove in this game—that they could score without the aid of Willie. This they accomplished against the 6-foot-6, 240-pound Radatz in the eighth. They did it in crisp fashion, on a single by the Cardinals' Bill White, a stolen base and an RBI single by the Cubs' Ron Santo.

It was not a good day for the usually dependable Richardson. The Yankee infielder not only committed the game's only error, which led to what proved to be the game-winning run, but also chilled rallies by hitting into inning-ending double plays in the sixth and ninth as the Americans went down to a 5-3 defeat.

There was a nostalgia-drenched moment in the Nationals' fifth. Making his 24th All-Star appearance—it turned out to be his last —was Stan Musial. Pinch-hitting for Bailey, Musial, who later in the summer announced his retirement effective at the end of the season, lined out to right fielder Al Kaline. Musial left behind an All-Star log of 20 hits in 63 at-bats for a .317 average. Included among those hits were six home runs, an All-Star Game record.

Willie Mays.

Earl Battey.

Brooks Robinson.

Willie Mays (24) heads home as Dick Groat's second-inning base hit finds its way past the American League's infield in the 1963 All-Star Game.

Bill White.

Dick Radatz.

Stan Musial. The 1963 contest was his 24th and last
All-Star Game.

Johnny on the Spot

Americans	AB.	R.	H.	RBI.	PO.	A.
Fregosi (Angels), ss	4	1	1	1	4	1
Oliva (Twins), rf	4	0	0	0	0	0
Radatz (Red Sox), p	1	0	0	0	0	0
Mantle (Yankees), cf	4	1	1	0	2	0
Hall (Twins), cf	0	0	0	0	0	0
Killebrew (Twins), lf	4	1	3	1	0	0
Hinton (Senators), lf	0	0	0	0	0	0
Allison (Twins), 1b	3	0	0	0	9	0
fPepitone (Yankees), 1b	0	0	0	0	1	0
Robinson (Orioles), 3b	4	0	2	2	1	2
Richardson (Yanks), 2b	4	0	1	0	0	4
Howard (Yankees), c	3	1	0	0	9	0
Chance (Angels), p	1	0	0	0	0	1
Wyatt (Athletics), p	0	0	0	0	0	1
bSiebern (Orioles)	1	0	0	0	0	0
Pascual (Twins), p	0	0	0	0	0	1
eColavito (Athletics), rf	2	0	1	0	0	0
Totals	35	4	9	4	26	10

Nationals	AB.	R.	H.	RBI.	PO.	A.
Clemente (Pirates), rf	3	1	1	0	1	0
Short (Phillies), p	0	0	0	0	0	1
Farrell (Colts), p	0	0	0	0	0	0
gWhite (Cardinals)	1	0	0	0	0	0
Marichal (Giants), p	0	0	0	0	0	0
Groat (Cardinals), ss	3	0	1	1	0	0
dCardenas (Reds), ss	1	0	0	0	1	0
Williams (Cubs), lf	4	1	1	1	1	0
Mays (Giants), cf	3	1	0	0	7	0
Cepeda (Giants), 1b	4	0	1	0	6	0
hFlood (Cardinals)	0	1	0	0	0	0
Boyer (Cardinals), 3b	4	1	2	1	0	2
Torre (Braves), c	2	0	0	0	5	0
Edwards (Reds), c	1	1	0	0	5	0
Hunt (Mets), 2b	3	0	1	0	1	0
iAaron (Braves)	1	0	0	0	0	0
Drysdale (Dodgers), p	0	0	0	0	0	3
aStargell (Pirates)	1	0	0	0	0	0
Bunning (Phillies), p	0	0	0	0	0	0
cCallison (Phillies), rf	3	1	1	3	0	0
Totals	34	7	8	6	27	6

American League .... 1 0 0 0 0 2 1 0 0 — 4
National League .... 0 0 0 2 1 0 0 0 4 — 7
Two out when winning run scored.

Americans	IP.	H.	R.	ER.	BB.	SO.
Chance	3	2	0	0	0	2
Wyatt	1	2	2	2	0	0
Pascual	2	2	1	1	0	1
Radatz (L)	2⅔	2	4	4	2	5

Nationals	IP.	H.	R.	ER.	BB.	SO.
Drysdale	3	2	1	0	0	3
Bunning	2	2	0	0	0	4
Short	1	3	2	2	0	1
Farrell	2	2	1	1	1	1
Marichal (W)	1	0	0	0	0	1

aGrounded out for Drysdale in third. bFlied out for Wyatt in fifth. cPopped out for Bunning in fifth. dRan for Groat in fifth. eDoubled for Pascual in seventh. fRan for Allison in eighth. gStruck out for Farrell in eighth. hRan for Cepeda in ninth. iStruck out for Hunt in ninth. E—Pepitone. LOB—Americans 7, Nationals 3. 2B—Groat, Colavito. 3B—Robinson. HR—Williams, Boyer, Callison. SB—Mays. SF—Fregosi. HBP—By Farrell (Howard). WP—Drysdale. PB—Torre. U—Sudol, Secory and Harvey (N.L.), Paparella, Chylak and Salerno (A.L.). T—2:37. A—50,844.

In a rally reminiscent of the American League's comeback in the 1941 All-Star Game, the Nationals, having started their inexorable roll, stole the 1964 game from their rivals. The dramatic ninth-inning burst, like the one in 1941, was capped by a three-run home run, this one by the Phillies' Johnny Callison.

The game was played on July 7 at Shea Stadium, new home of the New York Mets. The opposing managers were Walter Alston and Al Lopez, the latter replacing Ralph Houk, who had won the pennant with the Yankees in 1963 before being elevated to the general manager's job.

Lopez started Angels righthander Dean Chance and, befitting a man on his way to a Cy Young Award, Chance shut down the Nationals on two hits as he fired his way through three scoreless innings. Going against Chance was another gifted righthander from Southern California, Don Drysdale. The Dodger ace was scratched for an unearned run in the first inning, fashioned on a single by Jim Fregosi of the Angels, a passed ball and an RBI single by the Twins' muscular Harmon Killebrew, who had three hits in the game, one-third of his team's total.

When Jim Bunning took the mound for the Nationals in the fourth, it marked the first time a pitcher had worked both sides of the street in an All-Star Game. Bunning, now with the Phillies, had pitched in six of these games for the American League while serving as an envoy from Detroit. The tall righthander, who 16 days prior to the '64 classic had carved a different slice of history when he threw a perfect game at the Mets from this very mound, burned off two shutout innings against the Americans while his teammates were moving into the lead.

Kansas City Athletics righthander John Wyatt had followed Chance in the fourth and was welcomed by a couple of home runs. The first bomb was unloaded by the Cubs' Billy Williams, the second by the Cardinals' Ken Boyer. The Nationals made it 3-1 against the Twins' Camilo Pascual in the next inning on a single by Roberto Clemente and Dick Groat's RBI double.

Another Phillies pitcher, lefthander Chris Short, took over for the Nationals in the sixth and sailed right into rough waters.

Singles by Mickey Mantle and Killebrew were followed by a triple by Brooks Robinson, making it 3-3.

The Americans untied the game with a run in the seventh. Houston's Dick Farrell hit the Yankees' Elston Howard with a pitch to start the inning and Rocky Colavito, now with the A's, rotated Howard around to third with a double, from where the Yankee catcher scored on Fregosi's fly ball.

With the Red Sox's Dick Radatz bringing his imposing presence to the mound in the bottom of the seventh, the American League lead seemed reasonably secure, particularly when the big guy buzzed through the seventh and eighth, fanning four of the six men he faced.

After Juan Marichal retired the Americans in the ninth, the Nationals began jabbing at Radatz. After fouling off five two-strike pitches, leadoff man Willie Mays walked. With Orlando Cepeda at bat, Mays took off and daringly stole second. Cepeda then blooped one into short right. When Willie saw the ball drop out of the reach of second baseman Bobby Richardson, he dashed for third and stopped. But when first baseman Joe Pepitone, who had retrieved the ball, fired home, the ball took a radical hop over Howard's glove and Mays raced in with the tying run (while Cepeda advanced to second).

The significance of Mays' stolen base was underlined later by Richardson. "Because Willie was there (on second)," Richardson said, "I had to play closer to the bag to keep him from getting a big lead. If I had been in my normal position, I probably could have caught Cepeda's ball."

After Boyer popped out, Johnny Edwards of the Reds was

walked intentionally to set up a double play. Henry Aaron pinch-hit for the Mets' Ron Hunt and struck out. (The National League lineup obviously had become more and more robust, considering that Aaron's role had been reduced to that of a pinch-hitter.)

The next batter was Callison, who had pinch-hit in the fifth inning and remained in the game in right field. Radatz made one pitch to the lefthanded-hitting Callison and Johnny powdered it into the upper right-field stands—not far off the foul line—for a three-run homer and a dramatic 7-4 National League victory.

Callison's heroics had drawn the Nationals even at last in the All-Star series, which now stood 17-17 (with one tie). The 20-year National League tide was now in full motion.

Jim Bunning.

San Francisco superstar Willie Mays and Dodgers ace lefthander Sandy Koufax show off the engraved bowls and traveling bags presented to the participants of the 1964 All-Star Game.

Dean Chance.

Harmon Killebrew.

Billy Williams.

Orlando Cepeda.

Jim Fregosi.

Juan Marichal.

Johnny Callison connects for the three-run homer that brought a dramatic conclusion to the 1964 midsummer classic.

Shea Stadium, home of the New York Mets and the site of the 1964 All-Star Game.

National Pride

Nationals	AB.	R.	H.	RBI.	PO.	A.
Mays (Giants), cf	3	2	1	1	4	0
Aaron (Braves), rf	5	0	1	0	0	0
Stargell (Pirates), lf	3	2	2	2	1	0
fClemente (Pirates), lf	2	0	0	0	0	0
Allen (Phillies), 3b	3	0	1	0	0	1
Santo (Cubs), 3b	2	0	1	1	2	0
Torre (Braves), c	4	1	1	2	5	1
Banks (Cubs), 1b	4	0	2	0	11	0
Rose (Reds), 2b	2	0	0	0	1	5
Wills (Dodgers), ss	4	0	1	0	2	3
Cardenas (Reds), ss	0	0	0	0	0	0
Marichal (Giants), p	1	1	1	0	0	0
bRojas (Phillies)	1	0	0	0	0	0
Maloney (Reds), p	0	0	0	0	0	0
Drysdale (Dodgers), p	0	0	0	0	0	0
dF. Robinson (Reds)	1	0	0	0	0	0
Koufax (Dodgers), p	0	0	0	0	0	0
Farrell (Astros), p	0	0	0	0	0	0
gWilliams (Cubs)	1	0	0	0	0	0
Gibson (Cardinals), p	0	0	0	0	1	0
Totals	36	6	11	6	27	10

Americans	AB.	R.	H.	RBI.	PO.	A.
McAuliffe (Tigers), ss	3	2	2	2	3	0
McDowell (Indians), p	0	0	0	0	0	1
eOliva (Twins), rf	2	0	1	0	0	0
B. Robinson (Orioles), 3b	4	1	1	0	1	2
Alvis (Indians), 3b	1	0	0	0	0	0
Killebrew (Twins), 1b	3	1	1	2	7	1
Colavito (Indians), rf	4	0	1	1	1	0
Fisher (White Sox), p	0	0	0	0	1	1
hPepitone (Yankees)	1	0	0	0	0	0
Horton (Tigers), lf	3	0	0	0	2	0
Mantilla (Red Sox), 2b	2	0	0	0	1	1
Richardson (Yanks), 2b	2	0	0	0	2	1
Davalillo (Indians), cf	2	0	1	0	1	0
Versalles (Twins), ss	1	0	0	0	0	2
Battey (Twins), c	2	0	0	0	4	1
Freehan (Tigers), c	1	0	1	0	4	0
Pappas (Orioles), p	0	0	0	0	0	1
Grant (Twins), p	0	0	0	0	0	0
aKaline (Tigers)	1	0	0	0	0	0
Richert (Senators), p	0	0	0	0	0	0
cHall (Twins), cf	2	1	0	0	0	0
Totals	34	5	8	5	27	11

National League	3 2 0	0 0 0	1 0 0—6			
American League	0 0 0	1 4 0	0 0 0—5			

Nationals	IP.	H.	R.	ER.	BB.	SO.
Marichal	3	1	0	0	0	0
Maloney	1⅔	5	5	5	2	1
Drysdale	⅓	0	0	0	0	0
Koufax (W)	1	0	0	0	2	1
Farrell	1	0	0	0	1	0
Gibson	2	2	0	0	1	3

Americans	IP.	H.	R.	ER.	BB.	SO.
Pappas	1	4	3	3	1	0
Grant	2	2	2	2	1	3
Richert	2	1	0	0	0	2
McDowell (L)	2	3	1	1	1	2
Fisher	2	1	0	0	0	0

aGrounded out for Grant in third. bFlied out for Marichal in fourth. cWalked for Richert in fifth. dStruck out for Drysdale in sixth. eGrounded out for McDowell in seventh. fHit into force play for Stargell in seventh. gGrounded out for Farrell in eighth. hStruck out for Fisher in ninth. DP—Nationals 1, Americans 2. LOB—Americans 8, Nationals 7. 2B—Oliva. HR—Mays, Torre, Stargell, McAuliffe, Killebrew. SH—Rose. WP—Maloney. U—Stevens, DiMuro and Valentine (A.L.), Weyer, Williams and Kibler (N.L.). T—2:45. A—46,706.

An examination of the National League's starting lineup for the 1965 All-Star Game indicates that the older league's dominance in the midsummer attraction might not have been entirely logic-defying. That lineup, pitcher excluded, read:

Willie Mays, center field
Henry Aaron, right field
Willie Stargell, left field
Richie Allen, third base
Joe Torre, catcher
Ernie Banks, first base
Pete Rose, second base
Maury Wills, shortstop

The potency of the league's power pool was so lethal and so abundant at this time that some of the Nationals' non-starters included full-dimensional talents like Roberto Clemente and Frank Robinson. And not only did this abundantly stocked league stack dynamite bats, but in this particular game four of the six N.L. pitchers used by Phillies Manager Gene Mauch (who had replaced the Cardinals' Johnny Keane, now with the Yankees) were named Juan Marichal, Don Drysdale, Sandy Koufax and Bob Gibson. That's four future Hall of Fame pitchers—each in his prime, no less—coming at you in one game.

Despite the lopsided weight of talent (the American squad was described as one of the weakest teams ever to represent the league), the 36th All-Star Game, played at the Minnesota Twins' Metropolitan Stadium in Bloomington on July 13, was a good ball game, and a close one, the Nationals winning it 6-5.

Righthander Milt Pappas of the Orioles started for White Sox Manager Al Lopez's club. (Like Mauch, Lopez was managing in place of a pennant-winning man-ager no longer on the job, in this case the Yankees' Yogi Berra, who had been dismissed after the 1964 World Series.) It was Pappas who was victimized by the firestorm of that National League lineup, and quickly.

Mays led off the game by popping one a long way through the brilliant Minnesota sunshine into the left-center bleachers for a home run. The blow signaled the game's leitmotif. Stargell singled and then Torre hit one out.

Twins righthander Jim (Mudcat) Grant was pitching for the Americans at the start of the second inning, and he fared only slightly better. National League starter Marichal singled and Mays walked. Grant achieved momentary relief by getting Aaron to hit into a double play, but Stargell clubbed his team's third home run and it was 5-0, National League.

After Marichal had gone three scoreless innings, the Americans put on a spirited drive at the expense of hard-throwing right-hander Jim Maloney of Cincinnati. After scoring once in the bottom of the fourth, the Americans struck as furiously and unexpectedly as a summer squall.

With two out and nobody on in the fifth, Maloney walked the Twins' Jimmie Hall and yielded a homer to the Tigers' Dick McAuliffe. Brooks Robinson singled and the Twins' Harmon Killebrew thrilled the Minnesota crowd with a booming, game-tying home run. The blow kayoed Maloney, who was replaced by Drysdale.

The game remained 5-5 until the seventh. With Cleveland's Sam McDowell pitching for the Americans (having followed Washington's Pete Richert, who had gone two scoreless innings), the Nationals broke the tie and, considering their earlier cannonading, they did it rather modestly.

Mays walked against the fast-balling McDowell, went to third on Aaron's single and scored on Ron Santo's infield single. With Koufax having held the Americans in the sixth, the one-run lead was entrusted to Houston's Dick Farrell, who guarded it well for one inning, and then to Gibson, a man most possessive of late-inning leads.

Gibson, who had worked out of a runners-on-second-and-third jam in the eighth, demonstrated in the ninth just how tightly his fist could close upon a narrow lead. The Twins' Tony Oliva opened with a double, placing the tying run at second. Gibson then induced Cleveland's Max Alvis to pop up while attempting to sacrifice. With the tying run still on second, Gibson gave a sizzling example of his competitive zeal by striking out Killebrew and the Yankees' Joe Pepitone to end the game.

The National League's 6-5 triumph gave it the lead in the series for the first time, 18-17-1.

For Lopez, it was his fifth American League All-Star managerial assignment and his fifth loss. Since Al also had appeared in two losing games as a National League player (in 1934 and 1941), his was a perfect, in the unavailing sense, All-Star Game record.

Dick McAuliffe.

Joe Torre.

Willie Mays takes his rip.

Ron Santo.

The makings of a pitching staff: Don Drysdale (left) and Sandy Koufax.

A bird's-eye view of Metropolitan Stadium, home of the American League's Minnesota Twins and the site of the 1965 All-Star Game.

Tony Oliva.

Harmon Killebrew, power personified.

Bob Gibson.

Willie Stargell.

Nineteen victories in 20 games. That's the way it was going to be, and there were times when the National League even seemed to toy with its rival. On other occasions, the Nationals allowed the American League a brief smell of victory's aroma but not a bit of its taste. The Americans got such whiffs from 1965 through 1968, when the National League scored four consecutive one-run triumphs.

The 1966 game was played in 105 degrees of soul-burning St. Louis heat at new Busch Memorial Stadium, which had opened its gates only two months earlier. With spectators passing out in the stands, and with ice packs, smelling salts and oxygen available in the dugouts, the July 12 game was played in a most gingerly fashion, only three runs being scored.

National League Manager Walter Alston started his own ace, Sandy Koufax, while the Twins' Sam Mele nominated Detroit righthander Denny McLain. McLain, who would win 20 games that year and 31 two years later, gave a glimpse of impending greatness by retiring the National League buzz saws without so much as a flyspeck on his record —nine up, nine down.

Hotly Contested

Americans	AB.	R.	H.	RBI.	PO.	A.
McAuliffe (Tigers), ss	3	0	0	0	1	1
Stottlemyre (Yankees), p..	0	0	0	0	0	0
hColavito (Indians)............	1	0	0	0	0	0
Siebert (Indians), p............	0	0	0	0	0	1
Richert (Senators), p	0	0	0	0	0	0
Kaline (Tigers), cf.............	4	0	1	0	3	0
Agee (White Sox), cf.......	0	0	0	0	1	0
F. Robinson (Orioles), lf..	4	0	0	0	2	0
Oliva (Twins), rf..............	4	0	0	0	0	0
B. Robinson (Orioles), 3b..	4	1	3	0	4	4
Scott (Red Sox), 1b	2	0	0	0	4	1
eCash (Tigers), 1b............	2	0	0	0	4	0
Freehan (Tigers), c............	2	0	1	0	4	0
Battey (Twins), c	1	0	0	0	1	0
Knoop (Angels), 2b	2	0	0	0	3	1
gRichardson (Yanks), 2b..	2	0	0	0	1	1
McLain (Tigers), p............	1	0	0	0	0	1
Kaat (Twins), p	0	0	0	0	0	0
cKillebrew (Twins)	1	0	1	0	0	0
dFregosi (Angels), ss	2	0	0	0	0	1
Totals....................	35	1	6	0	28	11

Nationals	AB.	R.	H.	RBI.	PO.	A.
Mays (Giants), cf	4	1	1	0	3	0
Clemente (Pirates), rf	4	0	2	0	2	0
Aaron (Braves), lf	4	0	0	0	2	0
McCovey (Giants), 1b	3	0	0	0	10	1
Santo (Cubs), 3b...............	4	0	1	1	2	2
Torre (Braves), c	3	0	0	0	5	0
McCarver (Cardinals), c ..	1	1	1	0	1	0
Lefebvre (Dodgers), 2b	2	0	0	0	2	0
Hunt (Mets), 2b................	1	0	0	0	0	1
Cardenas (Reds), ss	2	0	0	0	2	2
fStargell (Pirates)	1	0	0	0	0	0
Wills (Dodgers), ss	1	0	1	1	1	1
Koufax (Dodgers), p.........	0	0	0	0	0	0
aFlood (Cardinals)	1	0	0	0	0	0
Bunning (Phillies), p	0	0	0	0	0	0
bAllen (Phillies)	1	0	0	0	0	0
Marichal (Giants), p.........	0	0	0	0	0	0
iHart (Giants)	1	0	0	0	0	0
Perry (Giants), p...............	0	0	0	0	0	0
Totals....................	33	2	6	2	30	7

American League............0 1 0 0 0 0 0 0 0 0—1
National League.............0 0 0 1 0 0 0 0 0 1—2
One out when winning run scored.

Americans	IP.	H.	R.	ER.	BB.	SO.
McLain............................	3	0	0	0	0	3
Kaat...............................	2	3	1	1	0	1
Stottlemyre.....................	2	1	0	0	1	0
Siebert...........................	2	0	0	0	0	1
Richert (L)......................	⅓	2	1	1	0	0

Nationals	IP.	H.	R.	ER.	BB.	SO.
Koufax	3	1	1	1	0	1
Bunning	2	1	0	0	0	2
Marichal.........................	3	3	0	0	0	2
Perry (W).......................	2	1	0	0	1	1

aGrounded out for Koufax in third. bStruck out for Bunning in fifth. cSingled for Kaat in sixth. dRan for Killebrew in sixth. eGrounded into double play for Scott in seventh. fFouled out for Cardenas in seventh. gGrounded out for Knoop in eighth. hFlied out for Stottlemyre in eighth. iStruck out for Marichal in eighth. DP—Nationals 1. LOB—Americans 5, Nationals 5. 2B—Clemente. 3B—B. Robinson. SH—Hunt. WP— Koufax, Perry. U—Barlick, Vargo and Engel (N.L.), Umont, Honochick and Neudecker (A.L.). T—2:19. A—49,936.

The Americans took a 1-0 edge against Koufax in the second inning. Brooks Robinson, who had half of the A.L.'s six hits, smashed a one-out liner to left field and wound up with a triple when Henry Aaron lost track of the ball in the white-shirted background and let it slip past him. Robinson scored a few moments later on a wild pitch.

The Nationals tied it against Twins lefthander Jim Kaat in the fourth inning. This was done in the shape of singles by Willie Mays, Roberto Clemente and Ron Santo. Santo's hit was a slow roll-

er along the third-base line, enough to score Mays from third. The year before, Willie had scored from third with the winning run on Santo's infield single. National League consistency.

After that it was a goose-egg toss for five innings, thanks to Jim Bunning, Juan Marichal and Gaylord Perry (Giants) for the Nationals and Kaat, Mel Stottlemyre (Yankees) and Sonny Siebert (Indians) for the Americans. The result was just what everyone needed: A 1-1 tie, extra innings and 105 degrees.

Fortunately, there was only one extra inning. With Washington's Pete Richert now on the mound, the Cardinals' Tim McCarver led off the bottom of the 10th with a single. The Mets' Ron Hunt sacrificed. Then Maury Wills, angry over his non-starter status, sent everyone toward cooler precincts with a base hit to right field, scoring McCarver with the winning run in the Nationals' 2-1 conquest.

"The heat didn't bother me that much. I could've played another 10 innings," said the ever-upbeat Mays, who seemed to keep cool when it was warm, get warm when it was cool and sizzle when a game was on the line.

Juan Marichal.

Mel Stottlemyre.

Maury Wills.

Brooks Robinson.

Ron Santo.

Denny McLain.

The 1966 honorary All-Star coaches: Ted Williams (left) and Casey Stengel.

Tim McCarver (left) is congratulated by Gaylord Perry after scoring the winning run in the bottom of the 10th inning of the 1966 All-Star Game. Willie Mays is at the right.

1967

A second straight 2-1, extra-inning All-Star Game was played in 1967, on July 11 at the California Angels' Anaheim Stadium. The 15-inning contest was the fifth—and longest—extra-inning game in the series and, curiously enough, the National League had won all of these long-running contests.

Both Walter Alston's Nationals and Hank Bauer's Americans rolled out pitcher after pitcher who delivered brilliantly—the Nationals, in fact, were shut out for 12 straight innings, the third through the 14th, while the Americans were blanked over the last nine. Thirty strikeouts were registered, which some of the hitters attributed to the shadows that fell after the late-afternoon start. The pitchers, of course, had their own explanations for the plethora of strikeouts.

A roll call of those tight-fisted pitchers reads like this: National League—Juan Marichal, three one-hit, shutout innings; the Cubs' Ferguson Jenkins, three innings, one run, six strikeouts; Bob Gibson, two shutout innings; the Phillies' Chris Short, two shutout innings; the Astros' Mike Cuellar, two shutout innings; Don Drysdale, two shutout innings, and Mets rookie Tom Seaver, the final zero. American League—the Twins' Dean Chance, three innings, one run; the Angels' Jim McGlothlin, two shutout innings; the White Sox's Gary Peters, three perfect innings; the Yankees' Al

Extra Perfect

Nationals	AB.	R.	H.	RBI.	PO.	A.
Brock (Cardinals), lf	2	0	0	0	1	0
cMays (Giants), cf	4	0	0	0	3	0
Clemente (Pirates), rf	6	0	1	0	6	0
Aaron (Braves), cf-lf	6	0	1	0	2	0
Cepeda (Cardinals), 1b	6	0	0	0	6	0
Allen (Phillies), 3b	4	1	1	1	0	2
Perez (Reds), 3b	2	1	1	1	0	3
Torre (Braves), c	2	0	0	0	4	1
Haller (Giants), c	1	0	0	0	7	0
gBanks (Cubs)	1	0	1	0	0	0
McCarver (Cardinals), c	2	0	2	0	7	1
Mazeroski (Pirates), 2b	4	0	0	0	7	1
Drysdale (Dodgers), p	0	0	0	0	0	0
kHelms (Reds)	1	0	0	0	0	0
Seaver (Mets), p	0	0	0	0	0	0
Alley (Pirates), ss	5	0	0	0	1	3
Marichal (Giants), p	1	0	0	0	0	0
Jenkins (Cubs), p	1	0	0	0	0	0
Gibson (Cardinals), p	0	0	0	0	0	1
fWynn (Astros)	1	0	1	0	0	0
Short (Phillies), p	0	0	0	0	0	1
iStaub (Astros)	1	0	1	0	0	0
Cuellar (Astros), p	0	0	0	0	0	0
jRose (Reds), 2b	1	0	0	0	1	0
Totals	51	2	9	2	45	13

Americans	AB.	R.	H.	RBI.	PO.	A.
B. Robinson (Orioles), 3b	6	1	1	1	0	6
Carew (Twins), 2b	3	0	0	0	2	3
McAuliffe (Tigers), 2b	3	0	0	0	3	2
Oliva (Twins), cf	6	0	2	0	4	0
Killebrew (Twins), 1b	6	0	0	0	15	1
Conigliaro (Red Sox), rf	6	0	0	0	4	0
Yastrzemski (Red Sox), lf	4	0	3	0	2	0
Freehan (Tigers), c	5	0	0	0	13	0
Petrocelli (Red Sox), ss	4	0	0	0	0	1
McGlothlin (Angels), p	0	0	0	0	0	0
bMantle (Yankees)	1	0	0	0	0	0
Peters (White Sox), p	0	0	0	0	0	1
dMincher (Angels)	1	0	1	0	0	0
eAgee (White Sox)	1	0	0	0	0	0
Downing (Yankees), p	0	0	0	0	0	0
hAlvis (Indians)	1	0	0	0	0	0
Hunter (Athletics), p	1	0	0	0	0	0
lBerry (White Sox)	1	0	0	0	0	0
Chance (Twins), p	0	0	0	0	0	0
aFregosi (Angels), ss	4	0	1	0	2	3
Totals	49	1	8	1	45	17

National League ....010 000 000 000 001 — 2
American League ......000 001 000 000 000 — 1

Nationals	IP.	H.	R.	ER.	BB.	SO.
Marichal	3	1	0	0	0	3
Jenkins	3	3	1	1	0	6
Gibson	2	2	0	0	0	2
Short	2	0	0	0	1	1
Cuellar	2	1	0	0	0	2
Drysdale (W)	2	1	0	0	0	2
Seaver	1	0	0	0	1	1

Americans	IP.	H.	R.	ER.	BB.	SO.
Chance	3	2	1	1	0	1
McGlothlin	2	1	0	0	0	2
Peters	3	0	0	0	0	4
Downing	2	0	0	0	0	2
Hunter (L)	5	4	1	1	0	4

aSingled for Chance in third inning. bStruck out for McGlothlin in fifth inning. cStruck out for Brock in sixth inning. dSingled for Peters in eighth inning. eRan for Mincher in eighth inning. fSingled for Gibson in ninth inning. gSingled for Haller in tenth inning. hGrounded into fielder's choice for Downing in tenth inning. iSingled for Short in eleventh inning. jFlied out for Cuellar in thirteenth inning. kLined into double play for Drysdale in fifteenth inning. lStruck out for Hunter in fifteenth inning. DP—Americans 2. LOB—Nationals 5, Americans 7. 2B —Yastrzemski, McCarver. HR—Allen, B. Robinson, Perez. SB—Aaron. SH—Fregosi, Freehan, Mazeroski. U—Runge (A.L.) plate, Secory (N.L.) first, DiMuro (A.L.) second, Burkhart (N.L.) third, Ashford (A.L.) left and Pelekoudas (N.L.) right. T—3:41. A—46,309.

Downing, two shutout innings, and the Athletics' Catfish Hunter, who pitched the last five and gave up only one run—but it was the winning run.

The National League pitchers yielded just eight hits, the Americans nine. In addition to this near-starvation diet, only two bases on balls were issued, both to the Red Sox's Carl Yastrzemski, who also picked up three hits in a performance that typified his Triple Crown season.

Each of the three runs scored in the long game was put on the scoreboard in a sudden and decisive manner. In the second inning, the Phillies' Richie Allen homered against Chance. In the sixth, Orioles third baseman Brooks Robinson tied the score when he hit one out off Jenkins. And there it remained until the top of the 15th, when the Reds' Tony Perez came up with one out and sent a Hunter pitch over the left-field fence for the game-winner. Perez had replaced Allen at third base in the 10th inning, meaning that the dynamite in this game was all packed into the third-base position.

For Allen, Robinson and Perez, the drives were the only home runs of their All-Star careers. In fact, Perez's homer, coming in his first midsummer classic, proved his only hit in seven All-Star Games.

It was the National League's fifth straight victory over the Americans, the longest winning streak in the series. The triumph also extended the Nationals' lead in games to 20-17-1. And a record television audience for a non-World Series baseball game witnessed the contest, thanks to the 4:15 p.m. start (Pacific time) that sent much of the game into the East and the Midwest during prime time.

Richie Allen.

Gary Peters.

Ferguson Jenkins.

Tony Perez is welcomed home by Tim McCarver after his game-winning 15th-inning home run.

Catfish Hunter.

Chris Short.

Carl Yastrzemski.

Brooks Robinson.

Armed Destruction

Americans	AB.	R.	H.	RBI.	PO.	A.
Fregosi (Angels), ss	3	0	1	0	1	6
Campan'ris (Athletics), ss.	1	0	0	0	1	0
Carew (Twins), 2b	3	0	0	0	2	2
Johnson (Orioles), 2b	1	0	0	0	1	1
Yastr'ski (Red Sox), cf-lf	4	0	0	0	0	0
Howard (Senators), rf	2	0	0	0	0	0
Oliva (Twins), rf	1	0	1	0	2	0
Horton (Tigers), lf	2	0	0	0	1	0
Azcue (Indians), c	1	0	0	0	5	0
Josephson (White Sox), c	0	0	0	0	0	0
Killebrew (Twins), 1b	1	0	0	0	4	0
Powell (Orioles), 1b	2	0	0	0	2	0
Freehan (Tigers), c	2	0	0	0	4	0
McLain (Tigers), p	0	0	0	0	0	0
McDowell (Indians), p	0	0	0	0	0	0
eMantle (Yankees)	1	0	0	0	0	0
Stottlemyre (Yankees), p..	0	0	0	0	0	0
John (White Sox), p	0	0	0	0	0	0
Robinson (Orioles), 3b	2	0	0	0	0	1
Wert (Tigers), 3b	1	0	1	0	1	0
Tiant (Indians), p	0	0	0	0	0	0
aHarrelson (Red Sox)	1	0	0	0	0	0
Odom (Athletics), p	0	0	0	0	0	0
Monday (Athletics), cf	2	0	0	0	0	0
Totals	30	0	3	0	24	10

Nationals	AB.	R.	H.	RBI.	PO.	A.
Mays (Giants), cf	4	1	1	0	0	0
Flood (Cardinals), lf	1	0	0	0	1	0
M. Alou (Pirates), lf	1	0	1	0	1	0
Javier (Cardinals), 2b	0	0	0	0	0	0
McCovey (Giants), 1b	4	0	0	0	10	0
Aaron (Braves), rf	3	0	1	0	0	0
Santo (Cubs), 3b	2	0	1	1	1	1
Perez (Reds), 3b	0	0	0	0	0	1
Helms (Reds), 2b	3	0	1	0	1	2
Reed (Braves), p	0	0	0	0	0	0
Koosman (Mets), p	0	0	0	0	0	0
Grote (Mets), c	2	0	0	0	3	0
Carlton (Cardinals), p	0	0	0	0	0	1
cStaub (Astros)	1	0	0	0	0	0
Seaver (Mets), p	0	0	0	0	0	0
F. Alou (Braves), lf	0	0	0	0	0	0
Kessinger (Cubs), ss	2	0	0	0	1	2
dWilliams (Cubs)	1	0	0	0	0	0
Cardenas (Reds), ss	0	0	0	0	0	1
Drysdale (Dodgers), p	1	0	0	0	0	1
Marichal (Giants), p	0	0	0	0	0	0
bHaller (Dodgers), c	2	0	0	0	6	0
Bench (Reds), c	0	0	0	0	2	0
Totals	27	1	5	0	27	9

American League	0 0 0	0 0 0	0 0 0—0			
National League	1 0 0	0 0 0	0 0 x—1			

Americans	IP.	H.	R.	ER.	BB.	SO.
Tiant (L)	2	2	1	0	2	2
Odom	2	0	0	0	2	2
McLain	2	1	0	0	2	1
McDowell	1	1	0	0	0	3
Stottlemyre	⅓	0	0	0	0	1
John	⅔	1	0	0	0	0

Nationals	IP.	H.	R.	ER.	BB.	SO.
Drysdale (W)	3	1	0	0	0	0
Marichal	2	0	0	0	0	3
Carlton	1	0	0	0	0	1
Seaver	2	2	0	0	0	5
Reed	⅔	0	0	0	0	1
Koosman	⅓	0	0	0	0	0

aFlied out for Tiant in third. bFlied out for Marichal in fifth. cPopped out for Carlton in sixth. dFlied out for Kessinger in sixth. eStruck out for McDowell in eighth. E—Killebrew. DP—Americans 2. LOB—Americans 3, Nationals 8. 2B—Fregosi, Helms, Oliva, Wert. SB—Aaron. WP—Tiant. U—Crawford (N.L.) plate, Napp (A.L.) first, Steiner (N.L.) second, Kinnamon (A.L.) third, Odom (A.L.) left and Wendelstedt (N.L.) right. T—2:10. A—48,321.

It was the Year of the Pitcher, when the American League batted a collective .230 for the season and the Nationals hit .243, when Denny McLain won 31 games for the Detroit Tigers and the Cardinals' Bob Gibson logged a 1.12 earned-run average, when the Dodgers' Don Drysdale pitched 58 consecutive scoreless innings, and when Carl Yastrzemski won the American League batting title with a .301 average. And right in spirit with this offensive languor was the All-Star Game, played July 9 at Houston's Astrodome.

For the third straight game, runs were as scarce as apples in the desert as pitchers commanded the game like so many martinets. The final score was 1-0. Making the whole thing thematically precise and esthetically correct, the run was unearned.

The game was played indoors and on artificial surface, All-Star "firsts" that were joined by another—the first 1-0 outcome in the series.

Cardinals Manager Red Schoendienst started Drysdale against Red Sox skipper Dick Williams' American Leaguers. For Drysdale, one of the great pitchers in All-Star Game annals, it was his record-equaling eighth appearance and record-tying fifth start. It also was Drysdale's final All-Star Game, and he left with a record 19⅓ innings pitched, an unmatched 19 strikeouts, a 2-1 won-lost mark and a 1.40 ERA.

The National League's shutout was fashioned by these pitchers: Drysdale, three innings of one-hit ball; Juan Marichal, two hitless innings; the Cardinals' Steve Carlton, one hitless inning; Tom Seaver, two innings of two-hit ball garnished with five strikeouts, and the Braves' Ron Reed and the Mets' Jerry Koosman, who combined for one hitless inning. In styling their shutout, the N.L. misers issued no walks, allowed just three hits (all doubles) and retired 20 consecutive American batters in one stretch.

In the three low-scoring games of 1966, 1967 and 1968, National League pitchers held the American Leaguers to a mere 17 hits in 34 innings and limited the A.L. to a composite batting average of .149, giving up just three walks along the way. The National hitters did slightly better—20 hits in 33 innings and a .180 average.

The American League also used six pitchers in the '68 classic, which was played at night (as the midsummer contest became a prime-time television attraction). Cleveland's Luis Tiant started and yielded the game's lone run in the first inning. Tiant pitched two innings and gave two hits, while his successors—Blue Moon Odom of the A's, McLain, Sam McDowell, Mel Stottlemyre and the White Sox's Tommy John—permitted only three the rest of the way.

Willie Mays, in the starting lineup only because of an injury to Pete Rose, led off the Nationals' half of the first inning by grounding a single to left. A pickoff attempt by Tiant got past first baseman Harmon Killebrew and sent Mays to second. Then, as he delivered a fourth ball to the Cardinals' Curt Flood, Tiant missed badly, the ball getting away for a wild pitch and Willie moving to third. With men on first and third and still no one out, Tiant induced the Giants' Willie McCovey to ground into a double play, but Mays scored with what proved to be the game's only run.

The closest the Americans came to scoring was in the seventh when the Twins' Tony Oliva hit one off the left-field fence that just missed being a home run. Oliva settled for a double, giving the American League its first baserunner since the first inning, but the A.L. eventually had to settle for its sixth straight loss.

Besides the masterful pitching, the '68 All-Star Game probably is best remembered because of a third-inning injury suffered by Minnesota's Killebrew. Stretching for a low throw, the Twins' star suffered a severe hamstring tear, was forced to leave the game and missed more than seven weeks of the regular season.

The first pitch of baseball's first indoor All-Star Game is delivered by Don Drysdale to Jim Fregosi at the Houston Astrodome.

Ron Santo is forced at second base in the sixth inning of the 1968 game. The man airborne is shortstop Bert Campaneris, who couldn't quite get Tommy Helms at first on the double play attempt.

Sudden Sam McDowell.

Luis Tiant.

Don Drysdale.

The camera focused on Denny McLain a lot in 1968, the year he won 31 games.

Tom Seaver.

An N.L. Explosion

Nationals	AB.	R.	H.	RBI.	PO.	A.
Alou (Pirates), cf	4	1	2	0	5	0
Kessinger (Cubs), ss	3	0	0	0	0	0
eMays (Giants)	1	0	0	0	0	0
Menke (Astros), ss	1	0	0	0	1	0
Aaron (Braves), rf	4	1	1	0	0	0
Singer (Dodgers), p	0	0	0	0	0	0
Beckert (Cubs), 2b	1	0	0	0	0	0
McCovey (Giants), 1b	4	2	2	3	2	0
L. May (Reds), 1b	1	0	0	0	3	0
Santo (Cubs), 3b	3	0	0	0	2	1
Perez (Reds), 3b	1	0	0	0	1	1
Jones (Mets), lf	4	2	2	0	3	0
Rose (Reds), lf	1	0	0	0	2	0
Bench (Reds), c	3	2	2	2	4	0
Hundley (Cubs), c	1	0	0	0	3	0
Millan (Braves), 2b	4	1	1	2	1	1
Koosman (Mets), p	0	0	0	0	0	0
Dierker (Astros), p	0	0	0	0	0	0
Niekro (Braves), p	0	0	0	0	0	1
Carlton (Cardinals), p	2	0	1	1	0	1
Gibson (Cardinals), p	0	0	0	0	0	0
dBanks (Cubs)	1	0	0	0	0	0
Clemente (Pirates), rf	1	0	0	0	0	0
Totals	40	9	11	8	27	5

Americans	AB.	R.	H.	RBI.	PO.	A.
Carew (Twins), 2b	3	0	0	0	0	2
Andrews (Red Sox), 2b	1	0	0	0	0	0
Jackson (Athletics), cf-rf	2	0	0	0	2	0
Yastrzemski (R. Sox), lf	1	0	0	0	1	0
F. Robinson (Orioles), rf	2	0	0	0	0	0
Blair (Orioles), cf	2	0	0	0	2	0
Powell (Orioles), 1b	4	0	1	0	9	1
Howard (Senators), lf	1	1	1	1	0	0
bSmith (Red Sox), lf-rf	2	0	0	0	0	0
Bando (Athletics), 3b	3	0	1	0	0	1
McDowell (Indians), p	0	0	0	0	0	0
Culp (Red Sox), p	0	0	0	0	0	0
fWhite (Yankees)	1	0	0	0	0	0
Petrocelli (Red Sox), ss	3	0	1	0	1	3
Fregosi (Angels), ss	1	0	0	0	0	0
Freehan (Tigers), c	2	1	2	2	4	0
Roseboro (Twins), c	1	0	0	0	6	0
gC. May (White Sox)	1	0	0	0	0	0
Stottlemyre (Yankees), p	0	0	0	0	1	0
Odom (Athletics), p	0	0	0	0	0	0
Knowles (Senators), p	0	0	0	0	0	0
aKillebrew (Twins)	1	0	0	0	0	0
McLain (Tigers), p	0	0	0	0	0	0
cMincher (Pilots)	1	0	0	0	0	0
McNally (Orioles), p	0	0	0	0	0	0
B. Robinson (Orioles), 3b	1	0	0	0	1	1
Totals	33	3	6	3	27	8

National League ....1 2 5 1 0 0 0 0 0—9
American League ....0 1 1 1 0 0 0 0 0—3

Nationals	IP.	H.	R.	ER.	BB.	SO.
Carlton (W)	3	2	2	2	1	2
Gibson	1	2	1	1	1	2
Singer	2	0	0	0	0	0
Koosman	1⅔	1	0	0	0	1
Dierker	⅓	1	0	0	0	0
Niekro	1	0	0	0	0	2

Americans	IP.	H.	R.	ER.	BB.	SO.
Stottlemyre (L)	2	4	3	2	0	1
Odom	⅓	5	5	4	0	0
Knowles	⅔	0	0	0	0	0
McLain	1	1	1	1	2	2
McNally	2	1	0	0	1	1
McDowell	2	0	0	0	0	4
Culp	1	0	0	0	0	2

aFlied out for Knowles in third. bRan for Howard in fourth. cStruck out for McLain in fourth. dLined out for Gibson in fifth. eFlied out for Kessinger in fifth. fStruck out for Culp in ninth. gStruck out for Roseboro in ninth. E—Howard, Petrocelli. LOB—Nationals 7, Americans 5. 2B—Millan, Carlton, Petrocelli. HR—Bench, Howard, McCovey 2, Freehan. WP—Stottlemyre. U—Flaherty (A.L.) plate, Donatelli (N.L.) first, Stewart (A.L.) second, Gorman (N.L.) third, Springstead (A.L.) left and Venzon (N.L.) right. T—2:38. A—45,259.

The American League almost got a reprieve in 1969. The All-Star Game scheduled for the night of July 22 at Washington's Robert F. Kennedy Stadium was washed down the drain by a torrential downpour. The skies held off the next afternoon, however, and the rescheduled game was played—much to the chagrin of Detroit Manager Mayo Smith and his American Leaguers.

In their last 40 innings preceding the 1969 game, the National Leaguers had scored only six runs (but still were unbeatable). By the end of the third inning of the contest in Washington, though, the Nationals already had scored eight runs and were coasting, thanks to a murderous assault on A.L. starter Mel Stottlemyre and his immediate successor, Blue Moon Odom. Denny McLain had been scheduled to start for the Americans, but with the evening postponement the Tiger right-hander had flown to Detroit to keep a morning dental appointment and didn't get back to the Senators' ball park until the second inning.

Red Schoendienst's Nationals started slowly and built momentum into an explosive third inning, led by the sweet, powerful sweep of Willie McCovey's bat.

The Nationals started as they had a year before, with an unearned run in the first inning. Unlike the previous year's game, they didn't stop there. The run came on a leadoff single by Pittsburgh's Matty Alou, an infield out, a wild pitch and a fly ball that was dropped by Washington left fielder Frank Howard.

The National Leaguers were more emphatic in the second inning. The Mets' Cleon Jones legged out an infield hit and then Johnny Bench sounded the game's keynote with a two-run homer off Stottlemyre, making it 3-0.

Against N.L. starter Steve Carlton, the Americans scored single runs in the second and third, on home runs by Howard and Detroit's Bill Freehan. (Howard's homer had broken a 19-inning American League drought.) By that time, however, the game was in a state of permanent disarray.

In the top of the third, the Nationals had crashed into the Athletics' Odom like a fleet of Mack trucks. The report from damage control read like this: Henry Aaron, single; McCovey, home run; Jones, safe on an error; Bench, single; the Braves' Felix Millan, two-run double, and pitcher Carlton, RBI double. At this juncture (one man on, one out, five runs in), the Senators' Darold Knowles came in and retired the side.

McLain made his belated appearance in the fourth and fed McCovey his second home run. This made it 9-2, Nationals. In the bottom of the inning, Freehan singled in a run off Bob Gibson.

Thereafter, the pitchers assumed control. Bill Singer of the Dodgers, Jerry Koosman of the Mets, Larry Dierker of the Astros and Phil Niekro of the Braves shut down the Americans, while the Orioles' Dave McNally, the Indians' Sam McDowell and Boston's Ray Culp did the same to the Nationals.

The National League came close to adding a couple of runs in the sixth when Bench drove a McNally pitch to deep left field. Carl Yastrzemski deprived Johnny of a second homer, though, with a leaping catch in front of the wall, Yastrzemski's glove reportedly extending some three feet above the barrier when he made the snag.

The American Leaguers went quietly to the end. With Juan Marichal and Tom Seaver sitting in the National League bullpen, the Americans probably reasoned there was no point in stirring any trouble in this game, which served as the centerpiece to Washington festivities noting the centennial of professional baseball.

The 9-3 triumph was the National League's seventh straight; it also was the Nationals' seventh consecutive errorless game, two statistics that no doubt bespeak their own moral.

At this point, the American League might well have reflected on the words of former A.L. star Charlie Gehringer after Carl Hubbell had fanned five straight American superstars in the 1934 game:

"It was starting to get embarrassing."

Willie McCovey.

Bill Freehan.

Felix Millan.

Matty Alou makes a head-long dive toward third base as Sal Bando awaits the late throw. Alou advanced on a wild pitch before scoring the National League's first run in the first inning of the 1969 All-Star Game. The umpire is Tom Gorman.

Big Frank Howard homers in the second inning of the 1969 classic.

Carl Yastrzemski robs Johnny Bench of a two-run homer in the sixth inning. It would have been Bench's second of the game.

Jerry Koosman.

1970

FIVE TO

1979

The Tide
Is Pouring

The National League won its eighth straight All-Star Game in 1970, and upon the American League's continuing embarrassment was ladled a galling portion of mortification. More than winning streaks, losing streaks seem to develop personalities of their own, becoming maddeningly creative in finding fresh bumps in the road that help perpetuate the streak. If this is to imply that losing is more ingenious than winning, well, in what other sport does the team in possession of the ball play defense?

The '70 All-Star Game was played at Cincinnati's new Riverfront Stadium on July 14. The opposing managers were Gil Hodges of the "Miracle Mets" and Baltimore's Earl Weaver. The feisty Weaver, managing in his first All-Star Game, was determined to be the man who would lead the American League out of the wilderness. And he would have done it, too—if baseball had been an eight-inning game.

The game, the first since 1957 to feature starting lineups (excluding pitchers) chosen through fans' balloting, was launched on prolonged notes of high-class pitching. Jim Palmer of the Orioles and Tom Seaver of the Mets each opened with three innings of one-hit, shutout ball. Cleveland's Sam McDowell then brought his blistering fastball into the game for the American side and hung three more circles on the scoreboard. Cincinnati lefthander Jim Merritt pitched two shutout innings for the Nationals, and then the Americans finally scored in the sixth against San Francisco's Gaylord Perry.

The ingredients of the game's maiden run consisted of a single by Cleveland's Ray Fosse, a sacrifice by McDowell and an RBI single by Carl Yastrzemski, who had

Collision Course

Americans	AB.	R.	H.	RBI.	PO.	A.
Aparicio (White Sox), ss....	6	0	0	0	1	4
Y'strz'mski (R. Sox), cf-1b.	6	1	4	1	8	0
F. Robinson (Orioles), rf-lf	3	0	0	0	1	0
Horton (Tigers), lf	2	1	2	0	1	0
Powell (Orioles), 1b	3	0	0	0	5	0
Otis (Royals), cf	3	0	0	0	2	0
Killebrew (Twins), 3b	2	0	1	0	0	0
bHarper (Brewers)	0	0	0	0	0	0
B. Robinson (Orioles), 3b ..	3	1	2	2	1	1
Howard (Senators), lf	2	0	0	0	0	0
Oliva (Twins), rf	2	0	1	0	0	0
D. Johnson (Orioles), 2b...	5	0	1	0	5	1
Wright (Angels), p	0	0	0	0	0	0
Freehan (Tigers), c	1	0	0	0	4	0
Fosse (Indians), c	2	1	1	1	7	0
Palmer (Orioles), p	1	0	0	0	0	0
McDowell (Indians), p	0	0	0	0	0	3
dA. Johnson (Angels)	1	0	0	0	0	0
J. Perry (Twins), p	0	0	0	0	0	0
fFregosi (Angels)	1	0	0	0	0	0
Hunter (Athletics), p	0	0	0	0	0	0
Peterson (Yankees), p	0	0	0	0	0	0
Stottlemyre (Yankees), p..	0	0	0	0	0	2
Alomar (Angels), 2b	1	0	0	0	0	0
Totals	44	4	12	4	35	11
Nationals	AB.	R.	H.	RBI.	PO.	A.
Mays (Giants), cf	3	0	0	0	3	0
G. Perry (Giants), p	0	0	0	0	0	2
eMcCovey (Giants), 1b	2	0	1	1	1	0
gOsteen (Dodgers), p	0	0	0	0	1	0
iTorre (Cardinals)	1	0	0	0	0	0
Allen (Cardinals), 1b	3	0	0	0	4	0
Gibson (Cardinals), p	0	0	0	0	0	0
hClemente (Pirates), rf...	1	0	0	1	2	0
Aaron (Braves), rf	2	0	0	0	1	0
Rose (Reds), rf-lf	3	1	1	0	3	0
Perez (Reds), 3b	3	0	0	0	1	1
Grabarkewitz (Dod.), 3b ..	3	0	1	0	0	1
Carty (Braves), lf	1	0	0	0	0	0
Hickman (Cubs), lf-1b	4	0	1	1	6	1
Bench (Reds), c	3	0	0	0	5	1
Dietz (Giants), c	2	1	1	1	2	0
Kessinger (Cubs), ss	2	0	2	0	0	0
Harrelson (Mets), ss	3	2	2	0	0	4
Beckert (Cubs), 2b	2	0	0	0	2	1
Gaston (Padres), cf	2	0	0	0	2	0
Seaver (Mets), p	0	0	0	0	0	0
aStaub (Expos)	1	0	0	0	0	0
Merritt (Reds), p	0	0	0	0	0	0
cMenke (Astros), 2b	0	0	0	0	2	1
Morgan (Astros), 2b	2	1	1	0	1	2
Totals	43	5	10	4	36	14

American League....0 0 0 0 0 1 1 2 0 0 0 0—4
National League .....0 0 0 0 0 0 1 0 3 0 0 1—5
Two out when winning run scored.

Americans	IP.	H.	R.	ER.	BB.	SO.
Palmer	3	1	0	0	1	3
McDowell	3	1	0	0	3	3
J. Perry	2	1	1	1	1	3
Hunter	⅓	3	3	3	0	0
Peterson	0*	1	0	0	0	0
Stottlemyre	1⅔	0	0	0	0	2
Wright (L)	1⅔	3	1	1	0	0

Nationals	IP.	H.	R.	ER.	BB.	SO.
Seaver	3	1	0	0	0	4
Merritt	2	1	0	0	0	1
G. Perry	2	4	2	2	1	0
Gibson	2	3	2	2	1	2
Osteen (W)	3	3	0	0	0	3

*Pitched to one batter in ninth.

aFlied out for Seaver in third. bRan for Killebrew in fifth. cWalked for Merritt in fifth. dHit into force play for McDowell in seventh. eGrounded into double play for G. Perry in seventh. fFlied out for J. Perry in ninth. gRan for McCovey in ninth. hHit sacrifice fly for Gibson in ninth. iGrounded out for Osteen in twelfth. DP—Americans 1, Nationals 1. LOB—Americans 9, Nationals 10. 2B—Oliva, Yastrzemski. 3B—B. Robinson. HR—Dietz. SH—McDowell. SF—Fosse, Clemente. HBP—J. Perry (Menke). U—Barlick (N.L.) plate, Rice (A.L.) first, Secory (N.L.) second, Haller (A.L.) third, Dezelan (N.L.) left, Goetz (A.L.) right. T—3:19. A—51,838.

four hits in the game (the first four-hit performance in the midsummer show since Ted Williams, Yastrzemski's predecessor as the Red Sox's left fielder, did it in 1946).

The Americans left another footprint on home plate against Perry in the seventh. This one was put together on a single by Brooks Robinson, a walk to Tony Oliva, an infield hit by the Orioles' Dave Johnson and a sacrifice fly by Fosse. That made it 2-0.

The Nationals made their way home for the first time in the seventh inning, doing so against Jim Perry, Minnesota's star righthander and Gaylord's brother (Jim won 24 games for the Twins in 1970, while Gaylord won 23 for the Giants). Hodges' team loaded the bases with none out, building the most menacing of all baseball threats in variety-show style: single, walk and hit batsman (starring, respectively, the Mets' Bud Harrelson, the Padres' Cito Gaston and the Astros' Denis Menke). Perry, however, extricated himself right at flood tide by getting the dangerous Willie McCovey to rap into a double play (at the cost of a run) and Richie Allen to strike out. At the end of seven, it was 2-1, American League.

In the eighth, the Americans cuffed around Bob Gibson for two runs. The Cardinals' glowering ace gave up singles to Yastrzemski and Detroit's Willie Horton and then a triple to Brooks Robinson. It was now 4-1, Americans, and remained that way as Jim Perry guided his team safely through the last of the eighth and Gibson did the same for the Nationals in the top of the ninth. But there had to be a last of the ninth, and those National League bushwhackers were lurking in the tall grass.

Weaver brought on the splendid Catfish Hunter to protect the three-run margin. It looked like money in the bank for the Americans; but, again, losing streaks have lives of their own.

There was nothing ambiguous about the National League's comeback against Hunter. Catfish was simply hooked and bronzed.

The Giants' Dick Dietz began with a home run. Harrelson singled and, after Gaston popped out, budding star Joe Morgan of the Astros singled Harrelson to second.

With the lefthanded-hitting McCovey coming up, Weaver brought on Yankees lefthander Fritz Peterson. McCovey sent a backfire charge into the strategy with a rip to center, the base hit scoring Harrelson and sending Morgan to third with the tying run. Weaver then brought in Yankees righthander Mel Stottlemyre as Hodges sent up a pretty nifty pinch-hitter—Roberto Clemente. Roberto hoisted a sacrifice fly and the game was tied, much to the glee of a highly animated National League squad, which had been on the verge of a shocking experience—losing an All-Star Game.

So, for the sixth time, an All-Star Game went into extra innings. Dodgers lefthander Claude Osteen worked a scoreless slate through the 10th, 11th and 12th innings. Angels lefthander Clyde Wright took over for Stottlemyre in the 11th and kept it going.

There were two out in the bottom of the 12th when lightning escaped from the National League bottle. The first sizzle of this electricity was a familiar charge named Peter Edward Rose, delegate from Cincinnati, who singled. Rose went to second on another single by the Dodgers' Billy Grabarkewitz. There then occurred one of the memorable get-togethers in All-Star Game annals.

The Cubs' Jim Hickman lined a single to center field, where strong-armed Amos Otis of the Royals raced in and fired home for a play on Rose.

Pete Rose running to first base on a grounder to the pitcher is a man trying to outrun destiny. Pete Rose coming around third carrying the winning run is like destiny itself. With Fosse blocking the plate and awaiting the throw, and with the galvanized Rose coming hellbent, it was not a moment for the squeamish.

The irresistible met the movable and Fosse, who should have been carrying collision insurance for this one, was bruisingly bowled over by the oncoming Rose and left dazed, resting on his knees and head, as Pete scored what was perhaps the archetypical run of his long career. The Nationals had done it again, 5-4.

By hammer and tongs, by theft and by guile, by pocket-picking and by direct assault, the National League had extended its winning streak. And the senior league was now an amazing 6 for 6 in extra-inning games.

Tom Seaver.

Dave Johnson.

Jim Palmer.

Carl Yastrzemski.

Dick Dietz.

Willie McCovey.

Claude Osteen.

Pete Rose collides (above) with American League catcher Ray Fosse, knocking both ball and glove loose while scoring the winning run in the 12th inning of the 1970 All-Star Game. Rose is embraced (below) by teammate Dick Dietz as the injured Fosse slumps in pain. N.L. coach Leo Durocher is in the background.

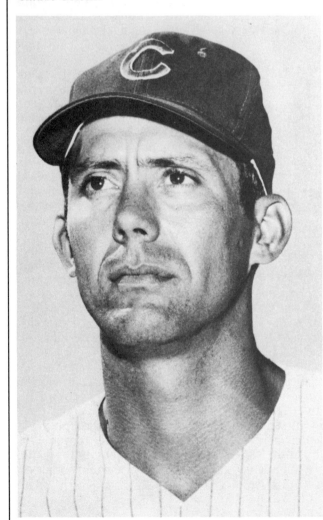

Jim Hickman.

1971

A Breakthrough

Nationals	AB.	R.	H.	RBI.	PO.	A.
Mays (Giants), cf	2	0	0	0	0	0
Clemente (Pirates), rf	2	1	1	1	0	0
Millan (Braves), 2b	0	0	0	0	1	1
Aaron (Braves), rf	2	1	1	1	0	0
May (Reds), 1b	1	0	0	0	6	0
Torre (Cardinals), 3b	3	0	0	0	1	0
fSanto (Cubs), 3b	1	0	0	0	0	1
Stargell (Pirates), lf	2	1	0	0	2	0
gBrock (Cardinals)	1	0	0	0	0	0
McCovey (Giants), 1b	2	0	0	0	4	0
Marichal (Giants), p	0	0	0	0	0	0
Kessinger (Cubs), ss	2	0	0	0	1	1
Bench (Reds), c	4	1	2	2	5	0
Beckert (Cubs), 2b	3	0	0	0	0	5
Rose (Reds), rf	0	0	0	0	0	0
Harrelson (Mets), ss	2	0	0	0	1	2
Jenkins (Cubs), p	0	0	0	0	0	0
cColbert (Padres)	1	0	0	0	0	0
Wilson (Astros), p	0	0	0	0	0	0
Ellis (Pirates), p	1	0	0	0	0	0
Davis (Dodgers), cf	1	0	1	0	2	0
eBonds (Giants), cf	1	0	0	0	0	0
Totals	31	4	5	4	24	11

Americans	AB.	R.	H.	RBI.	PO.	A.
Carew (Twins), 2b	1	1	0	0	1	2
Rojas (Royals), 2b	1	0	0	0	1	1
Murcer (Yankees), cf	3	0	1	0	1	0
Cuellar (Orioles), p	0	0	0	0	1	0
dBuford (Orioles)	1	0	0	0	0	0
Lolich (Tigers), p	0	0	0	0	0	3
Yastrzemski (R. Sox), lf	3	0	0	0	0	0
F. Robinson (Orioles), rf	2	1	1	2	2	0
Kaline (Tigers), rf	2	1	1	0	2	0
Cash (Tigers), 1b	2	0	0	0	7	0
Killebrew (Twins), 1b	2	1	1	2	4	0
B. Robinson (Orioles), 3b	3	0	1	0	1	3
Freehan (Tigers), c	3	0	0	0	6	1
Munson (Yankees), c	0	0	0	0	1	0
Aparicio (Red Sox), ss	3	1	1	0	1	2
Blue (Athletics), p	0	0	0	0	0	0
aJackson (Athletics)	1	1	1	2	0	0
Palmer (Orioles), p	0	0	0	0	0	0
bHoward (Senators)	1	0	0	0	0	0
Otis (Royals), cf	1	0	0	0	0	0
Totals	29	6	7	6	27	12

National League	0 2 0	0 0 0	0 1 0—4			
American League	0 0 4	0 0 2	0 0 x—6			

Nationals	IP.	H.	R.	ER.	BB.	SO.
Ellis (L)	3	4	4	4	1	2
Marichal	2	0	0	0	1	1
Jenkins	1	3	2	2	0	0
Wilson	2	0	0	0	1	2

Americans	IP.	H.	R.	ER.	BB.	SO.
Blue (W)	3	2	3	3	0	3
Palmer	2	1	0	0	0	2
Cuellar	2	1	0	0	1	2
Lolich	2	1	1	1	0	1

aHomered for Blue in third. bGrounded out for Palmer in fifth. cStruck out for Jenkins in seventh. dStruck out for Cuellar in seventh. eStruck out for Davis in eighth. fGrounded out for Torre in eighth. gBunted and was thrown out for Stargell in ninth. DP—Nationals 2, Americans 2. LOB—Nationals 2, Americans 2. HR—Bench, Aaron, Jackson, F. Robinson, Killebrew, Clemente. HBP—By Blue (Stargell). U—Umont (A.L.) plate, Pryor (N.L.) first, O'Donnell (A.L.) second, Harvey (N.L.) third, Denkinger (A.L.) right, Colosi (N.L.) left. T—2:05. A—53,559.

The American League finally won an All-Star Game again in 1971, and the Americans did it in manly style, coming from behind and standing toe-to-toe in a battle of haymaker punches. All of the runs in the American Leaguers' 6-4 win were scored on home runs, with each side unloading three long-distance shots.

The game was played at Detroit's Tiger Stadium on July 13. Vida Blue, Oakland's sensational young lefthander, started for Earl Weaver's Americans, while Reds Manager Sparky Anderson opened with Pittsburgh righthander Dock Ellis for the Nationals. Blue, who already had won 17 games in '71 and was on the way to both Cy Young Award and Most Valuable Player honors, was not at his purest during his stint, nor was Ellis, as four of the cannon shots were touched off in the first three innings.

After a 1-2-3 top of the first, Blue began the second by hitting Willie Stargell with a pitch. After striking out Willie McCovey, Vida was rocked by a Johnny Bench home run, making it 2-0, Nationals. When Henry Aaron belted one out in the third against Blue, it became 3-0 and American League adherents—and there were many in the Tigers' ball park—began sighing and shaking their heads. There it was again—the handwriting on the scoreboard.

The Americans showed some resilience in their half of the third, though, coming from behind for the first time since 1964 to take the lead. The Red Sox's Luis Aparicio led off with a single. Weaver then sent up Oakland's Reggie Jackson to hit for Blue. Playing in his fourth full major league season, Reggie had not yet become a household name; in this at-bat, however, he incised his name upon All-Star scrolls and upon the consciousness of all who were watching.

Connecting emphatically with an Ellis delivery, Reggie unloaded a shot of mammoth height and distance, a missile that struck a light tower on the roof in right-center, traveling by some estimates 520 feet. Always the chief admirer of his own work, Reggie paused for a moment to watch his prodigious clout climb toward its destiny, and then began his jour-

ney around the bases.

Ellis then walked the Twins' Rod Carew before retiring the following two batters. Up next was former National Leaguer Frank Robinson, now with the Orioles. Robinson sliced a shot into the lower right-field seats, giving the Americans a 4-3 edge and becoming the first man ever to homer for both sides in the All-Star Game (he had socked one for the Nationals in the second 1959 game while representing the Reds).

A pair of Baltimore pitchers, Jim Palmer and Mike Cuellar, held the Nationals scoreless from the fourth inning through the seventh while the Americans fattened their lead. After Juan Marichal had replaced Ellis and pitched shutout ball in the fourth and fifth, the Cubs' Ferguson Jenkins came on and fed a two-run homer to Harmon Killebrew in the sixth, making it 6-3.

In the Nationals' eighth, with Detroit lefthander Mickey Lolich now pitching, Roberto Clemente closed out the scoring with the game's record-tying sixth home run. And while Astros righthander Don Wilson pitched two strong shutout innings for the National League in the seventh and eighth, Lolich delivered a perfect top of the ninth to put the lid on the Americans' 6-4 win, their first victory since the second game of 1962.

If the American Leaguers had hoped this long-awaited success would mark a turnaround in their midsummer fortunes, they were to be sorely disappointed. Babes now in their cribs would be callow teen-agers before the American League won another of these games.

Henry Aaron.

Reggie Jackson admires his mammoth home run in the third inning of the 1971 All-Star Game.

Roberto Clemente.

Harmon Killebrew watches the flight of his sixth-inning home run.

Frank Robinson.

Johnny Bench.

After a one-year respite, the plague returned to the American League in 1972, this time to remain for 11 years.

The Nationals resumed the torment of their interleague brethren in a familiar style—coming from behind and winning in extra innings (and, in the process, playing errorless ball for the 10th straight game).

For the third consecutive year, Earl Weaver ran the American League squad. Pittsburgh's Danny Murtaugh managed the Nationals.

The game was played on July 25 at Atlanta Stadium, a park known as "the launching pad" for the friendly sendoff it gave to batted balls. Nevertheless, just two long ones were struck this night.

Bob Gibson started for the Nationals and sailed through two scoreless innings. He was followed by Pittsburgh righthander Steve Blass, who in his lone inning of work gave up the game's first run on a walk to the Tigers' Bill Freehan, a sacrifice and an RBI single by Rod Carew. A.L. starter Jim Palmer of Baltimore worked three innings of high-class shutout ball.

The Americans were held in check through the sixth inning by the Dodgers' Don Sutton and the Phillies' Steve Carlton, who was in the midst of a scintillating 27-10 season for a last-place ball club.

The Nationals took a 2-1 lead in their half of the sixth when Henry Aaron, playing in his home park, hit what he described after the game as "the most dramatic home run of my career" (to that point, anyway), a two-run shot off a familiar figure, Gaylord Perry, now with Cleveland. (Perry, the long-time Giant, had just come on to replace Mickey Lolich, who had spun two scoreless innings.)

Back to Reality

Americans	AB.	R.	H.	RBI.	PO.	A.
Carew (Twins), 2b	2	0	1	1	2	3
cRojas (Royals), 2b	1	1	1	2	3	1
Murcer (Yankees), cf	3	0	0	0	1	0
Scheinblum (Royals), rf	1	0	0	0	1	0
Jackson (Athletics), rf-cf	4	0	2	0	5	0
Allen (White Sox), 1b	3	0	0	0	4	0
Cash (Tigers), 1b	1	0	0	0	3	0
Yastrzemski (R. Sox), lf	3	0	0	0	3	0
Rudi (Athletics), lf	1	0	1	0	0	0
Grich (Orioles), ss	4	0	0	0	0	3
Robinson (Orioles), 3b	2	0	0	0	0	1
Bando (Athletics), 3b	2	0	0	0	1	1
Freehan (Tigers), c	1	1	0	0	3	0
Fisk (Red Sox), c	2	1	1	0	2	0
Palmer (Orioles), p	0	0	0	0	0	0
Lolich (Tigers), p	1	0	0	0	0	0
Perry (Indians), p	0	0	0	0	0	0
bSmith (Red Sox)	1	0	0	0	0	0
Wood (White Sox), p	0	0	0	0	0	0
dPiniella (Royals)	1	0	0	0	0	0
McNally (Orioles), p	0	0	0	0	0	1
Totals	33	3	6	3	28	10

Nationals	AB.	R.	H.	RBI.	PO.	A.
Morgan (Reds), 2b	4	0	1	1	3	5
Mays (Mets), cf	2	0	0	0	2	0
Cedeno (Astros), cf	2	1	1	0	0	0
Aaron (Braves), rf	3	1	1	2	0	0
Oliver (Pirates), rf	1	0	0	0	0	0
Stargell (Pirates), lf	1	0	0	0	0	0
Williams (Cubs), lf	2	1	1	0	0	0
Bench (Reds), c	2	0	0	0	3	0
Sanguillen (Pirates), c	2	0	1	0	6	0
May (Astros), 1b	4	0	1	1	13	2
Torre (Cardinals), 3b	3	0	1	0	1	2
Santo (Cubs), 3b	1	0	0	0	0	0
Kessinger (Cubs), ss	2	0	0	0	0	0
Carlton (Phillies), p	0	0	0	0	0	0
Stoneman (Expos), p	1	0	0	0	0	0
McGraw (Mets), p	0	0	0	0	0	0
eColbert (Padres)	0	1	0	0	0	0
Gibson (Cardinals), p	0	0	0	0	1	0
Blass (Pirates), p	0	0	0	0	0	0
aBeckert (Cubs)	1	0	0	0	0	0
Sutton (Dodgers), p	0	0	0	0	0	0
Speier (Giants), ss	2	0	0	0	1	5
Totals	33	4	8	4	30	14

American League...........0 0 1 0 0 0 0 2 0 0–3
National League...........0 0 0 0 0 2 0 0 1 1–4
One out when winning run scored.

Americans	IP.	H.	R.	ER.	BB.	SO.
Palmer	3	1	0	0	1	2
Lolich	2	1	0	0	0	1
Perry	2	3	2	2	0	1
Wood	2	2	1	1	1	1
McNally (L)	⅓	1	1	1	1	0

Nationals	IP.	H.	R.	ER.	BB.	SO.
Gibson	2	1	0	0	0	0
Blass	1	1	1	1	1	0
Sutton	2	1	0	0	0	2
Carlton	1	0	0	0	1	0
Stoneman	2	2	2	2	0	2
McGraw (W)	2	1	0	0	0	4

aFlied out for Blass in third. bStruck out for Perry in eighth. cHomered for Carew in eighth. dGrounded out for Wood in tenth. eWalked for McGraw in tenth. DP—Nationals 2, Americans 1. LOB—Nationals 5, Americans 3. 2B—Jackson, Rudi. HR—Aaron, Rojas. SB—Morgan. SH—Palmer, Speier. U—Landes (N.L.) plate, DiMuro (A.L.) first, Weyer (N.L.) second, Neudecker (A.L.) third, Dale (N.L.) left, Kunkel (A.L.) right. T—2:26. A—53,107.

Aaron's home run had sent the 50,000-plus spectators into a loud roar of approval for their hero. The ball cleared the left-field fence and landed close to a sign that noted the arrival point of Henry's 600th major league home run, struck during the previous season—off Gaylord Perry, then with San Francisco.

"I hit a spitter," Aaron said after the game, reviving the issue of Perry's alleged moist deliveries. "But not one of his best spitters." Perry's disclaimer was, "Fastball, inside." Whatever the pitch, it was surely dry by the time it came down.

Henry found himself upstaged, however, in the Americans' eighth, and by a most unlikely fellow. With Bill Stoneman of the Expos pitching for the Nationals, the Red Sox's Carlton Fisk singled and rode home on a pinch home run by the Royals' Cookie Rojas. Rojas, best-known for his defensive prowess, had batted for Carew (who was suffering from a rib-cage injury).

The American League took its 3-2 lead into the bottom of the ninth, with the White Sox's Wilbur Wood trying to protect the slim edge and give the Americans consecutive victories for the first time since 1957-1958. Wood couldn't nail it down.

Singles by the Cubs' Billy Williams and the Pirates' Manny Sanguillen put men on first and third with none out. Williams scored the tying run on a force-out. Wood then retired the side.

With the Mets' ebullient Tug McGraw holding the Americans scoreless in the 10th, the Nationals made it a return to old times in the bottom of the inning.

Baltimore's Dave McNally was on the mound now. The lefthander began by walking the Padres' Nate Colbert. The Giants' Chris Speier sacrificed him to second. The next batter was Joe Morgan, now a member of the Reds after an off-season Houston-Cincinnati trade, and Morgan brought the evening's proceedings to an abrupt, rousing end by stinging a single to right-center that easily scored Colbert.

The 4-3, 10-inning victory gave the National League a 7-for-7 record in extra-inning games, a startling statistic. It also raised the Nationals' series lead to 24-18-1, and they really hadn't gotten warm yet.

Bob Gibson.

Jim Palmer.

Gaylord Perry.

Henry Aaron.

Bill Freehan slides home safely in the third inning with the first run of the 1972 All-Star Game. Waiting for the throw is National League catcher Johnny Bench.

Joe Morgan.

Cookie Rojas.

Mickey Lolich.

National League players swarm around Joe Morgan after the little second baseman delivered the 10th-inning single that broke up the 1972 game. Winning pitcher Tug McGraw is putting on his jacket (right).

The scoreboard at new Royals Stadium in Kansas City was 12 stories high and illuminated with 16,000 lights that winked and flashed as various displays of animated characters grinned and gamboled through them. From behind the center-field fence, a row of fountains gushed plumes and geysers of water high into the air under the transposing contemplation of multi-colored spotlights. It was an elegant, dazzling show, and the more than 40,000 fans loved it.

There also was a ball game there on the night of July 24, but for American League fans, the lights and the fountains carried the night.

Dick Williams' American Leaguers scored first, in the second inning, but then it was all Sparky Anderson and his talent-laden Nationals. Each manager employed seven pitchers in a ball game that turned into a brutally clear-cut demonstration of National League superiority.

The Americans scored on a double by Reggie Jackson and a single by Royals favorite Amos Otis. Thereafter they managed just three more hits and no runs off the assorted deliveries of the Cardinals' Rick Wise (the N.L. starter), the Dodgers' Claude Osteen and Don Sutton, the Phillies' Wayne Twitchell, the Pirates' Dave Giusti, the Mets' Tom Seaver and a third Dodger, Jim Brewer.

The Nationals collected two runs in the third inning and went on scoring steadily and modestly through the sixth, building a 7-1 lead that proved the final score. The Astros' Cesar Cedeno and the

Lights Out

Nationals	AB.	R.	H.	RBI.	PO.	A.
Rose (Reds), lf	3	1	0	0	1	0
Twitchell (Phillies), p	0	0	0	0	0	0
Giusti (Pirates), p	0	0	0	0	0	0
jMota (Dodgers), lf	1	0	0	0	0	0
Brewer (Dodgers), p	0	0	0	0	2	2
Morgan (Reds), 2b	3	2	1	0	2	2
Johnson (Braves), 2b	1	0	0	0	1	1
Cedeno (Astros), cf	3	0	1	1	3	0
Russell (Dodgers), ss	2	0	0	0	0	2
Aaron (Braves), 1b	2	0	1	1	3	1
Torre (Cards), 1b-3b	3	0	0	0	5	0
Williams (Cubs), rf	2	0	1	0	0	0
Bonds (Giants), rf	2	1	2	2	0	0
Bench (Reds), c	3	1	1	1	3	1
fSimmons (Cards), c	1	0	0	0	1	1
Santo (Cubs), 3b	1	1	1	0	0	1
hColbert (Padres)	1	0	0	0	0	0
Fairly (Expos), 1b	0	0	0	0	4	0
Speier (Giants), ss	2	0	0	0	1	1
dStargell (Pirates), lf	1	0	0	0	1	0
iMays (Mets)	1	0	0	0	0	0
Seaver (Mets), p	0	0	0	0	0	1
Watson (Astros), lf	0	0	0	0	0	0
Wise (Cardinals), p	0	0	0	0	1	0
aEvans (Braves)	0	0	0	0	0	0
Osteen (Dodgers), p	0	0	0	0	0	1
Sutton (Dodgers), p	0	0	0	0	0	1
eDavis (Dodgers), cf	2	1	2	2	1	0
Totals	34	7	10	7	27	12

Americans	AB.	R.	H.	RBI.	PO.	A.
Campan'ris (Athletics), ss.	3	0	0	0	1	2
Brinkman (Tigers), ss	1	0	0	0	1	1
Carew (Twins), 2b	3	0	0	0	5	1
Rojas (Royals), 2b	0	0	0	0	1	1
Mayberry (Royals), 1b	3	0	1	0	8	0
Jackson (Athletics), rf	4	1	1	0	0	0
Blair (Orioles), cf	0	0	0	0	1	0
Otis (Royals), cf	2	0	2	1	0	0
May (Brewers), cf-rf	2	0	0	0	0	0
Murcer (Yankees), lf	3	0	0	0	0	1
Fisk (Red Sox), c	2	0	0	0	3	0
Munson (Yankees), c	2	0	0	0	5	1
Robinson (Orioles), 3b	2	0	0	0	1	3
Bando (Athletics), 3b	1	0	0	0	0	1
Nelson (Rangers), 3b	0	0	0	0	1	0
kHorton (Tigers)	1	0	0	0	0	0
Hunter (Athletics), p	0	0	0	0	0	0
Holtzman (Athletics), p	0	0	0	0	0	0
Blyleven (Twins), p	0	0	0	0	0	0
bBell (Indians)	1	0	1	0	0	0
Singer (Angels), p	0	0	0	0	0	1
cKelly (White Sox)	1	0	0	0	0	0
Ryan (Angels), p	0	0	0	0	0	0
gSpencer (Rangers)	1	0	0	0	0	0
Lyle (Yankees), p	0	0	0	0	0	0
Fingers (Athletics), p	0	0	0	0	0	0
Totals	32	1	5	1	27	12

National League	0	0	2	1	2	2	0	0	0—7
American League	0	1	0	0	0	0	0	0	0—1

Nationals	IP.	H.	R.	ER.	BB.	SO.
Wise (W)	2	2	1	1	0	1
Osteen	2	2	0	0	1	1
Sutton	1	0	0	0	0	0
Twitchell	1	1	0	0	0	1
Giusti	1	0	0	0	0	0
Seaver	1	0	0	0	1	0
Brewer	1	0	0	0	1	2

Americans	IP.	H.	R.	ER.	BB.	SO.
Hunter	1⅓	1	0	0	0	1
Holtzman	⅔	1	0	0	0	0
Blyleven (L)	1	2	2	2	2	0
Singer	2	3	3	3	1	2
Ryan	2	2	2	2	2	2
Lyle	1	1	0	0	0	1
Fingers	1	0	0	0	0	0

aWalked for Wise in third. bTripled for Blyleven in third. cPopped out for Singer in fifth. dStruck out for Speier in sixth. eHomered for Sutton in sixth. fStruck out for Bench in seventh. gFlied out for Ryan in seventh. hFouled out for Santo in eighth. iStruck out for Stargell in eighth. jHit into force play for Giusti in eighth. kStruck out for Nelson in ninth. DP—Americans 1. LOB—Nationals 6, Americans 7. 2B—Jackson, Morgan, Mayberry, Bonds. 3B—Bell. HR—Bench, Bonds, Davis. SB—Otis. SH—Osteen. PB—Fisk. U—Chylak (A.L.) plate, Burkhart (N.L.) first, Barnett (A.L.) second, W. Williams (N.L.) third, Luciano (A.L.) left, Engel (N.L.) right. T—2:45. A—40,849.

Braves' Henry Aaron singled in runs in the third, Johnny Bench banged a solo homer in the fourth, the Giants' Bobby Bonds hit a two-run homer in the fifth and the Dodgers' Willie Davis

slammed a two-run shot in the sixth. Not big, not dramatic, but nastily steady, and more than enough.

Catfish Hunter started for the Americans but had to leave in the second inning when Billy Williams' line drive caused a hairline fracture of his right thumb. Oakland teammate Ken Holtzman replaced Hunter (who was sidelined for almost four weeks) and, combined, they pitched two scoreless innings. Yielding the National League runs were Minnesota's Bert Blyleven and California fastballers Bill Singer and Nolan Ryan. Two of baseball's all-time-best relief pitchers, the Yankees' Sparky Lyle and Oakland's Rollie Fingers, finished up for the A.L.

In Anderson's opinion, the National League's best player wasn't voted to the starting lineup by the fans. So, Sparky inserted the talented athlete, Bonds, just as soon as he could, in the fourth inning. And the power-hitting, swift-running Bonds responded flawlessly, hitting his home run and stretching a routine single into a daring double in the seventh that drew a loud round of applause from the appreciative fans.

The game marked the 24th and final All-Star Game appearance of Willie Mays (who finished his career that year with the Mets), reduced now to a pinch-hitting role (he struck out in the eighth inning). Perhaps the greatest all-around performer in All-Star history, Willie left behind a .307 batting average, a record 20 runs scored and a record 23 hits that included three home runs, three triples and two doubles, plus a variety of spectacular defensive plays. He had indeed been, as one teammate put it, "The Star of Stars."

In opening its margin in games to 25-18-1, the National League had played its 11th consecutive game of errorless ball. Both teams, in fact, played errorless ball for the fourth straight year.

It was the 40th anniversary of the first All-Star Game played at Comiskey Park in 1933. As part of the celebration, a roundup of surviving players from that first game served as honored guests. The former greats included Carl Hubbell, Bill Hallahan, Lefty Gomez, Dick Bartell, Lefty Grove, Joe Cronin, Jimmie Dykes and Charlie Gehringer. No doubt many of the old American Leaguers couldn't help thinking that times had changed. Indeed they had.

Bobby Bonds.

Willie Davis.

The American Leaguers take the field as Kansas City's new 12-story, crown-shaped scoreboard posts the starting lineup. The new Royals Stadium water spectacular can be seen on both sides of the scoreboard.

Rollie Fingers.

Amos Otis.

Buddy Bell slides into third base with a triple in the third inning of the 1973 All-Star Game. Ron Santo is the third baseman and Whitey Herzog is the American League coach.

Johnny Bench connects for a home run against Bill Singer in the fourth inning of the 1973 midsummer classic. Carlton Fisk is the catcher and Nestor Chylak is the umpire.

Claude Osteen.

N.L. Manager Sparky Anderson congratulates pitcher Jim Brewer, who retired the A.L. in the ninth inning. Cardinal Joe Torre (left) looks on.

Easy Pickings

Americans	AB.	R.	H.	RBI.	PO.	A.
Carew (Twins), 2b	1	1	0	0	0	1
Grich (Orioles), 2b	3	0	1	0	0	2
Campan'ris (Athletics), ss.	4	0	0	0	2	3
Jackson (Athletics), rf	3	0	0	0	3	0
Allen (White Sox), 1b	2	0	1	1	2	0
Yastrz'ski (Red Sox), 1b	1	0	0	0	5	0
Murcer (Yankees), cf	2	0	0	0	0	0
Hendrick (Indians), cf	2	0	1	0	3	0
Burroughs (Rangers), lf	0	0	0	0	1	0
Rudi (Athletics), lf	2	0	0	0	1	0
B. Robinson (Orioles), 3b	3	0	0	0	0	0
hMayberry (Royals)	1	0	0	0	0	0
Fingers (Athletics), p	0	0	0	0	0	0
Munson (Yankees), c	3	1	1	0	7	0
Perry (Indians), p	0	0	0	0	0	0
bKaline (Tigers)	1	0	0	0	0	0
Tiant (Red Sox), p	0	0	0	0	0	0
dF. Robinson (Angels)	1	0	0	0	0	0
Hunter (Athletics), p	0	0	0	0	0	0
Chalk (Angels), 3b	1	0	0	0	0	0
Totals	30	2	4	1	24	6
Nationals	AB.	R.	H.	RBI.	PO.	A.
Rose (Reds), lf	2	0	0	0	1	0
Brett (Pirates), p	0	0	0	0	0	0
cBrock (Cardinals)	1	1	1	0	0	0
Smith (Cardinals), rf	2	1	1	1	0	0
Morgan (Reds), 2b	2	0	1	1	3	4
gCash (Phillies), 2b	1	0	0	0	0	1
Aaron (Braves), rf	2	0	0	0	0	0
Cedeno (Astros), cf	2	0	0	0	2	0
Bench (Reds), c	3	1	2	0	7	0
Grote (Mets), c	0	0	0	0	1	0
Wynn (Dodgers), cf-rf	3	1	1	0	0	0
Matlack (Mets), p	0	0	0	0	0	0
Grubb (Padres), lf	1	0	0	0	0	0
Garvey (Dodgers), 1b	4	1	2	1	6	2
Cey (Dodgers), 3b	2	0	1	2	0	0
eSchmidt (Phillies), 3b	0	1	0	0	0	1
Bowa (Phillies), ss	2	0	0	0	2	0
fPerez (Reds)	1	0	0	0	0	0
Kessinger (Cubs), ss	1	1	1	1	1	0
Mess'rsmith (Dodgers), p	0	0	0	0	2	1
aGarr (Braves), lf	3	0	0	0	0	0
McGlothen (Cardinals), p	0	0	0	0	0	0
Marshall (Dodgers), p	1	0	0	0	0	1
Totals	33	7	10	6	27	10

American League ...... 0 0 2 0 0 0 0 0 0—2
National League ......0 1 0 2 1 0 1 2 x—7

Americans	IP.	H.	R.	ER.	BB.	SO.
Perry	3	3	1	1	0	4
Tiant (L)	2	4	3	2	1	0
Hunter	2	2	1	1	1	3
Fingers	1	1	2	2	1	0
Nationals	IP.	H.	R.	ER.	BB.	SO.
Messersmith	3	2	2	2	3	4
Brett (W)	2	1	0	0	1	0
Matlack	1	1	0	0	1	0
McGlothen	1	0	0	0	0	1
Marshall	2	0	0	0	1	2

aStruck out for Messersmith in third. bFouled out for Perry in fourth. cSingled for Brett in fifth. dHit into force play for Tiant in sixth. eWalked for Cey in sixth. fStruck out for Bowa in sixth. gFlied out for Morgan in seventh. hGrounded out for B. Robinson in eighth. E—Bench, Munson. LOB—Americans 8, Nationals 6. 2B—Cey, Munson, Morgan, Garvey. 3B—Kessinger. HR—Smith. SB—Carew, Brock. SH—Perry. SF—Morgan. WP—Fingers. U—Sudol (N.L.) plate, Frantz (A.L.) first, Vargo (N.L.) second, Anthony (A.L.) third, Kibler (N.L.) left, Maloney (A.L.) right. T—2:37. A—50,706.

For the second straight year, the National League All-Stars had an easy time of it against the American Leaguers. Not only did Yogi Berra's squad cruise to a 7-2 victory in the 1974 game, played at Three Rivers Stadium, Pittsburgh, it did so while using five pitchers who had never worked in an All-Star Game.

Berra's pitchers for the July 23 game were starter Andy Messersmith of the Dodgers, lefthanders Ken Brett of the Pirates and Jon Matlack of the Mets, and then Lynn McGlothen of the Cardinals and Mike Marshall of the Dodgers (who established a major league record for avid work habits by pitching in 106 games that year). Also being filtered into the National League lineup for the first time were two future All-Star perennials, Steve Garvey of the Dodgers and Mike Schmidt of the Phillies. The rich were getting richer.

Cleveland's Gaylord Perry started for Dick Williams' American Leaguers, and at the end of three innings the A.L. held a 2-1 lead. The margin would have been greater if not for a pivotal defensive play at first base by Garvey. The piece of leathered larceny occurred in the third, after the Americans had scored their two runs and had men on first and second and two out. The Yankees' Bobby Murcer smashed one toward right field, but Garvey made a great stop and threw to Messersmith covering to get the out.

Garvey, who was not listed on the All-Star ballot but who made the starting lineup by a write-in vote, stood out as the winners' key man. In the second inning, he singled with two out and came in on Dodger teammate Ron Cey's double. In the fourth, with Johnny Bench and the Dodgers' Jim Wynn on base with singles, Garvey doubled in one run and set up another.

At the end of four innings, it was 3-2 in favor of the Nationals, who gradually pulled away. No American League pitcher emerged from the game without a stubbed toe. Perry, Luis Tiant of the Red Sox, Catfish Hunter and Rollie Fingers each was massaged lightly as the Nationals methodically expanded their lead.

The Cardinals' Reggie Smith hit the game's only home run, a bases-empty shot off Hunter in the seventh.

Smith's blast was sandwiched between Joe Morgan's sacrifice fly for the National League in the fifth inning and Don Kessinger's run-scoring triple for the N.L. in the eighth. Kessinger scored on a wild pitch by Fingers.

Berra, whose logic has often been obscured by malaprops and abstruse semantics, was a model of precision and lucidity as he explained the reason for the game's outcome.

"We had the better team," said the Mets' manager, whose N.L. troops nonetheless proved they were human by committing the first National League error since the second All-Star Game of 1962 (when the Nationals had four misplays).

Steve Garvey.

Ron Cey.

Mike Marshall.

Reggie Smith.

Don Kessinger.

Rod Carew.

Thurman Munson.

Reggie Smith gets a glad hand from coach Red Schoendienst after hitting a seventh-inning home run.

The Other Shoe Drops

Nationals	AB	R	H	RBI	PO	A
Rose (Reds), rf-lf	4	0	2	1	4	0
Carter (Expos), lf	0	0	0	0	1	0
Brock (Cardinals), lf	3	1	1	0	2	0
Murcer (Giants), rf	2	0	0	0	1	0
Jones (Padres), p	0	0	0	0	0	1
Morgan (Reds), 2b	4	0	1	0	0	1
Cash (Phillies), 2b	1	0	0	0	0	0
Bench (Reds), c	4	0	1	1	10	1
Garvey (Dodgers), 1b	3	1	2	1	4	1
iPerez (Reds), 1b	1	0	0	0	1	1
Wynn (Dodgers), cf	2	1	1	1	1	0
Smith (Cardinals), cf-rf	2	1	1	0	0	0
Cey (Dodgers), 3b	3	0	1	0	0	1
Seaver (Mets), p	0	0	0	0	0	0
Matlack (Mets), p	0	0	0	0	0	0
jOliver (Pirates), cf	1	1	1	0	0	0
Concepcion (Reds), ss	2	0	1	0	1	1
hLuzinski (Phillies)	1	0	0	0	0	0
Bowa (Phillies), ss	0	1	0	0	2	0
Reuss (Pirates), p	1	0	0	0	0	0
bWatson (Astros)	1	0	0	0	0	0
Sutton (Dodgers), p	0	0	0	0	0	0
Madlock (Cubs), 3b	2	0	1	2	0	0
Totals	37	6	13	6	27	8

Americans	AB	R	H	RBI	PO	A
Bonds (Yankees), cf	3	0	0	0	0	1
Scott (Brewers), 1b	2	0	0	0	5	0
Carew (Twins), 2b	5	0	1	0	3	1
Munson (Yankees), c	2	0	1	0	1	1
dW'h'gt'n (Athletics), cf-lf	1	0	1	0	1	0
Jackson (Athletics), rf	3	0	1	0	2	0
Dent (White Sox), ss	1	0	0	0	0	1
Rudi (Athletics), lf	3	0	1	0	5	0
eHendrick (Indians), rf	1	1	1	0	0	0
Nettles (Yankees), 3b	4	0	1	0	2	2
Tenace (Athletics), 1b-c	3	1	0	0	4	0
Camp'eris (Athletics), ss	2	0	2	0	3	2
fLynn (Red Sox), cf	2	0	0	0	1	0
Blue (Athletics), p	0	0	0	0	0	0
aAaron (Brewers)	1	0	0	0	0	0
Busby (Royals), p	0	0	0	0	0	0
cHargrove (Rangers)	1	0	0	0	0	0
Kaat (White Sox), p	0	0	0	0	0	0
gYastrzemski (Red Sox)	1	1	1	3	0	0
Hunter (Yankees), p	0	0	0	0	0	0
Gossage (White Sox), p	0	0	0	0	0	0
kMcRae (Royals)	1	0	0	0	0	0
Totals	36	3	10	3	27	9

National League ....0 2 1 0 0 0 0 0 3—6
American League ....0 0 0 0 0 3 0 0 0—3

Nationals	IP	H	R	ER	BB	SO
Reuss	3	3	0	0	0	2
Sutton	2	3	0	0	0	1
Seaver	1	2	3	3	1	2
Matlack (W)	2	2	0	0	0	4
Jones	1	0	0	0	0	1

Americans	IP	H	R	ER	BB	SO
Blue	2	5	2	2	0	1
Busby	2	4	1	1	0	0
Kaat	2	0	0	0	0	0
Hunter (L)	2*	3	2	2	0	2
Gossage	1	1	1	1	0	0

*Pitched to two batters in ninth.

aLined out for Blue in second. bFlied out for Reuss in fourth. cFlied out for Busby in fourth. dRan for Munson in fifth. eRan for Rudi in sixth. fFlied out for Campaneris in sixth. gHomered for Kaat in sixth. hStruck out for Concepcion in seventh. iStruck out for Garvey in eighth. jDoubled for Matlack in ninth. kGrounded out for Gossage in ninth. E—Concepcion, Tenace. LOB—Nationals 6, Americans 8. 2B—Oliver. HR—Garvey, Wynn, Yastrzemski. SB—Brock, Washington, Hendrick, Nettles. SF—Rose. HBP—By Reuss (Munson), by Gossage (Bowa). Balk—Busby. PB—Bench. U—Haller (A.L.) plate, Pelekoudas (N.L.) first, Springstead (A.L.) second, Froemming (N.L.) third, Goetz (A.L.) left, McSherry (N.L.) right. T—2:35. A—51,480.

Like the practiced tormentor it had become, the National League gave its rival a glimpse of the promised land in 1975, then at the last moment closed the drapes.

Played at Milwaukee's County Stadium on July 15, the 46th All-Star Game was a good one, but those fatalists among the pro-American League crowd—the contest attracted 51,480 fans—sat waiting for the other shoe to drop. It dropped in the ninth inning, right on the necks of the home team, with the Americans losing for the 12th time in 13 games.

Oakland Manager Alvin Dark, running the American squad, chose A's standout Vida Blue as his starting pitcher and followed with Kansas City's Steve Busby, the White Sox's Jim Kaat, the Yankees' Catfish Hunter and White Sox speedballer Goose Gossage. Only Kaat escaped without damage.

Dodgers skipper Walter Alston started Pittsburgh's Jerry Reuss, then came on with his own Don Sutton, followed by the Mets' Tom Seaver and Jon Matlack, and finished up with sinkerballing lefthander Randy Jones of the Padres. All except Seaver fared well.

The Nationals roiled the waters first with back-to-back home runs by Dodger teammates Steve Garvey and Jim Wynn off Blue in the second.

In the third inning, the Cardinals' Lou Brock, who had stolen a major league record 118 bases the year before, gave the crowd a demonstration of his art. Against Busby, Brock opened with a single and then bedeviled the Royals' righthander into committing a balk. Lou quickly showed that Busby's concern had been legitimate by stealing third, from where he scored on Johnny Bench's single, giving the Nationals a 3-0 lead.

The Americans' pitching tightened up after that, with Busby, Kaat and Hunter holding the Nationals scoreless until the ninth. Meanwhile, in the sixth inning, the Americans had suddenly thrown a lightning bolt into the night. With Seaver having just arrived on the mound, Oakland's Joe Rudi and Gene Tenace got aboard via a single and a walk. Boston's Carl Yastrzemski pinch-hit for Kaat and drove a long home run to right-center, tying the score.

The tie remained in place through the eighth inning, then the boilers of inevitability began rumbling. The Cardinals' Reggie Smith opened the ninth by looping one into left-center that Oakland's Claudell Washington dropped after a long run, Smith being credited with a single. The Pirates' Al Oliver was sent up to hit for Matlack (who had pitched skillfully in the seventh and eighth, fanning four). Oliver came through with a double into the left-field corner, sending Smith to third.

At this point, needing strikeouts, Dark removed Hunter in favor of Gossage. The batter was the Phillies' Larry Bowa, a good contact hitter. But it was Gossage who made contact, hitting Bowa with a pitch to load the bases. That brought Goose eye-to-eye with the Cubs' Bill Madlock, who would win the National League batting championship that year with a .354 average. Madlock quickly showed what emerging batting titlists are made of (through 1986, he had won four crowns) by banging a single into left field to score two runs. A third came in on Pete Rose's sacrifice fly, making it 6-3, Nationals.

San Diego's Jones came in to pitch in the bottom of the ninth and rubbed out three batters in a row, wrapping up another National League victory. The American League, which at one time had led the series 12-4, was now down 27-18-1.

Along with Yastrzemski's home run, the crowd particularly enjoyed one other moment in the game. It came in the second inning when the Milwaukee Brewers' Henry Aaron, nearing the end of a long and historic big-league career that he had begun with the Milwaukee Braves, was called upon to pinch-hit. Henry lined out softly to shortstop, con-

cluding his appearances as an All-Star performer. It was Aaron's 24th game (23 with the National League), leaving him in a tie for most games with Stan Musial and Willie Mays. Henry, however, had not been as dominant in All-Star play as the other two, leaving behind a statistical sheet showing just two home runs and a .194 batting average.

Bill Madlock.

Lou Brock.

Jim Kaat.

Jim Wynn.

The bat has splintered and the ball looks flat. Altogether, a disappointing final All-Star appearance for Henry Aaron, who made an out as a pinch-hitter for the American League in the second inning of the 1975 game.

Al Oliver.

Carl Yastrzemski.

Jon Matlack.

Bert Campaneris.

Same Old Routine

Americans	AB.	R.	H.	RBI.	PO.	A.
LeFlore (Tigers), lf	2	0	1	0	2	0
Yastrzemski (R. Sox), lf	2	0	0	0	0	0
Carew (Twins), 1b	3	0	0	0	9	2
Brett (Royals), 3b	2	0	0	0	0	1
Money (Brewers), 3b	1	0	0	0	0	1
Munson (Yankees), c	2	0	0	0	4	0
Fisk (Red Sox), c	1.	0	0	0	1	0
dChambliss (Yankees)	1	0	0	0	0	0
Lynn (Red Sox), cf	3	1	1	1	0	0
eOtis (Royals)	1	0	0	0	0	0
Harrah (Rangers), ss	2	0	0	0	0	0
Belanger (Orioles), ss	1	0	0	0	1	1
Patek (Royals), ss	0	0	0	0	0	0
Staub (Tigers), rf	2	0	2	0	1	0
Tiant (Red Sox), p	0	0	0	0	0	0
cWynegar (Twins)	0	0	0	0	0	0
Tanana (Angels), p	0	0	0	0	1	0
Grich (Orioles), 2b	2	0	0	0	1	1
Garner (Athletics), 2b	1	0	0	0	1	1
Fidrych (Tigers), p	0	0	0	0	1	0
aMcRae (Royals)	1	0	0	0	0	0
Hunter (Yankees), p	0	0	0	0	0	0
bRivers (Yankees), rf	2	0	1	0	2	0
Totals	29	1	5	1	24	8

Nationals	AB.	R.	H.	RBI.	PO.	A.
Rose (Reds), 3b	3	1	2	0	0	1
Oliver (Pirates), rf-lf	1	0	0	0	1	0
Garvey (Dodgers), 1b	3	1	1	1	6	0
Cash (Phillies), 2b	1	1	1	0	1	1
Morgan (Reds), 2b	3	1	1	0	2	3
Perez (Reds), 1b	0	0	0	0	2	0
Foster (Reds), cf-rf	3	1	1	3	0	0
Montefusco (Giants), p	0	0	0	0	0	0
Russell (Dodgers), ss	1	0	0	0	1	2
Luzinski (Phillies), lf	3	0	0	0	0	0
Griffey (Reds), rf	1	1	1	1	1	0
Bench (Reds), c	2	0	1	0	1	0
Cedeno (Astros), cf	2	1	1	2	1	0
Kingman (Mets), rf	2	0	0	0	1	0
Boone (Phillies), c	2	0	0	0	5	0
Concepcion (Reds), ss	2	0	1	0	2	3
Bowa (Phillies), ss	1	0	0	0	2	1
Rhoden (Dodgers), p	0	0	0	0	0	0
Cey (Dodgers), 3b	0	0	0	0	0	0
Jones (Padres), p	1	0	0	0	1	1
Seaver (Mets), p	1	0	0	0	0	0
Schmidt (Phillies), 3b	1	0	0	0	0	0
Forsch (Astros), p	0	0	0	0	0	0
Totals	33	7	10	7	27	12

American League	0 0 0	1 0 0	0 0 0—1			
National League	2 0 2	0 0 0	0 3 x—7			

Americans	IP.	H.	R.	ER.	BB.	SO.
Fidrych (L)	2	4	2	2	0	1
Hunter	2	2	2	2	0	3
Tiant	2	1	0	0	0	1
Tanana	2	3	3	3	1	0

Nationals	IP.	H.	R.	ER.	BB.	SO.
Jones (W)	3	2	0	0	1	1
Seaver	2	2	1	1	0	1
Montefusco	2	0	0	0	2	2
Rhoden	1	1	0	0	0	0
Forsch	1	0	0	0	0	1

aGrounded out for Fidrych in third. bStruck out for Hunter in fifth. cWalked for Tiant in seventh. dGrounded out for Fisk in ninth. eStruck out for Lynn in ninth. DP—Americans 1, Nationals 3. LOB — Americans 4, Nationals 3. 3B—Garvey, Rose. HR—Foster, Lynn, Cedeno. SB—Carew. PB—Munson. U—Wendelstedt (N.L.) plate, Neudecker (A.L.) first, Olsen (N.L.) second, Denkinger (A.L.) third, Davidson (N.L.) left, Evans (A.L.) right. T—2:12. A—63,974.

The dictionary defines "routine" as a customary or regular course of procedure, one that is unvarying or habitual.

The annual major league All-Star Game was turning into a routine affair. The 1976 game, played on July 13 at Philadelphia (to help celebrate the nation's Bicentennial), was reminiscent of the 1973 and 1974 games, won by the Nationals by 7-1 and 7-2 scores. The Nationals opted for the 7-1 score this time.

The Americans did have the game's most colorful and talked-about performer in righthanded pitcher Mark Fidrych. The Detroit Tigers' youngster, midway through a spectacular rookie season, had charmed his way into the hearts of baseball fans by his refreshingly uninhibited personality and by his antics on the mound, which included talking to himself between pitches and sometimes speaking to the ball.

American League Manager Darrell Johnson of the Red Sox started Fidrych against Padres lefthander Randy Jones, selected by Cincinnati's Sparky Anderson. Jones was succeeded by Tom Seaver, the Giants' John Montefusco, the Dodgers' Rick Rhoden and the Astros' Ken Forsch, the five pitchers conspiring to hold the opposition to five hits and one run—a homer by Boston's Fred Lynn off Seaver in the fourth.

Five members of Cincinnati's Big Red Machine—one of the greatest teams of all time—were voted to the starting lineup: Pete Rose at third base, Joe Morgan at second, George Foster in center field, Johnny Bench behind the plate and Dave Concepcion at shortstop. The Reds' representatives did just fine, too, going 6 for 13 at the plate.

The Nationals got Fidrych talking to himself right off the bat at Veterans Stadium. Rose opened the N.L. first with a single and Steve Garvey got a triple when his drive bounced away from Detroit right fielder Rusty Staub, never the most agile of fielders. Garvey came in on Foster's grounder and, bingo, it was 2-0 for the National League.

Fidrych pitched out of a jam in the second and then left the game, replaced by the Yankees' Catfish Hunter, an otherwise great pitcher who often stumbled in All-Star competition. Hunter was immediately stung by Cincinnati Inc.—Morgan singled and Foster homered, making it 4-0.

Hunter was followed by Luis Tiant and then Angels lefthander Frank Tanana, who was milked for three runs in the eighth inning. The Phillies' Dave Cash singled and the Reds' Tony Perez walked. The Dodgers' Bill Russell grounded into a double play, Cash going to third. Ken Griffey, the seventh Cincinnati player to get into the game, followed with a run-scoring single. The Astros' Cesar Cedeno then poked a final finger into the American League eye with a two-run homer, boosting the score to 7-1.

The 63,974 fans, primarily National League partisans, went home satisfied but hardly surprised. It had been, after all, just a routine All-Star Game.

George Foster.

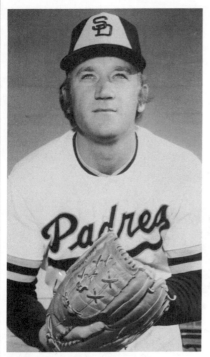

Randy Jones.

Pete Rose.

Luis Tiant.

Pete Rose gets back to third base in the fifth inning of the 1976 All-Star Game as George Brett fields Steve Garvey's grounder and prepares to throw him out at first.

Shortstop Bill Russell leaps over Mickey Rivers and gets off the throw to first base to double up Carl Yastrzemski in eighth-inning action.

Cesar Cedeno.

Mark Fidrych.

Fred Lynn.

Ho Hum!

Nationals	AB.	R.	H.	RBI.	PO.	A.
Morgan (Reds), 2b	4	1	1	1	1	0
Trillo (Cubs), 2b	1	0	0	0	0	1
Garvey (Dodgers), 1b	3	1	1	1	1	0
Montanez (Braves), 1b	2	0	0	0	6	1
Parker (Pirates), rf	3	1	1	0	2	0
Templeton (Cards), ss	1	1	1	0	1	2
Foster (Reds), cf	3	1	1	1	2	0
Morales (Cubs), cf	0	1	0	0	1	0
Luzinski (Phillies), lf	2	1	1	2	0	0
Winfield (Padres), lf	2	0	2	2	1	0
Cey (Dodgers), 3b	2	0	0	0	0	0
Seaver (Reds), p	0	0	0	0	0	1
eSmith (Dodgers)	1	0	1	0	0	0
fSchmidt (Phillies)	0	0	0	0	0	0
R. Reuschel (Cubs), p	0	0	0	0	0	0
Stearns (Mets), c	0	0	0	0	2	0
Bench (Reds), c	2	0	0	0	4	0
Lavelle (Giants), p	0	0	0	0	0	0
cRose (Reds), 3b	2	0	0	0	0	1
Concepcion (Reds), ss	1	0	0	0	1	1
Valentine (Expos), rf	1	0	0	0	0	0
Sutton (Dodgers), p	0	0	0	0	0	1
Simmons (Cardinals), c	3	0	0	0	5	0
Gossage (Pirates), p	0	0	0	0	0	0
Totals	33	7	9	7	27	8

Americans	AB.	R.	H.	RBI.	PO.	A.
Carew (Twins), 1b	3	1	1	0	7	0
Scott (Red Sox), 1b	2	1	1	2	4	0
Randolph (Yankees), 2b	5	0	1	1	2	6
Brett (Royals), 3b	2	0	0	0	2	1
Campbell (Red Sox), p	0	0	0	0	0	0
dFairly (Blue Jays)	1	0	0	0	0	0
Lyle (Yankees), p	0	0	0	0	0	0
gMunson (Yankees)	1	0	0	0	0	0
Yastrzemski (R. Sox), cf	2	0	0	0	0	0
Lynn (Red Sox), cf	1	1	0	0	2	0
Zisk (White Sox), lf	3	0	2	2	0	0
Singleton (Orioles), rf	0	0	0	0	0	0
Jackson (Yankees), rf	2	0	1	0	0	0
Rice (Red Sox), rf-lf	2	0	1	0	1	0
Fisk (Red Sox), c	2	0	0	0	6	1
Wynegar (Twins), c	2	1	1	0	3	0
Burleson (Red Sox), ss	2	0	0	0	0	0
Campan'ris (Rangers), ss	1	1	0	0	0	1
Palmer (Orioles), p	0	0	0	0	0	0
Kern (Indians), p	0	0	0	0	0	0
aJones (Mariners)	1	0	0	0	0	0
Eckersley (Indians), p	0	0	0	0	0	1
bHisle (Twins)	1	0	0	0	0	0
LaRoche (Angels), p	0	0	0	0	0	0
Nettles (Yankees), 3b	2	0	0	0	0	1
Totals	35	5	8	5	27	11

National League	4 0 1	0 0 0	0 2 0	—7		
American League	0 0 0	0 0 2	1 0 2	—5		

Nationals	IP.	H.	R.	ER.	BB.	SO.
Sutton (W)	3	1	0	0	1	4
Lavelle	2	1	0	0	0	2
Seaver	2	4	3	2	1	2
R. Reuschel	1	0	0	0	0	0
Gossage	1	1	2	2	1	2

Americans	IP.	H.	R.	ER.	BB.	SO.
Palmer (L)	2*	5	5	5	1	3
Kern	1	0	0	0	0	2
Eckersley	2	0	0	0	0	1
LaRoche	1	1	0	0	1	0
Campbell	1	0	0	0	1	2
Lyle	2	3	2	2	0	1

*Pitched to one batter in third.

aFlied out for Kern in third. bFlied out for Eckersley in fifth. cFlied out for Lavelle in sixth. dStruck out for Campbell in seventh. eSingled for Seaver in eighth. fRan for Smith in eighth. gStruck out for Lyle in ninth. E—Templeton. DP—Nationals 1, Americans 1. LOB—Nationals 4, Americans 7. 2B—Foster, Winfield, Zisk, Templeton. HR—Morgan, Luzinski, Garvey, Scott. SH—Sutton. WP—Palmer, Lyle. HBP—By Lyle (Morales), by R. Reuschel (Singleton). U—Kunkel (A.L.) plate, Harvey (N.L.) first, Phillips (A.L.) second, Stello (N.L.) third, Pulli (N.L.) left, Brinkman (A.L.) right. T—2:34. A—56,683.

To the list of verities such as sunrise and sunset, and death and taxes, another had been added: The National League wins in the All-Star Game. If you had doubts about the latter, you were in for a rude jolt at the outset of the 1977 game, played in that dominion of American League monarchs, Yankee Stadium, on July 19. Neither the ghosts of Ruth and Gehrig nor the living shadows of DiMaggio and Mantle could inspire the American Leaguers or intimidate the Nationals.

Sparky Anderson's N.L. team struck quickly at Billy Martin's contingent. With Orioles great Jim Palmer on the mound for the Americans, Joe Morgan began tolling the bell for the home team by leading off the game with a home run. Pittsburgh's Dave Parker singled and scored on George Foster's double, and then Philadelphia's pillar of muscles, Greg Luzinski, cracked a home run. So, it was 4-0, Nationals, and the final notes of "The Star-Spangled Banner" had barely floated off.

In the third inning, Steve Garvey, always at his best in these games, finished off Palmer with a home run, making it 5-0. The American League's "0" was courtesy of the Dodgers' Don Sutton, who pitched shutout ball for the opening three innings, allowing one hit and striking out four. Giants lefthander Gary Lavelle worked the next two innings in high style (no runs, one hit, two strikeouts) and, going into the bottom of the sixth, it was still 5-0, Nationals. (Cleveland right-handers Jim Kern and Dennis Eckersley and Angels lefthander Dave LaRoche had held the Nationals through the top of the sixth.)

The Americans then tried to create some semblance of a ball game. They scuffed Tom Seaver (now with Cincinnati) for two runs on a single by Rod Carew, a walk to Fred Lynn and a double by the White Sox's Richie Zisk. An inning later, the Yankees' Willie Randolph warmed the hearts of the 56,000-plus home-towners looking on with an RBI single, bringing in an unearned run against Seaver and making it a 5-3 game.

The National League seemed to have a "look but don't touch" attitude in these games. Translated into All-Star Game argot, it meant "score, American League, but don't come too close."

So, facing the Yankees' Sparky Lyle in the eighth inning, the Nationals quickly turned a 5-3 game into a 7-3 game. The Cardinals' Garry Templeton doubled and Lyle then hit the Cubs' Jerry Morales with a pitch, putting men on first and second. A wild pitch moved the runners up and Dave Winfield, then with the San Diego Padres, brought them home with a single.

After the Cubs' Rick Reuschel pitched a scoreless eighth for the Nationals, the Pirates' Goose Gossage came on in the ninth. Gossage was another star pitcher who seldom had much luck in these games, no matter which league he pitched for. Goose did nail it down for the National League, but not before giving up a two-run homer to Boston's George Scott, making it a 7-5 final.

The American League, after losing its sixth straight and falling for the 14th time in 15 games, could mutter that two of its top pitchers had been unable to suit up because of physical problems —California's Frank Tanana and Detroit's Mark Fidrych. (Fidrych's colorful comet had just about come to earth. The glory days of this talented and engaging young pitcher's brief career were now in the past, due to injuries.) When Martin asked the Angels' Nolan Ryan to substitute for Tanana, fastballer Ryan, irked at not having been selected in the first place, refused. Martin, a demon for having the last word, fumed and announced that he would never select Ryan for any future games.

The unavailability of Tanana and Fidrych (and Ryan, too) perhaps didn't really matter to the Americans. As the Nationals' Anderson put it, "The only reason we're here is to kick living hell out of those guys."

Dave Winfield.

Dennis Eckersley.

Joe Morgan gets a warm reception from Steve Garvey after hitting a first-inning home run in the 1977 All-Star Game. The catcher is Carlton Fisk and the umpire is Bill Kunkel.

Greg Luzinski.

Don Sutton.

Dave Parker scores a first-inning run, beating catcher Carlton Fisk's diving tag, as Greg Luzinski watches. The umpire is Bill Kunkel.

George Scott.

Sparky Lyle.

Richie Zisk.

Sooner or Later

Americans	AB.	R.	H.	RBI.	PO.	A.
Carew (Twins), 1b	4	2	2	0	6	1
Brett (Royals), 3b	3	1	2	2	0	2
Gossage (Yankees), p	0	0	0	0	0	0
Rice (Red Sox), lf	4	0	0	0	2	0
Lemon (White Sox), lf	0	0	0	0	0	0
Zisk (Rangers), rf	2	0	1	0	0	0
Evans (Red Sox), rf	1	0	0	0	3	0
Fisk (Red Sox), c	2	0	0	1	4	0
Sundberg (Rangers), c	0	0	0	0	2	1
fThompson (Tigers), cf	1	0	0	0	0	0
Lynn (Red Sox), cf	4	0	1	0	3	0
Money (Brewers), 2b	2	0	0	0	1	1
White (Royals), 2b	1	0	0	0	1	2
gPorter (Royals)	1	0	0	0	0	0
Patek (Royals), ss	3	0	1	0	1	1
Palmer (Orioles), p	1	0	0	0	1	0
Keough (A's), p	0	0	0	0	0	0
bHowell (Blue Jays)	1	0	0	0	0	0
Sorensen (Brewers), p	0	0	0	0	0	1
cHisle (Brewers)	1	0	1	0	0	0
Kern (Indians), p	0	0	0	0	0	0
Guidry (Yankees), p	0	0	0	0	0	0
Nettles (Yankees), 3b	0	0	0	0	0	1
Totals	31	3	8	3	24	10

Nationals	AB.	R.	H.	RBI.	PO.	A.
Rose (Reds), 3b	4	0	1	0	1	0
dLopes (Dodgers), 2b	1	0	1	1	0	1
Morgan (Reds), 2b	3	1	0	0	2	1
Clark (Giants), rf	1	0	0	0	0	0
Foster (Reds), cf	2	1	0	0	2	0
Luzinski (Phillies), lf	2	0	1	1	0	0
Fingers (Padres), p	0	0	0	0	0	1
eStargell (Pirates)	1	0	0	0	0	0
Sutter (Cubs), p	0	0	0	0	0	0
Niekro (Braves), p	0	0	0	0	0	0
Garvey (Dodgers), 1b	3	1	2	2	7	1
Simmons (Cardinals), c	3	0	1	0	4	1
Concepcion (Reds), ss	0	1	0	0	2	0
Monday (Dodgers), rf	2	0	0	0	1	0
Rogers (Expos), p	0	0	0	0	0	0
Winfield (Padres), lf	2	1	1	0	1	0
Bowa (Phillies), ss	3	1	2	0	2	4
Boone (Phillies), c	1	1	1	2	3	1
Pocoroba (Braves), c	0	0	0	0	0	0
Blue (Giants), p	0	0	0	0	0	1
aSmith (Dodgers), rf	3	0	0	0	1	0
Cey (Dodgers), 3b	1	0	0	0	1	0
Totals	32	7	10	6	27	11

American League .... 2 0 1 0 0 0 0 0 0—3
National League .... 0 0 3 0 0 0 0 4 x—7

Americans	IP.	H.	R.	ER.	BB.	SO.
Palmer	2⅔	3	3	3	4	4
Keough	⅓	1	0	0	0	0
Sorensen	3	1	0	0	0	0
Kern	⅔	1	0	0	1	1
Guidry	⅓	1	0	0	0	0
Gossage (L)	1	4	4	4	1	1

Nationals	IP.	H.	R.	ER.	BB.	SO.
Blue	3	5	3	3	1	2
Rogers	2	2	0	0	0	2
Fingers	2	1	0	0	0	1
Sutter (W)	1⅔	0	0	0	0	2
Niekro	⅓	0	0	0	0	0

aStruck out for Blue in third. bGrounded out for Keough in fourth. cSingled for Sorensen in seventh. dRan for Rose in seventh. eFlied out for Fingers in seventh. fFlied out for Sundberg in ninth. gFouled out for White in ninth. E—Lemon. DP—Americans 1. LOB—Americans 4, Nationals 7. 2B—Brett, Rose. 3B—Carew 2, Garvey. SB—Bowa, Brett. SF—Fisk, Brett. WP—Rogers, Gossage. PB—Sundberg. U—Pryor (N.L.) plate, Chylak (A.L.) first, Tata (N.L.) second, Deegan (A.L.) third, Runge (N.L.) left, McCoy (A.L.) right. T—2:37. A—51,549.

Rod Carew leads off the All-Star Game with a triple and George Brett follows with a double. Brett later scores on Carlton Fisk's sacrifice fly. After the top of the first inning, the American League is in front, 2-0. Third inning: Carew again leads off with a triple and scores on a sacrifice fly by Brett. The Americans' dugout at San Diego Stadium is a fun house of cheering and chatter and back-slapping. American League President Lee MacPhail is smiling in his flag-draped box, sharing all of the buoyant good feeling produced by a 3-0 lead. Tonight, at last, his players will throw off the National League noose.

Final score: National League 7, American League 3.

National League retaliation for the Americans' defiance of the proper order of things came with little delay. Larry Bowa of the Phillies opened the Nationals' third with a single. Two outs later, Jim Palmer, operating under the American League All-Star Game Hex, stepped completely out of character by walking, in succession, the Reds' Joe Morgan and George Foster, and then the Phillies' Greg Luzinski, forcing in a run. Palmer then found the plate and Steve Garvey made him regret it by stroking a game-tying, two-run single. Oakland's Matt Keough replaced the A.L. starter and retired the side.

It had been a rocky road for both starters in the July 11 contest. Yielding Carew's brace of triples and all three American League runs was Vida Blue of the San Francisco Giants, who was starting his third All-Star Game. (Blue's previous two starts had been for the American League when he was a member of the Oakland A's. He had been rocked on both of those occasions, too.)

After the third inning, the two teams settled in and played four scoreless innings, Lary Sorensen of the Brewers delivering three of them for the Americans and Jim Kern and Ron Guidry collaborating on the other. For the National League, Montreal ace Steve Rogers and San Diego's own Rollie Fingers worked two shutout innings apiece, and then the Cubs' Bruce Sutter split-fingered the Americans into submission in the eighth.

In the bottom of the eighth, American League Manager Billy Martin brought in one of the game's toughest relief pitchers, Goose Gossage, now with Billy's Yankees. With the game still tied, 3-3, and an array of righthanded hitters coming up for the Nationals, it seemed like a good move. Gossage, however, promptly paid truth to the adage, "He who prospers during the season does not necessarily do likewise in the All-Star Game."

Gossage, possessor of a fastball capable of burning its way into a bank vault, ran into an inning that was a pure nightmare. Garvey greeted him with a triple (Steve's eighth hit in 16 All-Star at-bats). Gossage then wild-pitched Garvey home with the tie-breaking run. The Reds' Dave Concepcion walked and this was followed by a single by the Padres' Dave Winfield, which brought cheers from the local clientele. When the White Sox's Chet Lemon misplayed the ball in left field, Concepcion and Winfield each moved up a base. The Phillies' Bob Boone then rapped a single up the middle, knocking in two runs. Boone later scored on a bloop hit by the Dodgers' Davey Lopes, making it 7-3, the score by which the game was laid to rest.

In the Americans' ninth, Sutter retired the first two batters. At this point, National League skipper Tom Lasorda, nothing if not a sentimentalist, removed Sutter and put in 39-year-old knuckleballer Phil Niekro of the Braves, reasoning that it might be the popular veteran's last All-Star Game. (Little did the Dodgers' pilot know that Niekro would still be pitching in the mid-1980s —and even later. On the other hand, while Niekro was named to All-Star teams in 1982 and 1984, the '78 pitching stint had remained his last All-Star appearance entering the 1987 season.)

Niekro got his man, the Royals' Darrell Porter, on a pop foul and thereby applied the varnish to another National League triumph.

Some prominent players, pleading various aches and pains, had begged out of the '78 game. Martin's American League squad was minus two of Billy's Yankee stars, Reggie Jackson and Thurman Munson, plus Carl Yastrzemski; Lasorda's team was without Johnny Bench.

Whatever the makeup of the squads, it was now seven straight victories for the Nationals and 15 out of 16, with the overall bottom line in the series now reading 30-18-1.

Rod Carew.

George Brett.

Carlton Fisk.

Steve Garvey.

The starting pitchers for the 1978 All-Star Game: Jim Palmer (left) for the American League and Vida Blue for the National League.

Lary Sorensen.

Bob Boone.

Bruce Sutter.

Steve Rogers.

Lucky Seven

Nationals	AB.	R.	H.	RBI.	PO.	A.
Lopes (Dodgers), 2b	3	0	1	0	4	1
iMorgan (Reds), 2b	1	1	0	0	1	1
Parker (Pirates), rf	3	0	1	1	0	2
Garvey (Dodgers), 1b	2	1	0	0	5	0
Perry (Padres), p	0	0	0	0	0	0
Sambito (Astros), p	0	0	0	0	0	0
Reynolds (Astros), ss	2	0	0	0	0	1
Schmidt (Phillies), 3b	3	2	2	1	1	1
Cey (Dodgers), 3b	1	0	0	0	2	1
Parrish (Expos), 3b	0	0	0	0	0	0
Foster (Reds), lf	1	0	1	1	0	0
Matthews (Braves), lf	2	0	0	0	2	0
jMazzilli (Mets), cf	1	1	1	1	2	0
Winfield (Padres), cf-lf	5	1	1	1	3	0
Boone (Phillies), c	2	1	1	0	0	0
Carter (Expos), c	2	0	1	1	6	1
Bowa (Phillies), ss	2	0	0	0	1	3
LaCoss (Reds), p	0	0	0	0	0	0
kHernandez (Cardinals)	1	0	0	0	0	0
Sutter (Cubs), p	0	0	0	0	0	1
Carlton (Phillies), p	0	0	0	0	0	0
aBrock (Cardinals)	1	0	1	0	0	0
Andujar (Astros), p	0	0	0	0	0	0
cClark (Giants)	1	0	0	0	0	0
Rogers (Expos), p	0	0	0	0	0	0
eRose (Phillies), 1b	2	0	0	0	2	0
Totals	35	7	10	7	27	12

Americans	AB.	R.	H.	RBI.	PO.	A.
Smalley (Twins), ss	3	0	0	0	2	2
Grich (Angels), 2b	1	0	0	0	2	0
Brett (Royals), 3b	3	1	0	0	1	2
Nettles (Yankees), 3b	1	0	1	0	1	2
Baylor (Angels), lf	4	2	2	1	1	0
Kern (Rangers), p	0	0	0	0	0	0
Guidry (Yankees), p	0	0	0	0	0	0
lSingleton (Orioles)	1	0	0	0	0	0
Rice (Red Sox), rf-lf	5	0	1	0	3	0
Lynn (Red Sox), cf	1	1	1	2	0	0
Lemon (White Sox), cf	2	1	0	0	2	0
Yastrzemski (R. Sox), 1b	3	0	2	1	5	1
fBurleson (Red Sox), ss	2	1	0	0	0	1
Porter (Royals), c	3	0	1	0	2	0
Downing (Angels), c	1	0	1	0	3	0
White (Royals), 2b	2	0	0	0	2	3
gBochte (Mariners), 1b	1	0	1	1	2	0
Ryan (Angels), p	0	0	0	0	0	0
bCooper (Brewers)	0	0	0	0	0	0
Stanley (Red Sox), p	0	0	0	0	1	0
dKemp (Tigers)	1	0	0	0	0	0
Clear (Angels), p	0	0	0	0	0	0
hJackson (Yankees), rf	1	0	0	0	0	0
Totals	35	6	10	5	27	10

National League ..... 2 1 1 0 0 1 0 1 1—7
American League ..... 3 0 2 0 0 1 0 0 0—6

Nationals	IP.	H.	R.	ER.	BB.	SO.
Carlton	1	2	3	3	1	0
Andujar	2	2	2	1	1	0
Rogers	2	0	0	0	0	2
Perry	0*	3	1	1	0	0
Sambito	⅔	0	0	0	1	0
LaCoss	1⅓	1	0	0	0	0
Sutter (W)	2	2	0	0	2	3

Americans	IP.	H.	R.	ER.	BB.	SO.
Ryan	2	5	3	3	1	2
Stanley	2	1	1	1	0	0
Clear	2	2	1	1	1	0
Kern (L)	2⅔	2	2	2	3	3
Guidry	⅓	0	0	0	1	0

*Pitched to three batters in sixth.

aSingled for Carlton in second. bWalked for Ryan in second. cGrounded out for Andujar in fourth. dLined out for Stanley in fourth. eGrounded into double play for Rogers in sixth. fRan for Yastrzemski in sixth. gSingled for White in sixth. hGrounded into force play for Clear in sixth. iStruck out for Lopes in seventh. jHomered for Matthews in eighth. kStruck out for LaCoss in eighth. lGrounded out for Guidry in ninth. E—Schmidt. DP—Americans 2. LOB—Nationals 8, Americans 9. 2B—Foster, Baylor, Schmidt, Winfield, Porter, Rice. 3B—Schmidt. HR—Lynn, Mazzilli. SF—Bochte. SF—Parker. WP—Andujar. HBP—By Andujar (Lemon). Balk—Kern. U—Maloney (A.L.) plate, Weyer (N.L.) first, Bremigan (A.L.) second, W. Williams (N.L.) third, Cooney (A.L.) left, Rennert (N.L.) right. T—3:11. A—58,905.

The National League was getting it down to a science now, even to the point of knowing just how many runs it would take to subdue its hapless opponent. The number the Nationals hit upon was 7. If you don't believe this, just check out the scores of their victories from 1973 through 1978: 7-1, 7-2, 6-3 (something went wrong here), 7-1, 7-5, 7-3. They used their magic number again in 1979, but this time cut it a bit fine, winning by a 7-6 score in the 50th All-Star Game.

There was a measure of consolation for the American League as it lost its eighth in a row and 16th of the last 17: It was a good, competitive ball game, with some solid hitting and some exciting play in the field, particularly from Pittsburgh's Dave Parker, who electrified the crowd of nearly 59,000 at Seattle's Kingdome with a pair of outfield assists that flew across the diamond with such stunning abruptness and accuracy as to qualify him for a Cy Young Award.

Ragged performances were turned in by most of the pitchers in the 1979 All-Star Game, especially members of Bob Lemon's American League staff, although several of Tom Lasorda's Nationals also had some of their deliveries flattened and laminated.

The starting pitchers for the July 17 game were two of baseball's notables, the Phillies' Steve Carlton, owner of one of the game's most diabolical sliders, and the California Angels' Nolan Ryan, a man with a fastball so swift it should have been given a ballistics test. Nolan, on his way to leading the American League in strikeouts for the seventh time in eight years, started off in true Ryanesque style, fanning Davey Lopes and Parker. Ryan then walked Steve Garvey; this was followed by a resounding triple by Mike Schmidt and a double by George Foster. It was quickly 2-0, National League. Here-we-go-again time.

This was a feisty American League contingent, however, and it came right back, taking the skid out of a few of Carlton's vaunted sliders. Steve walked Kansas City's George Brett with one out in the first and Brett promptly beat it around the bases on a double by the Angels' Don Baylor. Boston's Fred Lynn, a heavy hitter in these games, followed by hoisting one over the fence in right-center, giving the Americans a 3-2 edge.

The Nationals tied the score in the top of the second on three singles and Parker's sacrifice fly. Against Boston's Bob Stanley, they took a 4-3 lead in the third on a Schmidt double and two ground balls.

The Americans, apparently highly resolved this evening, moved ahead, 5-4, in the bottom of the third. This was achieved against Houston's Joaquin Andujar on the rather ragged assortment of a single by Baylor, a wild pitch, a groundout, a hit batsman, Carl Yastrzemski's run-scoring single and a Schmidt throwing error. The Americans were taking whatever they could get, any way they could get it.

Two scoreless innings ensued, with Montreal's Steve Rogers turning in two innings of hitless ball for the Nationals. American Leaguers Stanley and Mark Clear (Angels) worked a runless inning apiece.

Both sides scored in the sixth. The Nationals did it against Clear on a double by the Padres' Dave Winfield and a single by Montreal's Gary Carter. This tied it at 5-5. The Americans quickly untied it against the Padres' Gaylord Perry, with the go-ahead run scoring on a pinch single by Bruce Bochte, Seattle's lone representative in the game. Bochte's hit set off a display of vocal fireworks that threatened the stability of the Kingdome's roof. It took two more pitchers, the Astros' Joe Sambito and the Reds' Mike La-

Coss, to subdue the Americans in the inning. The Nationals were soon to get some solid hurling—from right fielder Parker.

In the Americans' seventh, Boston's Jim Rice popped one down the line in right that Parker lost in the lights. When Rice tried to make a triple out of it, Parker shot him down with a long and precise peg to Dodgers third baseman Ron Cey. With the A.L. trying to expand on its 6-5 lead and Rice having been the leadoff man in the inning, the throw proved crucial—for both clubs.

The Nationals tied it in the eighth when the Mets' Lee Mazzilli stroked an opposite-field home run just over the fence in left. Rangers righthander Jim Kern, who threw the pitch, said later that the ball "went 317 feet down a 316-foot line." Nevertheless, there remains no such thing as a too-short home run.

In the last of the eighth, Parker again went to work defensively,

this time cutting down a man right at the pay window. The man was the Angels' Brian Downing, who had led off the inning with a single against the Cubs' Bruce Sutter, newly arrived on the scene. A sacrifice bumped Downing 90 feet along, and Reggie Jackson then was walked intentionally. One out later, the Yankees' Graig Nettles rifled a single to right, and Parker rifled the ball right back. With Downing barreling home and catcher Carter blocking the plate, Parker's throw came in on a sizzling line, all the way in the air. The skillful Carter forced Downing to the inside of the plate and applied the inning-ending tag as Downing made a head-first dive into the dirt.

After that bit of pulsating excitement, the Nationals went on to score the winning run in the ninth in a most passive way. Kern walked the Reds' Joe Morgan and balked him to second. He then walked Parker intentionally and

Cey unintentionally, loading the bases. At this point (there were two out), the Yankees' Ron Guidry came in and proceeded to walk Mazzilli, giving the Nationals a 7-6 lead.

Sutter wiped out the Americans in the bottom of the ninth and it was over, a game that had a little bit of everything and a full dose of the usual—another National League victory. The American Leaguers, however, had taken a giant step in the right direction—they had shown that they could *almost* win.

On another front, the Phillies' Pete Rose played the last four innings of the game at first base and thereby added a significant achievement to his already starry career. First base was the record-setting fifth position that the noted hustler had played in All-Star Game competition, Pete previously having performed at second base, third base, right field and left field.

Fred Lynn and Jim Rice, the 1-2 punch of the Boston Red Sox.

Pete Rose.

Gary Carter.

Don Baylor.

Gary Carter tags out Brian Downing at the plate in the eighth inning of the 1979 game. The throw came from right fielder Dave Parker.

Dave Parker.

Mike Schmidt.

Lee Mazzilli.

Nolan Ryan.

1980

SIX

T O

1987

The Nationals Still In Control

Nobody's Perfect

Americans	AB.	R.	H.	RBI.	PO.	A.
Randolph (Yankees), 2b	4	0	2	0	0	3
Stieb (Blue Jays), p	0	0	0	0	0	0
Trammell (Tigers), ss	0	0	0	0	0	0
Carew (Angels), 1b	2	1	2	0	4	0
Cooper (Brewers), 1b	1	0	0	0	6	0
Lynn (Red Sox), cf	3	1	1	2	2	0
Bumbry (Orioles), cf	1	0	0	0	2	0
Jackson (Yankees), rf	2	0	1	0	0	0
aLandreaux (Twins), rf	1	0	0	0	1	0
Oglivie (Brewers), lf	2	0	0	0	1	0
Oliver (Rangers), lf	1	0	0	0	0	0
Gossage (Yankees), p	0	0	0	0	0	0
Fisk (Red Sox), c	2	0	0	0	5	0
Porter (Royals), c	1	0	0	0	0	1
Henderson (A's), lf	1	0	0	0	0	0
Nettles (Yankees), 3b	2	0	0	0	0	1
Bell (Rangers), 3b	2	0	0	0	0	2
Dent (Yankees), ss	2	0	1	0	0	1
John (Yankees), p	1	0	0	0	0	1
Farmer (White Sox), p	0	0	0	0	0	0
Grich (Angels), 2b	0	0	0	0	0	1
Stone (Orioles), p	1	0	0	0	0	0
Yount (Brewers), ss	2	0	0	0	3	2
Parrish (Tigers), c	1	0	0	0	0	0
Totals	32	2	7	2	24	12

Nationals	AB.	R.	H.	RBI.	PO.	A.
Lopes (Dodgers), 2b	1	0	0	0	0	2
Garner (Pirates), 2b	2	1	1	0	1	3
Smith (Dodgers), cf	2	0	0	0	0	0
Hendrick (Cardinals), cf	2	0	1	1	0	0
Sutter (Cubs), p	0	0	0	0	0	0
Parker (Pirates), rf	2	0	0	0	0	0
Winfield (Padres), rf	2	0	0	1	2	0
Garvey (Dodgers), 1b	2	0	0	0	7	0
bHernandez (Cards), 1b	2	0	2	0	5	0
Bench (Reds), c	1	0	0	0	5	0
Stearns (Mets), c	1	0	0	0	5	0
cRose (Phillies)	1	0	0	0	0	0
Bibby (Pirates), p	0	0	0	0	0	0
Murphy (Braves), cf	1	0	0	0	0	0
Kingman (Cubs), lf	1	0	0	0	0	0
Griffey (Reds), lf	3	1	2	1	0	0
Reitz (Cardinals), 3b	2	0	0	0	1	0
Reuss (Dodgers), p	0	0	0	0	0	0
Concepcion (Reds), ss	1	1	0	0	0	2
Russell (Dodgers), ss	2	0	0	0	0	2
Carter (Expos), c	1	0	0	0	1	0
Richard (Astros), p	0	0	0	0	0	0
Welch (Dodgers), p	1	0	0	0	0	1
Knight (Reds), 3b	1	1	1	0	0	1
Totals	31	4	7	3	27	11

American League	0	0	0	0 2 0	0 0 0—2
National League	0	0	0	0 1 2	1 0 x—4

Americans	IP.	H.	R.	ER.	BB.	SO.
Stone	3	0	0	0	0	3
John (L)	2⅓	4	3	3	0	1
Farmer	⅔	1	0	0	0	0
Stieb	1	1	1	0	2	0
Gossage	1	1	0	0	0	0

Nationals	IP.	H.	R.	ER.	BB.	SO.
Richard	2	1	0	0	2	3
Welch	3	5	2	2	1	4
Reuss (W)	1	0	0	0	0	3
Bibby	1	1	0	0	0	0
Sutter (S)	2	0	0	0	1	1

Game-winning RBI—Winfield.
aRan for Jackson in fifth. bSingled for Garvey in sixth. cGrounded into double play for Stearns in sixth. E—Randolph 2. DP—Americans 1, Nationals 1. LOB—Americans 7, Nationals 5. 2B—Carew. HR —Lynn, Griffey. SB—Carew, Knight, Garner. WP —Welch, Stieb 2. PB—Porter. U—Kibler (N.L.) plate, Barnett (A.L.) first, Colosi (N.L.) second, McKean (A.L.) third, Dale (N.L.) left, Garcia (A.L.) right. T—2:33. A—56,088.

There seemed only one sure way for the American League to go out and finally win one of these things, one undeniable, dead-certain way—not allow a National League runner to get aboard, not a single, solitary one. With this impeccable blueprint drawn up, American League pitchers set out to follow the plan in the 1980 All-Star Game, played on July 8 at Dodger Stadium in Los Angeles.

Baltimore's Steve Stone started for the Americans and he adhered strictly to the guidelines, delivering three perfect innings (the first such performance by an All-Star starter since Denny McLain turned the trick in 1966). When Stone was through, Manager Earl Weaver sent in the Yankees' Tommy John, who followed the blueprint for another inning and two-thirds, until there were two out in the bottom of the fifth.

At this point, the score was 2-0 in favor of the American League. In the Americans' fifth, Boston's Fred Lynn had followed a single by the Angels' Rod Carew with a home run. This blow was struck against the Dodgers' Bob Welch, who had just pitched two shutout innings after the Astros' J.R. Richard had opened with two scoreless frames.

Then, in the Nationals' fifth, after the first 14 of his teammates had been retired, the Reds' Ken Griffey turned one of John's pitches into a souvenir and it was 2-1.

Griffey's homer was the key that unlocked John, for in the sixth the Nationals began slapping Tommy around. With one out, singles by the Reds' Ray Knight, the Pirates' Phil Garner and the Cardinals' George Hendrick tied the score. John left, replaced by the White Sox's Ed Farmer.

Dave Winfield, playing his last year for the San Diego Padres, greeted Farmer by blistering a ground ball that handcuffed his future teammate, Yankees second baseman Willie Randolph. Garner scored the go-ahead run for the National League on the play, and Randolph was charged with an error—a tough one, some people thought. (Winfield nevertheless was credited with an RBI.)

The Nationals scored a most uninspired run against the Blue Jays' Dave Stieb in the seventh. It came about like this: Griffey singled. Reds teammate Dave Concepcion forced him at second. Concepcion advanced to second on a wild pitch and stayed there when Gary Carter grounded out. Knight walked, and when ball four got away from the Royals' Darrell Porter, Concepcion went to third. With Garner batting, Knight stole second. Stieb then threw a wild pitch, scoring Concepcion.

From the sixth inning on, National League Manager Chuck Tanner of the Pirates got one-hit, shutout pitching from the Dodgers' Jerry Reuss (who struck out the side in his one inning of work), the Pirates' Jim Bibby and the Cubs' Bruce Sutter.

The Nationals' 4-2 triumph— they didn't need seven runs this time—was their ninth straight victory and 17th in 18 years. There was only one thing for the puzzled and frustrated American Leaguers to say about it all:

"It's only an exhibition game."

Reggie Jackson: One of many mystified and frustrated American Leaguers.

The starting pitchers for the 1980 All-Star Game: The playful J.R. Richard (left) for the National League and Steve Stone for the American.

Ken Griffey watches the flight of his fifth-inning home run.

Willie Randolph.

Fred Lynn.

J.R. Richard.

Keith Hernandez.

Having just taken the toss from shortstop Dave Concepcion (left), second baseman Phil Garner forces the sliding Willie Randolph and fires to first base to double Cecil Cooper. The action occurred in the seventh inning of the 1980 game.

As far as the American League was concerned, one of baseball's most hallowed articles of legislation, the law of averages, had been repealed. After all, the numbers 32-18-1 reflected the National League's won-lost-tied record in the 51 All-Star Games played through 1980. And, even more humiliating, the figures 17-1 and 9-0 showed the Nationals' series dominance since 1963 and 1972, respectively.

The American League almost got a reprieve in 1981, and the law of averages had nothing to do with it. Because of the major league players' strike that began on June 12 and kept teams out of regular-season action until August 10, the All-Star Game scheduled at Cleveland on July 14 was called off. After the strike was settled on July 31, however, it was decided to play the game on August 9 as a gala prelude to the resumption of regularly scheduled league games.

Because of the ill will and disenchantment generated among the public by the long midsummer strike, people from the front offices to the playing fields were wondering how the return of big-league baseball would be received. The All-Star Game was considered a good test. Well, baseball was welcomed back—and no one should have been surprised—resoundingly, by an All-Star Game record crowd of 72,086. And the fans saw a good ball game, too.

Managers Dallas Green (Phillies) of the Nationals and Jim Frey (Royals) of the Americans should have hired a couple of crowd-control experts, because there were record numbers on the field, too (a series-high 56 players were used, a record 29 by the Nationals). Fifteen of these players were pitchers (another record), eight of them for the Nationals (another

Back to Work

Nationals	AB.	R.	H.	RBI.	PO.	A.
Rose (Phillies), 1b	3	0	1	0	5	0
Hooton (Dodgers), p	0	0	0	0	0	0
Ruthven (Phillies), p	0	0	0	0	0	0
kGuerrero (Dodgers)	1	0	0	0	0	0
Blue (Giants), p	0	0	0	0	0	0
Madlock (Pirates), 3b	1	0	0	0	0	1
Concepcion (Reds), ss	3	0	0	0	0	0
Smith (Padres), ss	0	0	0	0	1	0
Parker (Pirates), rf	3	1	1	1	1	0
Easler (Pirates), rf	1	1	0	0	0	0
Schmidt (Phillies), 3b	4	1	2	2	0	2
Ryan (Astros), p	0	0	0	0	0	0
Garner (Pirates), 2b	0	0	0	0	0	0
Foster (Reds), lf	2	0	0	0	0	0
Baker (Dodgers), lf	2	0	1	0	2	0
lRaines (Expos), lf	0	0	0	0	1	0
Dawson (Expos), cf	4	0	1	0	4	0
Carter (Expos), c	3	2	2	2	5	1
Benedict (Braves), c	1	0	0	0	3	0
Lopes (Dodgers), 2b	0	0	0	0	1	0
Trillo (Phillies), 2b	2	0	0	0	1	1
mBuckner (Cubs)	1	0	0	0	0	0
Sutter (Cardinals), p	0	0	0	0	0	0
Valenzuela (Dodgers), p	0	0	0	0	0	1
aYoungblood (Mets)	1	0	0	0	0	0
Seaver (Reds), p	0	0	0	0	0	2
Knepper (Astros), p	0	0	0	0	0	1
eKennedy (Padres)	1	0	0	0	0	0
Garvey (Dodgers), 1b	2	0	1	0	3	1
Totals	35	5	9	5	27	10

Americans	AB.	R.	H.	RBI.	PO.	A.
Carew (Angels), 1b	3	0	1	0	12	0
gMurray (Orioles), 1b	2	0	0	0	2	1
Randolph (Yankees), 2b	3	0	1	0	0	5
hSimmons (Brewers)	1	0	1	1	0	0
iWhite (Royals), 2b	1	0	0	0	1	0
Brett (Royals), 3b	3	0	0	0	0	1
Norris (A's), p	0	0	0	0	0	0
jOliver (Rangers)	1	0	0	0	0	0
Davis (Yankees), p	0	0	0	0	0	0
Fingers (Brewers), p	0	0	0	0	1	0
Stieb (Blue Jays), p	1	0	0	0	1	1
Winfield (Yankees), cf	4	0	0	0	1	0
Singleton (Orioles), lf	3	2	2	1	0	0
Burleson (Angels), ss	1	0	0	0	1	3
Jackson (Yankees), rf	1	0	0	0	0	0
cEvans (Red Sox), rf	2	1	1	0	2	0
Fisk (White Sox), c	3	1	1	0	4	0
Diaz (Indians), c	1	0	0	0	2	0
Dent (Yankees), ss	2	0	2	0	0	2
fLynn (Angels)	1	0	1	1	0	0
Armas (A's), lf	1	0	0	0	0	0
Morris (Tigers), p	0	0	0	0	0	0
bPaciorek (Mariners)	1	0	1	0	0	0
Barker (Indians), p	0	0	0	0	0	0
dThomas (Brewers)	1	0	0	0	0	0
Forsch (Angels), p	0	0	0	0	0	0
Bedl (Rangers), 3b	1	0	0	1	1	2
Totals	37	4	11	4	27	16

National League	0 0 0	0 1 1	1 2 0—5		
American League	0 1 0	0 0 3	0 0 0—4		

Nationals	IP.	H.	R.	ER.	BB.	SO.
Valenzuela	1	2	0	0	0	0
Seaver	1	3	1	1	0	1
Knepper	2	1	0	0	2	3
Hooton	1⅔	5	3	3	0	1
Ruthven	⅓	0	0	0	0	0
Blue (W)	1	0	0	0	0	1
Ryan	1	0	0	0	0	1
Sutter (S)	1	0	0	0	0	1

Americans	IP.	H.	R.	ER.	BB.	SO.
Morris	2	2	0	0	1	2
Barker	2	0	0	0	0	1
Forsch	1	1	1	1	0	0
Norris	1	2	1	1	0	1
Davis	1	1	1	1	0	1
Fingers (L)	⅓	2	2	2	2	0
Stieb	1⅔	1	0	0	1	1

Game-winning RBI—Schmidt.

aFouled out for Valenzuela in second. bSingled for Morris in second. cWalked for Jackson in fourth. dPopped out for Barker in fourth. eGrounded out for Knepper in fifth. fSingled for Dent in sixth. gGrounded out for Carew in sixth. hSingled for Randolph in sixth. iRan for Simmons in sixth. jFlied out for Norris in sixth. kStruck out for Ruthven in seventh. lRan for Baker in eighth. mGrounded out for Trillo in ninth. E—Schmidt, Fingers. LOB—Nationals 7, Americans 9. 2B—Dent, Schmidt, Garvey. HR—Singleton, Carter 2, Parker, Schmidt. SB—Dawson, Smith. SF—Bell. WP—Blue. U—Haller (A.L.) plate, Vargo (N.L.) first, DiMuro (A.L.) second, Engel (N.L.) third, Kosc (A.L.) left, Quick (N.L.) right. T—2:59. A—72,086.

mark). The Nationals tied still another mark by belting four home runs.

Fernando Valenzuela, the Dodgers' sensational rookie left-hander, started for the National League against the Tigers' Jack Morris. The game's first run was scored by the Americans in the second inning when Baltimore's Ken Singleton hit a home run, the only long one of the game for the A.L. He connected off the Reds' Tom Seaver.

After Morris and Cleveland's Len Barker had shut out the Nationals through the first four innings and the Astros' Bob Knepper had stymied the Americans through innings three and four, the visitors tied the score in the fifth. This was done quickly and efficiently by the Expos' Gary Carter, who led off by hitting the first pitch thrown by the Angels' Ken Forsch for a one-way ride. An inning later, the Pirates' Dave Parker homered off Oakland's Mike Norris and it was 2-1, Nationals.

The Americans made a spirited comeback in their sixth, roughing up the Dodgers' Burt Hooton. Singles by Singleton, the Red Sox's Dwight Evans and the White Sox's Carlton Fisk loaded the bases. Frey then sent up the Angels' Fred Lynn as a pinch-hitter and this lethal All-Star performer came through with a base hit to right, tying the game. A sacrifice fly by the Rangers' Buddy Bell and a pinch single by Milwaukee's Ted Simmons made it 4-2, Americans.

The long-balling Nationals were soon on their way back, however. Again hitting the first pitch of the inning, Carter shot one out off the Yankees' Ron Davis in the seventh, making Carter the fifth man in All-Star history to hit two home runs in one game.

With the Phillies' Dick Ruthven and the Giants' Vida Blue

holding the Americans at bay through the seventh inning, the Nationals dropped their final bomb in the eighth. The man on the mound for the A.L. was now Milwaukee's Rollie Fingers, who went on to Most Valuable Player and Cy Young Award honors that year. In this inning, Rollie pitched completely out of character.

Fingers started by walking San Diego's Ozzie Smith. With the Pirates' Mike Easler at bat, Ozzie stole second and when the throw went into center field, Smith set out for third. The relay came back and Ozzie was tagged out in a rundown. Fingers then walked Easler. That brought Mike Schmidt to the plate and the Phillies' slugger pounded a home run over the center-field fence. The Nationals had slipped ahead, 5-4. Dave Stieb replaced Fingers later in the inning and closed things down.

The Astros' Nolan Ryan pitched a perfect bottom of the eighth, and Stieb kept it a one-run game with a scoreless top of the ninth.

Bruce Sutter, now with the Cardinals, came on in his patented closer's role in the last of the ninth. Sutter retired the first man and then faced Stieb. Stieb? Yes, because Frey had run out of hitters and it was too late to send out for one. Sutter, not averse to shooting fish in a barrel, fanned Stieb on three pitches, then polished off the final batter as the National League won its 10th straight All-Star Game.

Baseball was officially back, its traditions flying like flags in the breeze.

Cleveland Stadium, the site of the 1981 All-Star Game.

Dave Parker.

The starting pitchers for the 1981 game: Fernando Valenzuela (left) for the National League and Jack Morris for the American.

Mike Schmidt.

Gary Carter.

Bruce Sutter.

Fred Lynn leaps over Eddie Murray's grounder to Steve Garvey in the sixth inning of the 1981 classic.

Dwight Evans.

Ken Singleton.

11 and Counting

Americans	AB.	R.	H.	RBI.	PO.	A.
Henderson (A's), lf	4	1	3	0	3	0
Lynn (Angels), cf	2	0	0	0	0	0
Wilson (Royals), cf	2	0	0	0	1	0
mHrbek (Twins)	1	0	0	0	0	0
Brett (Royals), 3b	2	0	2	0	0	0
cBell (Rangers), 3b	3	0	0	0	0	1
Jackson (Angels), rf	1	0	0	1	3	0
Winfield (Yankees), rf	2	0	1	0	0	0
Cooper (Brewers), 1b	2	0	1	0	5	0
fMurray (Orioles), 1b	1	0	0	0	4	0
Yount (Brewers), ss	3	0	0	0	0	2
Grich (Angels), 2b	1	0	0	0	2	2
gYastrzemski (Red Sox)	1	0	0	0	0	0
Quisenberry (Royals), p	0	0	0	0	0	0
kMcRae (Royals)	0	0	0	0	0	0
Fingers (Brewers), p	0	0	0	0	0	0
Fisk (White Sox), c	2	0	0	0	2	0
Parrish (Tigers), c	2	0	1	0	2	3
Eckersley (Red Sox), p	1	0	0	0	0	0
bThornton (Indians)	1	0	0	0	0	0
Clancy (Blue Jays), p	0	0	0	0	0	0
Bannister (Mariners), p	0	0	0	0	0	0
White (Royals), 2b	1	0	0	0	2	1
lOglivie (Brewers)	1	0	0	0	0	0
Totals	33	1	8	1	24	9

Nationals	AB.	R.	H.	RBI.	PO.	A.
Raines (Expos), lf	1	0	0	0	0	0
Carlton (Phillies), p	0	0	0	0	0	1
eHorner (Braves)	1	0	0	0	0	0
Soto (Reds), p	0	0	0	0	0	0
jThompson (Pirates)	1	0	0	0	0	0
Valenzuela (Dodgers), p	0	0	0	0	0	0
Minton (Giants), p	0	0	0	0	0	0
Howe (Dodgers), p	0	0	0	0	0	0
Hume (Reds), p	0	0	0	0	0	0
Rose (Phillies), 1b	1	0	0	1	4	0
Oliver (Expos), 1b	2	1	2	0	2	0
Dawson (Expos), cf	4	0	1	0	4	0
Schmidt (Phillies), 3b	1	0	0	0	0	0
Knight (Astros), 3b	3	0	0	0	1	4
Carter (Expos), c	3	0	1	1	7	0
hPena (Pirates), c	1	0	0	0	3	0
Stearns (Mets), c	0	0	0	0	0	0
Murphy (Braves), rf	2	1	0	0	2	0
Concepcion (Reds), ss	3	1	1	2	1	1
iO. Smith (Cardinals), ss	0	0	0	0	0	1
Trillo (Phillies), 2b	2	0	1	0	0	1
dSax (Dodgers), 2b	1	0	1	0	2	0
Rogers (Expos), p	0	0	0	0	0	0
aJones (Padres)	1	1	1	0	0	0
Baker (Dodgers), lf	2	0	0	0	0	0
L. Smith (Cardinals), lf	0	0	0	0	1	0
Totals	29	4	8	4	27	8

American League .... 1 0 0   0 0 0   0 0 0—1
National League .... 0 2 1   0 0 1   0 0 x—4

Americans	IP.	H.	R.	ER.	BB.	SO.
Eckersley (L)	3	2	3	3	2	1
Clancy	1	0	0	0	0	0
Bannister	1	1	0	0	0	0
Quisenberry	2	3	1	1	0	1
Fingers	1	2	0	0	0	0

Nationals	IP.	H.	R.	ER.	BB.	SO.
Rogers (W)	3	4	1	1	0	2
Carlton	2	1	0	0	2	4
Soto	2	3	0	0	0	4
Valenzuela	⅔	0	0	0	2	0
Minton	⅔	0	0	0	1	0
Howe	⅓	0	0	0	0	0
Hume (S)	⅓	0	0	0	0	0

Game-winning RBI—Concepcion.
aTripled for Rogers in third. bStruck out for Eckersley in fourth. cStruck out for Brett in fifth. dRan for Trillo in fifth. eFlied out for Carlton in fifth. fFlied out for Cooper in sixth. gStruck out for Grich in sixth. hRan for Carter in sixth. iRan for Concepcion in seventh. jGrounded out for Soto in seventh. kWalked for Quisenberry in eighth. lFlied out for White in ninth. mFlied out for Wilson in ninth. E—Sax, Henderson, Bell. DP—Nationals 1. LOB—Americans 11, Nationals 4. 2B—Oliver, Parrish. 3B—Jones. HR—Concepcion. SB—Raines, Pena, Henderson. SF—Jackson, Rose. WP—Rogers. U—Harvey (N.L.) plate, Springstead (A.L.) first, McSherry (N.L.) second, McKeon (A.L.) third, Montague (N.L.) left, Reilly (A.L.) right. T—2:53. A—59,057.

Perhaps, some people thought, if the All-Star Game were played in another country, the American League would win. That theory was put to the test in 1982, when the 53rd game of the series was contested at Montreal's Olympic Stadium.

After one inning, it seemed that going through customs had been a good idea for the A.L. as Billy Martin's team jumped to a 1-0 lead. Oakland's Rickey Henderson led off the July 13 game with a single and, one out later, George Brett singled him to second. Montreal's own Steve Rogers, the Nationals' starter, wild-pitched the runners up a notch while pitching to the Angels' Reggie Jackson. Reggie then brought in Henderson with a sacrifice fly.

The Americans never scored another run.

The Nationals, guided by Tom Lasorda, took only until the second inning to adjust to the Canadian climate. With two out, A.L. starter Dennis Eckersley of the Red Sox walked Atlanta's Dale Murphy and then, just to show how the gods were regarding these games, a most unlikely customer stepped up and popped a home run. Dave Concepcion, with just one homer in 328 at-bats thus far that season, hit one down the left-field line and out.

"A hanging slider," explained Eckersley, using a lament echoed by many a home run victim.

Concepcion wasn't startled by his homer. In fact, he had predicted it to National League teammate Manny Trillo.

"We tease around a lot," Concepcion said, "but I told him I was going to do it and I did it."

Despite getting at least one man on base in every inning but the second, the Americans were continually thwarted. This was the result of some handsome pitching by Rogers, Steve Carlton (two innings, four strikeouts), Cincinnati's Mario Soto (also two innings and four strikeouts) and bits and pieces of innings by Fernando Valenzuela, the Giants' Greg Minton, the Dodgers' Steve Howe and the Reds' Tom Hume as Lasorda alternated lefthanders and righthanders, depending on Martin's lineup moves.

The Nationals scored a third run against Eckersley in the third inning when San Diego's Ruppert Jones tripled and scored on Pete Rose's sacrifice fly. A couple of Montreal stars thrilled the almost 60,000 customers in the sixth, collaborating on the game's final run. Al Oliver doubled and came in on Gary Carter's single, the hits coming off Kansas City submariner Dan Quisenberry. Dan had followed Toronto's Jim Clancy and Seattle's Floyd Bannister, each of whom had pitched a noiseless inning.

The American Leaguers made a run at Soto in the seventh, putting men on second and third with one out, but Mario blew out the candles by fanning the Royals' Willie Wilson and the Rangers' Buddy Bell.

What little glory lay in the dust for the American League belonged to Henderson, who had three hits and a stolen base, and Detroit's Lance Parrish. The Tiger catcher not only doubled for his team's only extra-base hit, but he also threw out three National Leaguers trying to steal.

For the Nationals, their 4-1 victory was their 11th in a row and 19th in the last 20 games. The American League? Well, it had assumed the status of a Christmas tree—trimmed once a year.

Dave Concepcion: An unlikely hero.

Rickey Henderson.

Dave Winfield is forced out at second base by Steve Sax in the sixth inning of the 1982 All-Star Game. The upended Sax threw the ball into the dugout trying for the double play.

Lance Parrish.

Mario Soto.

1983

Major league baseball celebrated the All-Star Game's 50th anniversary by playing the 1983 game in the park where it all began on July 6, 1933. Fifty years to the day after the first "Dream Game" was held, baseball's best players were back at Chicago's Comiskey Park.

Maybe it was the inspiration of the occasion, maybe it was the impetus of launching the game's second half-century, or maybe it was the admonishing gestures of some old and noble ghosts named Ruth and Gehrig and Simmons that were lurking in the corridors of the Comiskey antiquities. Whatever it was, the American League won, easily and thunderously, posting along the way a couple of robust "mosts" and one explosive "first." The "mosts" were runs—a record-setting 13 for the game and an unprecedented seven in one inning; the All-Star "first" was a bases-loaded home run.

The final score was 13-3. Not only did the Americans end their 11-game losing streak, but they did it emphatically and impressively, blowing the Nationals out of contention early and keeping them out.

National League Manager Whitey Herzog of the Cardinals used seven pitchers, all but starter Mario Soto being All-Star Game first-timers; American League skipper Harvey Kuenn used five hurlers. The Americans machine-gunned a 15-hit attack, the brunt of which was absorbed by the Giants' Atlee Hammaker in a nightmarish third inning.

The game began with an exhibition of bumbling play on both sides. With Toronto's Dave Stieb starting for the Americans, the Dodgers' Steve Sax led off with a roller along the first-base line that Stieb picked up and threw away, allowing Sax to reach base. Sax then stole second. The Expos' Tim

The A.L. Unloads

Nationals	AB.	R.	H.	RBI.	PO.	A.
Sax, (Dodgers), 2b	3	1	1	1	2	0
Hubbard, (Braves), 2b	1	0	1	0	0	0
Raines, (Expos), lf	3	0	0	0	2	0
dMadlock, (Pirates), 3b	1	0	0	0	0	0
Dawson, (Expos), cf	3	0	0	0	3	0
Dravecky, (Padres), p	0	0	0	0	0	1
Perez, (Braves), p	0	0	0	0	0	0
Orosco, (Mets), p	0	0	0	0	0	0
gBench, (Reds)	1	0	0	0	0	0
L. Smith, (Cubs), p	0	0	0	0	1	0
Oliver, (Expos), 1b	2	1	1	0	2	1
Evans, (Giants), 1b	1	0	0	0	2	1
Murphy, (Braves), rf	3	0	1	1	0	0
Guerr'ro, (Dodgers), 3b-lf	1	0	0	0	0	0
Schmidt, (Phillies), 3b	3	0	0	0	0	0
Benedict, (Braves), c	1	0	1	0	5	0
Carter, (Expos), c	2	0	0	0	3	0
Durham, (Cubs), rf	2	0	0	0	0	0
O. Smith, (Cardinals), ss	2	1	1	0	0	0
McGee, (Cardinals), cf	2	0	1	0	2	0
Soto, (Reds), p	1	0	0	0	2	0
Hammaker, (Giants), p	0	0	0	0	0	0
Dawley, (Astros), p	0	0	0	0	0	0
bThon, (Astros), ss	3	0	1	0	0	2
Totals	35	3	8	2	24	5

Americans	AB.	R.	H.	RBI.	PO.	A.
Carew, (Angels), 1b	3	2	2	1	3	0
Murray, (Orioles), 1b	2	0	0	0	4	0
Yount, (Brewers), ss	2	1	0	1	0	1
Ripken, (Orioles), ss	0	0	0	0	1	0
Lynn, (Angels), cf	3	1	1	4	1	0
Wilson, (Royals), cf	1	0	1	1	2	0
Rice, (Red Sox), lf	4	1	2	1	1	0
Oglivie, (Brewers), rf	1	0	0	0	0	0
Young, (Mariners), p	0	0	0	0	0	0
Quisenberry, (Royals), p	0	0	0	0	0	0
Brett, (Royals), 3b	4	2	2	1	1	5
Simmons, (Brewers), c	2	0	0	0	4	0
Parrish, (Tigers), c	2	0	0	1	0	0
hCooper, (Brewers)	1	1	1	0	0	0
Boone, (Angels), c	0	0	0	0	1	0
Winfield, (Yankees), rf	3	2	3	1	3	0
Kittle, (White Sox), lf-rf	2	1	1	0	1	0
Trillo, (Indians), 2b	3	1	1	0	3	1
eWhitaker, (Tigers), 2b	1	1	1	2	1	0
Stieb, (Blue Jays), p	0	0	0	0	0	2
aDeCinces (Angels)	1	0	0	0	0	0
Honeycutt, (Rangers), p	0	0	0	0	0	0
cWard, (Twins)	1	0	0	0	0	0
Stanley, (Red Sox), p	0	0	0	0	0	1
fYastrzemski, (Red Sox)	1	0	0	1	0	0
Henderson, (A's), lf	1	0	0	1	0	0
Totals	38	13	15	13	27	10

National League	1 0 0	1 1 0	0 0 0— 3
American League	1 1 7	0 0 0	2 2 x—13

Nationals	IP.	H.	R.	ER.	BB.	SO.
Soto (L)	2	2	2	0	2	2
Hammaker	⅔	6	7	7	1	0
Dawley	1⅓	1	0	0	0	1
Dravecky	2	1	0	0	0	2
Perez	⅔	3	2	2	1	1
Orosco	⅓	0	0	0	0	1
L. Smith	1	2	2	1	0	1

Americans	IP.	H.	R.	ER.	BB.	SO.
Stieb (W)	3	0	1	0	1	4
Honeycutt	2	5	2	2	0	0
Stanley	2	2	0	0	0	0
Young	1	0	0	0	0	1
Quisenberry	1	1	0	0	0	1

Game-winning RBI—Yount.

aFlied out for Stieb in third. bSingled for Dawley in fifth. cFlied out for Honeycutt in fifth. dFlied out for Raines in seventh. eTripled for Trillo in seventh. fStruck out for Stanley in seventh. gPopped out for Orosco in eighth. hSingled for Parrish in eighth. E—Stieb, Carew, Schmidt, Sax, Guerrero. DP—Americans 2. LOB—Nationals 6, Americans 9. 2B—Winfield, Oliver, Wilson, Brett. 3B—Brett. HR—Rice, Lynn. SB—Sax, Raines. SH—Stieb. SF—Brett, Yount, Whitaker. PB—Benedict. U—Maloney (A.L.) plate, Wendelstedt (N.L.) first, Hendry (A.L.) second, Quick (N.L.) third, Shulock (A.L.) left, Pallone (N.L.) right. T—3:05. A—43,801.

Raines, seeing a good thing here, also hit one to Stieb and again there was a misplay as the pitcher's throw zipped past first baseman Rod Carew, who lost it in the setting sun. Sax scored on the play and Raines sprinted to third base.

Two little rollers, two errors, one run. American League fans

were getting ready for a long game. With Raines on third and none out, Stieb bulled his way through, striking out Andre Dawson, walking Al Oliver and then fanning Dale Murphy and Mike Schmidt.

In the bottom of the first, the Americans tied it on a Carew single, a Fred Lynn walk, Jim Rice's "double-play" grounder that Schmidt muffed and a sacrifice fly by George Brett. This was at the expense of the Reds' Soto, who was to give up another unearned run in the second inning. This was registered by a Dave Winfield double, a throwing error by Sax and a sacrifice fly by the Brewers' Robin Yount.

After Stieb had kept the Nationals buttoned up through the third, the Americans broke out in the bottom of the inning, ending 11 years worth of frustration and embarrassment with a mighty clanging of the anvil.

Hammaker, whose 1.70 earned-run average was leading the National League at the moment, took over in the third. The Red Sox's Rice gave him a look into the immediate future with a home run. Brett did almost as well, tripling to center. After the Brewers' Ted Simmons popped out, Winfield singled in Brett, making it 4-1, Americans. Cleveland's Manny Trillo singled Winfield to second. Hammaker got the second out, but then the flames began rising around the lefthander.

Carew singled home Winfield, Trillo going to third and Carew taking second on the throw to the plate. This opened up first base, and with the righthanded-hitting Yount up next, followed by the lefthanded-hitting Lynn, Herzog ordered Yount walked, filling the bases.

Having the batter ahead of you walked intentionally always is a red flag in the face, and Lynn saw it. "I take it personally when someone is walked ahead of me," he said later. Fred answered the affront by rocketing a 2-2 Hammaker pitch into the right-field bleachers for the first grand slam in All-Star history (a rather curious statistic, considering this was the 54th game of the series). Lynn's commanding blow completed a seven-run inning and relegated the American League's six-run inning of 1934 to the No. 2 spot in the record books.

Hammaker was relieved of further responsibility by the Astros' Bill Dawley, who along with the Padres' Dave Dravecky held off the Americans through the sixth. The Nationals had scored single runs in the fourth and fifth against the Rangers' Rick Honeycutt, the first coming on an Oliver double and a Murphy single and the second on singles by Ozzie Smith (Cardinals), Dickie Thon (Astros) and Sax, which made it 9-3.

After Honeycutt left, the Nationals were blanked over the final four innings by Bob Stanley, Seattle's Matt Young and the nether-world deliveries of Dan Quisenberry.

The American League, no doubt haunted by past events and still not feeling totally secure, did not let up. In the seventh, the Americans rattled Atlanta's Pascual Perez for two runs, the damaging blows being a triple by Detroit's Lou Whitaker and a double by Kansas City's Willie Wilson. The Mets' Jesse Orosco came in and rescued Perez.

In the eighth, against Cubs smokeballer Lee Smith, the Americans hammered home the final nails in the N.L. coffin with two more runs, bringing their total to 13, topping by one the figure achieved by their ancestors in the 1946 game.

The 11-year drought was over for the American League, and only two of its players had memories of winning one of these games—Carew and Carl Yastrzemski, the latter retiring at the end of the '83 season after appearing in his 14th All-Star Game. For the National League participants, only Johnny Bench, also retiring that year after 12 All-Star appearances, could remember what it was like to lose one of these games. (Carew, Yastrzemski and Bench were all starters in the last previous game won by the A.L., the 1971 classic.)

The 1983 star clearly was Lynn, whose big smash continued his knack of supplying high production in the midsummer games. Lynn now had struck four homers and driven in 10 runs in 20 All-Star at-bats. Only Ted Williams had a higher All-Star RBI count, with 12 in 46 at-bats. Stan Musial matched Lynn's 10 RBIs, but "The Man" had 63 All-Star at-bats. And while Musial still led all hitters with six All-Star homers, Lynn's four tied him with Williams for the American League lead.

George Brett.

Dave Stieb.

Rod Carew.

Dave Winfield.

Cal Ripken finds Glenn Hubbard's seventh-inning hit too hot to handle.

Steve Sax.

Fred Lynn gets a warm greeting from his American League teammates after hitting the first grand slam in All-Star Game history in the third inning of the 1983 classic.

Jim Rice.

Bob Stanley.

Back on Track

Americans	AB.	R.	H.	RBI.	PO.	A.
Whitaker (Tigers), 2b	3	0	2	0	0	5
Garcia (Blue Jays), 2b	1	0	0	0	1	0
Carew (Angels), 1b	2	0	0	0	5	0
Murray (Orioles), 1b	2	0	1	0	3	0
Ripken (Orioles), ss	3	0	0	0	0	0
Griffin (Blue Jays), ss	0	0	0	0	0	1
gMattingly (Yankees)	1	0	0	0	0	0
Winfield (Yankees), lf-rf	4	0	1	0	2	1
Re. Jackson (Angels), rf	2	0	0	0	0	0
Henderson (A's), lf-cf	2	0	0	0	0	0
Brett (Royals), 3b	3	1	1	1	3	0
Caudill (A's), p	0	0	0	0	0	0
W. Hernandez (Tigers), p	0	0	0	0	0	0
Parrish (Tigers), c	2	0	0	0	3	1
Sundberg (Brewers), c	1	0	0	0	6	0
Lemon (Tigers), cf	2	0	1	0	0	0
fRice (Red Sox), lf	1	0	0	0	1	0
Stieb (Blue Jays), p	0	0	0	0	0	0
bThornton (Indians)	1	0	1	0	0	0
Morris (Tigers), p	0	0	0	0	0	1
dA. Davis (Mariners)	1	0	0	0	0	0
Dotson (White Sox), p	0	0	0	0	0	0
Bell (Rangers), 3b	1	0	0	0	0	1
Totals	32	1	7	1	24	10

Nationals	AB.	R.	H.	RBI.	PO.	A.
Gwynn (Padres), lf	3	0	1	0	0	0
Raines (Expos), lf	1	0	0	0	4	0
Sandberg (Cubs), 2b	4	0	1	0	0	0
Garvey (Padres), 1b	3	1	1	0	5	1
K. Hernandez (Mets), 1b	1	0	0	0	1	0
Murphy (Braves), cf	3	1	2	1	0	0
Schmidt (Phillies), 3b	3	0	0	0	0	4
Wallach (Expos), 3b	1	0	0	0	0	0
Strawberry (Mets), rf	2	0	1	0	0	0
Washington (Braves), rf	2	0	1	0	1	0
Carter (Expos), c	2	1	1	1	9	0
J. Davis (Cubs), c	1	0	0	0	1	0
Gossage (Padres), p	0	0	0	0	0	0
O. Smith (Cardinals), ss	3	0	0	0	3	0
Lea (Expos), p	0	0	0	0	0	1
aC. Davis (Giants)	1	0	0	0	0	0
Valenzuela (Dodgers), p	0	0	0	0	0	0
cMumphrey (Astros)	1	0	0	0	0	0
Gooden (Mets), p	0	0	0	0	1	0
eBrenly (Giants)	1	0	0	0	0	0
Soto (Reds), p	0	0	0	0	0	0
Pena (Pirates), c	0	0	0	0	2	0
Totals	32	3	8	2	27	6

American League ....0 1 0 0 0 0 0 0 0—1
National League ....1 1 0 0 0 0 0 1 x—3

Americans	IP.	H.	R.	ER.	BB.	SO.
Stieb (L)	2	3	2	1	0	2
Morris	2	2	0	0	1	2
Dotson	2	2	0	0	1	2
Caudill	1	0	0	0	0	3
W. Hernandez	1	1	1	1	0	1

Nationals	IP.	H.	R.	ER.	BB.	SO.
Lea (W)	2	3	1	1	0	2
Valenzuela	2	2	0	0	0	3
Gooden	2	1	0	0	0	3
Soto	2	0	0	0	0	1
Gossage (S)	1	1	0	0	0	2

Game-winning RBI—Carter.
aLined out for Lea in second. bSingled for Stieb in third. cStruck out for Valenzuela in fourth. dStruck out for Morris in fifth. eStruck out for Gooden in sixth. fStruck out for Lemon in eighth. gFlied out for Griffin in ninth. E—Jackson, Parrish. DP—Nationals 1. LOB—Americans 4, Nationals 7. 2B—Whitaker, Murray, Washington, Winfield. HR—Brett, Carter, Murphy. SB—Sandberg, Strawberry, Gwynn, O. Smith. U—Weyer (N.L.) plate, Clark (A.L.) first, Rennert (N.L.) second, Merrill (A.L.) third, Brocklander (N.L.) left , Roe (A.L.) right. T—2:29. A—57,756.

If the American League hoped its long-awaited 1983 victory was a harbinger of better days, the hope vaporized a year later. The scene was Candlestick Park, San Francisco's infamous cave of winds, where 23 years earlier a gust of wind had nudged Stu Miller into everlasting fame. There were some gusts there again on July 10, 1984, but they came most noticeably from Dwight Gooden's fastball.

A year after the Americans had bloated the scorebooks with 13 runs, they were back in the lower pastures, tilted on the wrong side of a 3-1 score, pitched to death by Fernando Valenzuela, Gooden and Mario Soto.

Disdaining a "revenge" motive (it would have seemed churlish after losing only once in 12 years), the Nationals played with modest offensive efficiency, content to let their pitchers do the talking.

National League skipper Paul Owens of the Phillies gave his starting pitching assignment to the Expos' Charlie Lea; Joe Altobelli of the Orioles nominated Dave Stieb, making the Blue Jays' ace the Americans' starter for the second straight year.

With two out in the bottom of the first, the Padres' Steve Garvey singled to right and went to second when the Angels' Reggie Jackson misplayed the ball. Dale Murphy followed with a hit to left. Garvey raced Dave Winfield's strong throw to the plate, where he found Detroit's estimable Lance Parrish standing guard. The throw and Garvey made simultaneous arrivals and as Parrish tried to secure the ball, Garvey bowled him over. The ball rolled away, the National League had a 1-0 lead and Parrish had an error.

In the second inning, George Brett balanced things with a home run over the center-field fence. Thus inspired, the Expos' Gary Carter came up in the bottom of the same inning and put one out for his third All-Star Game homer, edging his club back in front, 2-1.

Valenzuela took over for the National League in the third and benefited from a sharply turned double play. Cleveland's Andre Thornton and Detroit's Lou Whitaker touched him for singles, putting runners on first and third with none out. Rod Carew then chopped a high bouncer to Garvey at first. With Thornton breaking down the line, Garvey quickly sized up the situation and saw he had a chance to make a big thing out of this. He stepped on first to retire Carew and then fired home, where Carter tagged out the sliding Thornton. Altobelli said later, with rueful admiration, "That was a great play for a first baseman."

In the fourth, Valenzuela put on an exhibition that enchanted the sensibilities of baseball historians. It had been 50 years to the day since Carl Hubbell had screwballed to earth five of the game's great hitters, striking out, in succession, Babe Ruth, Lou Gehrig, Jimmie Foxx, Al Simmons and Joe Cronin. A piece of living history, Hubbell was on hand to throw out the ceremonial first ball of this game. As if to honor the old master, Valenzuela, baseball's most gifted proponent of the delivery Hubbell had made famous, struck out three big hitters of his own in succession—Dave Winfield, Reggie Jackson and George Brett.

How much further along this route Fernando might have traveled we'll never know, for an inning later he passed the torch to the Mets' 19-year-old Gooden, the youngest player ever to appear in an All-Star Game.

Gooden had become the sensation of the National League in '84, firing a fastball that blistered the air and a big, fast-breaking curve that seemed to swoop down from the heavens. Gooden did no less than Valenzuela. In the fifth, Dwight faced and fanned Detroit's Lance Parrish and Chet Lemon and then Seattle's Alvin Davis. The six consecutive strikeouts racked up by the two young pitchers (Valenzuela was 23) rubbed out Hubbell's All-Star Game record of five straight.

The Americans never did score again, not against Gooden (who went one more inning, with no strikeouts), Mario Soto and finally the Padres' Goose Gossage. The fastballs thrown by those three gave the American League batters whiplash. All told, 21 strikeouts were recorded in the contest—a record for a nine-inning All-Star Game—and 11 of them were by National League pitchers. The Americans also received good pitching from Detroit's Jack Morris, the White Sox's Richard Dotson and Oakland's Bill Caudill, who fanned the side in order in the seventh, the third time in the game that such a buzzing had taken place.

The game's final run came in the eighth, when Murphy homered off Detroit's Willie Hernandez, providing the Nationals with the always-popular "insurance run."

The Nationals' 3-1 victory, which for some people restored the cosmic order that had been disturbed the year before, put the series bottom line at 35-19-1.

Gary Carter receives the plaudits of his National League teammates after hitting a second-inning home run in the 1984 All-Star Game.

Dwight Gooden.

Fernando Valenzuela.

Eddie Murray.

George Brett.

Mario Soto.

Jack Morris.

Dale Murphy connects for his eighth-inning homer, giving the National League an insurance run in its 3-1 victory.

Homerless Dome

Nationals	AB.	R.	H.	RBI.	PO.	A.
Gwynn (Padres), lf	1	0	0	0	1	0
Cruz (Astros), lf	1	0	0	0	2	0
fRaines (Expos), lf	0	1	0	0	0	0
Herr (Cardinals), 2b	3	1	1	0	0	1
Ryan (Astros), p	1	0	0	0	0	0
Pena (Pirates), c	1	0	0	0	4	1
Garvey (Padres), 1b	3	0	1	1	5	0
Clark (Cardinals), 1b	1	0	0	0	4	0
Murphy (Braves), cf	3	0	1	0	1	0
McGee (Cardinals), cf	2	0	1	2	1	0
Strawberry (Mets), rf	1	2	1	0	3	0
Parker (Reds), rf	2	0	0	0	1	0
Nettles (Padres), 3b	2	0	0	0	0	1
Wallach (Expos), 3b	2	1	1	0	1	1
Kennedy (Padres), c	2	0	1	1	0	0
Virgil (Phillies), c	1	0	1	2	3	0
Valenzuela (Dodgers), p	0	0	0	0	0	0
eRose (Reds)	1	0	0	0	0	0
Reardon (Expos), p	0	0	0	0	0	1
gWilson (Phillies)	1	0	0	0	0	0
Gossage (Padres), p	0	0	0	0	0	0
Smith (Cardinals), ss	4	0	0	0	1	3
Hoyt (Padres), p	1	0	0	0	0	0
bTempleton (Padres)	1	0	1	0	0	0
Sandberg (Cubs), 2b	1	1	0	0	0	3
Totals	35	6	9	6	27	11

Americans	AB.	R.	H.	RBI.	PO.	A.
Henderson (Yankees), cf	3	1	1	0	1	0
Molitor (Brewers), 3b-cf	1	0	0	0	0	0
Whitaker (Tigers), 2b	2	0	0	0	1	1
Garcia (Blue Jays), 2b	2	0	1	0	0	3
Brett (Royals), 3b	1	0	0	1	2	1
Bradley (Mariners), cf	1	0	0	0	1	0
Petry (Tigers), p	0	0	0	0	0	0
Hernandez (Tigers), p	0	0	0	0	0	0
Murray (Orioles), 1b	3	0	0	0	5	2
Brunansky (Twins), rf	1	0	0	0	0	0
Ripken (Orioles), ss	3	0	1	0	2	1
Trammell (Tigers), ss	1	0	0	0	0	0
Winfield (Yankees), rf	3	0	1	0	0	0
Moore (Angels), p	0	0	0	0	0	1
Boggs (Red Sox), 3b	0	0	0	0	0	0
Rice (Red Sox), lf	3	0	0	0	1	0
Fisk (White Sox), c	2	0	0	0	2	0
Whitt (Blue Jays), c	0	0	0	0	2	0
dWard (Rangers)	1	0	0	0	0	0
Gedman (Red Sox), c	1	0	0	0	4	0
Morris (Tigers), p	0	0	0	0	1	0
Key (Blue Jays), p	0	0	0	0	0	0
aBaines (White Sox)	1	0	1	0	0	0
Blyleven (Indians), p	0	0	0	0	1	2
cCooper (Brewers)	0	0	0	0	0	0
Stieb (Blue Jays), p	0	0	0	0	0	0
Mattingly (Yankees), 1b	1	0	0	0	4	0
Totals	30	1	5	1	27	11

National League ....0 1 1 0 2 0 0 0 2—6
American League ....1 0 0 0 0 0 0 0 0—1

Nationals	IP.	H.	R.	ER.	BB.	SO.
Hoyt (W)	3	2	1	0	0	0
Ryan	3	2	0	0	2	2
Valenzuela	1	0	0	0	1	1
Reardon	1	1	0	0	0	1
Gossage	1	0	0	0	1	2

Americans	IP.	H.	R.	ER.	BB.	SO.
Morris (L)	2⅔	5	2	2	1	1
Key	⅓	0	0	0	0	0
Blyleven	2	3	2	2	1	2
Stieb	1	0	0	0	1	2
Moore	2	0	0	0	0	1
Petry	⅓	0	2	2	3	1
Hernandez	⅔	1	0	0	1	2

Game-winning RBI—Garvey.
aSingled for Key in third. bSingled for Hoyt in fourth. cWalked for Blyleven in fifth. dLined out for Whitt in seventh. eGrounded out for Valenzuela in eighth. fWalked for Cruz in ninth. gStruck out for Reardon in ninth. E—Kennedy. DP—Nationals 1. LOB—Nationals 10, Americans 7. 2B—Herr, Murphy, Wallach, McGee. SB—Henderson, Strawberry, Winfield, Cruz, Garcia. SF—Brett. HBP—By Blyleven (Strawberry). WP—Valenzuela. U—McCoy (A.L.) plate, Kibler (N.L.) first, Bremigan (A.L.) second, C. Williams (N.L.) third, Coble (A.L.) left, Marsh (N.L.) right. T—2:54. A—54,960.

The 56th All-Star Game was played July 16 at the Hubert H. Humphrey Metrodome in Minneapolis, and after it was over, the American League was starting to experience a familiar apprehension. With almost scornful ease, the Nationals had clocked the Americans for the 21st time in 23 tries.

Sparky Anderson's American Leaguers were starved out on five hits and one first-inning run (unearned, no less) by a quintet of top-drawer National League pitchers: LaMarr Hoyt of the Padres, Nolan Ryan of the Astros, Fernando Valenzuela of the Dodgers, Jeff Reardon of the Expos and Goose Gossage of the Padres. Three of Anderson's seven pitchers took a scuffing—starter Jack Morris of Sparky's Detroit club, Bert Blyleven of Cleveland and Dan Petry of the Tigers.

Oddly, considering that the lineups were stacked with the game's top hitters and the contest was played in a park referred to as the "Homer Dome" because of the bleachers' propensity for inhaling fly balls, no home runs were hit.

"The American League has a lot of big boppers, guys who can hit the ball out of the park," said Hoyt, formerly with the A.L.'s Chicago White Sox. "But you can pitch to free swingers. The National League has the great athletes . . . we have guys who can hit for average, ht the long ball, run and throw."

Dick Williams' Nationals spotted the home team a run in the first inning. The Yankees' Rickey Henderson singled, stole second, went to third on a bad throw and scored on George Brett's sacrifice fly.

The Nationals tied it against Morris in the second inning in textbook style: a single by the Mets' Darryl Strawberry, a stolen base and an RBI single by San Diego's Terry Kennedy. In the third, the Nationals slipped ahead as the Cardinals' Tommy Herr doubled and came in on Steve Garvey's single. Then, in the fifth, the methodical National Leaguers punched up two more. Strawberry was struck by a Blyleven pitch, Montreal's Tim Wallach doubled him to third and the Phillies' Ozzie Virgil scored Strawberry and Wallach with a single. It was now 4-1, Nationals.

Dave Stieb and the Angels' Donnie Moore kept the National League at bay for three innings, but in the ninth the Nationals got two more runs. Both were charged to Petry, who went looking for trouble by walking the Cubs' Ryne Sandberg, the Expos' Tim Raines and the Cardinals' Jack Clark. Petry, facing a bases-loaded, one-out situation, was excused in favor of Detroit teammate Willie Hernandez, who allowed a two-run, ground-rule double by the Cards' Willie McGee. McGee's hit produced the last runs of the night.

In the 6-1 triumph, National League pitchers did not permit an extra-base hit to a team whose roster included Rickey Henderson, Lou Whitaker, George Brett, Eddie Murray, Cal Ripken, Alan Trammell, Wade Boggs, Dave Winfield, Jim Rice, Don Mattingly and Harold Baines.

"And don't forget," said N.L. skipper Williams, dropping some salt where it would hurt most, "we didn't even use Dwight Gooden."

Nolan Ryan.

Willie McGee.

Darryl Strawberry.

Somebody has just lifted a high fly during batting practice before the 1985 All-Star Game and following the ball's flight are (left to right) Jim Rice, Tom Brunansky, Carlton Fisk and Cal Ripken.

LaMarr Hoyt.

Ozzie Virgil.

Bubbly center fielder Rickey Henderson fields a ball during early-inning action.

Donnie Moore.

The American Way

Americans	AB.	R.	H.	RBI.	PO.	A.
Puckett (Twins), cf	3	0	1	0	5	0
Henderson (Yankees), lf	3	0	0	0	2	0
Moseby (Blue Jays), lf	0	0	0	0	0	0
Boggs (Red Sox), 3b	3	0	1	0	0	1
hJacoby (Indians), 3b	1	0	0	0	1	1
Parrish (Tigers), c	3	0	0	0	4	0
iRice (Red Sox)	1	0	0	0	0	0
Gedman (Red Sox), c	0	0	0	0	1	1
Joyner (Angels), 1b	1	0	0	0	3	1
bMattingly (Yankees), 1b.	3	0	0	0	7	0
Ripken (Orioles), ss	4	0	0	0	0	1
Fernandez (Blue Jays), ss	0	0	0	0	0	0
Winfield (Yankees), rf	1	1	1	0	0	0
cBarfield (Blue Jays), rf	3	0	0	0	2	0
Whitaker (Tigers), 2b	2	1	1	2	0	3
fWhite (Royals), 2b	2	1	1	1	1	1
Clemens (Red Sox), p	1	0	0	0	1	0
Higuera (Brewers), p	1	0	0	0	0	0
gBaines (White Sox)	1	0	0	0	0	0
Hough (Rangers), p	0	0	0	0	0	0
Righetti (Yankees), p	0	0	0	0	0	0
Aase (Orioles), p	0	0	0	0	0	0
Totals	33	3	5	3	27	9

Nationals	AB.	R.	H.	RBI.	PO.	A.
Gwynn (Padres), lf	3	0	0	0	1	0
Sax (Dodgers), 2b	1	0	1	1	0	1
Sandberg (Cubs), 2b	3	0	0	0	0	2
Scott (Astros), p	0	0	0	0	0	0
Fernandez (Mets), p	0	0	0	0	0	0
jG. Davis (Astros)	1	0	0	0	0	0
Krukow (Giants), p	0	0	0	0	0	1
Hernandez (Mets), 1b	4	0	0	0	5	0
Carter (Mets), c	3	0	0	0	9	0
J. Davis (Cubs), c	1	0	1	0	3	0
kPena (Pirates)	0	0	0	0	0	0
Strawberry (Mets), rf	2	0	1	0	1	0
Parker (Reds), rf	2	0	1	0	0	0
Schmidt (Phillies), 3b	1	0	0	0	0	0
Brown (Giants), 3b	2	1	1	0	1	0
Murphy (Braves), cf	2	0	0	0	2	0
C. Davis (Giants), cf	1	0	0	0	0	0
O. Smith (Cardinals), ss	1	0	0	0	3	2
dBrooks (Expos), ss	2	1	0	0	1	0
Gooden (Mets), p	0	0	0	0	0	0
aBass (Astros)	1	0	0	0	0	0
Valenzuela (Dodgers), p	0	0	0	0	0	0
eRaines (Expos), lf	2	0	0	0	1	0
Totals	32	2	5	1	27	6

American League	0	2 0	0 0 0	1 0 0	—3
National League	0 0 0	0 0 0	0 2 0	—2

Americans	IP.	H.	R.	ER.	BB.	SO.
Clemens (W)	3	0	0	0	0	2
Higuera	3	1	0	0	1	2
Hough	1⅔	2	2	1	0	3
Righetti	⅔	2	0	0	0	0
Aase	⅔	0	0	0	0	0

Nationals	IP.	H.	R.	ER.	BB.	SO.
Gooden (L)	3	3	2	2	0	2
Valenzuela	3	1	0	0	0	5
Scott	1	1	1	1	0	2
Fernandez	1	0	0	0	2	3
Krukow	1	0	0	0	0	0

Game-winning RBI—Whitaker.

aGrounded out for Gooden in third. bStruck out for Joyner in fourth. cStruck out for Winfield in fourth. dGrounded out for O. Smith in fifth. eFlied out for Valenzuela in sixth. fHomered for Whitaker in seventh. gGrounded out for Higuera in seventh. hStruck out for Boggs in eighth. iStruck out for Parrish in eighth. jFouled out for Fernandez in eighth. kRan for J. Davis in ninth. E—Sandberg. DP—Americans 1. LOB—Americans 5, Nationals 4. 2B—Winfield, Brown. HR—Whitaker, White. SB—Puckett, Moseby, Sax. WP—Hough. PB —Gedman. Balks—Gooden, Hough. U—Froemming (N.L.) plate, Palermo (A.L.) first, Runge (N.L.) second, Reed (A.L.) third, Gregg (N.L.) left and McClelland (A.L.) right. T—2:28. A—45,774.

It would not have been unreasonable for the American League to have wondered if it had been put on very slim rations in All-Star play—one victory per decade. The Americans' last three victories, as they went into the 1986 game on July 15 at Houston's Astrodome, had come in 1962, 1971 and 1983. Succinctly, A.L. successes were few and far between. Palm trees in the desert.

This year, however, the Americans had a nearly unbeatable pitcher going for them—for the first three innings, at least. That man was the Red Sox's Roger Clemens, who boasted a 15-2 record at the All-Star Game break, already had struck out a record 20 batters in a nine-inning game and was on his way to Most Valuable Player and Cy Young Award honors—plus any other trophies, plaques, ribbons and cut-glass bowls that were to be bestowed in the postseason.

Clemens, a high school star in suburban Houston and a standout at the University of Texas, had come home to start the All-Star Game for Kansas City Manager Dick Howser's American League club. Clemens stayed right in character, blazing through three perfect innings.

The Americans coupled such sound pitching with second-base power and came away with a 3-2 triumph in the 1986 game. In the second inning, Detroit's Lou Whitaker followed a Dave Winfield double with a home run off N.L. starter Dwight Gooden. In the seventh, with the game still 2-0, Kansas City's Frank White popped what proved to be the game-winner when he drove one of Astro pitcher Mike Scott's pitches over the wall in left-center.

The Nationals came within one run in the eighth inning, with a bit of assistance from the vagaries of Charlie Hough's knuckleballs.

After Milwaukee lefthander Ted Higuera (en route to 20 victories in his second big-league season) had followed Clemens' perfect outing with three innings of one-hit, scoreless pitching, Hough took over. The Texas Rangers' righthander had one of the best knucklers in baseball, although Red Sox catcher Rich Gedman soon would have other words to describe it. Hough worked a 1-2-3 seventh, but the eighth inning was a different matter.

The Giants' Chris Brown led off the Nationals' eighth with a double. When San Francisco's Chili Davis struck out on a Hough butterfly, the ball eluded Gedman, who recovered in time to throw out Davis at first, with Brown going to third on the wild pitch. Montreal's Hubie Brooks fanned on another knuckler, but the ball again took an impish leap away from Gedman and went wandering off on its own. With Brown trying to score on the passed ball, Hough rushed in to cover the plate but was too late. Brooks reached first. A balk sent him to second.

Hough, apparently still determined to strike out people no matter the risks, registered his third strikeout of the inning (but only the second out) against Tim Raines, and this time Gedman stayed with the pitch. A hit by the Dodgers' Steve Sax scored Brooks, making it 3-2, Americans. Much to Gedman's relief, Howser brought in Dave Righetti and the Yankees' lefthander retired the side.

The National League tried to tie it in the ninth—and came close. The Nationals put men on first and third with one out. At this point, Howser brought in Baltimore's ace reliever, Don Aase. Aase induced Brown to hit a checked-swing grounder to the Royals' White, who stepped on second and then threw on to first for a game-ending double play. The Americans had won, 3-2, scoring their second All-Star triumph in four years (a pretty heady statistic, considering that the junior league's won-lost-tied record from 1960 through 1986 stood at 4-25-1).

The National League was not without its moment of glory in the 1986 game, however. This was supplied by Fernando Valenzuela, who had wowed 'em two years earlier. This time, the Dodgers' lefthander was even better. Taking the mound in the fourth inning, he struck out, in order, Don Mattingly, Cal Ripken and Jesse Barfield. Then, in the fifth, he continued on, tying Carl Hubbell's All-Star record of five consecutive strikeouts by fanning Whitaker and Higuera. The Twins' Kirby Puckett ended the embarrassment by grounding out.

In hurling three innings of one-hit ball, Fernando ran his All-Star Game history to 7⅔ scoreless innings, sequined with nine strikeouts.

Overall, National League pitchers fanned 12 batters, tying the record for a nine-inning All-Star Game (the Mets' Sid Fernandez struck out the side in his one inning of work). Nevertheless, the night belonged to the American League—to Clemens, Higuera and those home run-hitting second basemen.

Roger Clemens.

Lou Whitaker.

Don Aase.

Fernando Valenzuela.

Frank White.

Charlie Hough.

1987

Not-So-Lively Ball

Nationals	AB.	R.	H.	RBI.	PO.	A.
Davis (Reds), lf	3	0	0	0	1	0
Raines (Expos), lf	3	0	3	2	1	0
Sandberg (Cubs), 2b	2	0	0	0	0	2
Samuel (Phillies), 2b	4	0	0	0	7	2
Dawson (Cubs), cf-rf	3	0	1	0	3	0
Reuschel (Pirates), p	0	0	0	0	0	0
Leonard (Giants), rf	2	0	0	0	0	0
Schmidt (Phillies), 3b	2	0	1	0	0	1
Wallach (Expos), 3b	3	0	0	0	0	2
Clark (Cardinals), 1b	3	0	0	0	7	1
Hernandez (Mets), 1b	2	0	1	0	4	2
Strawberry (Mets), rf	2	0	0	0	0	0
Diaz (Reds), c	1	0	0	0	1	0
Virgil (Braves), c	2	1	1	0	7	0
Carter (Mets), c	1	0	0	0	1	0
Hershiser (Dodgers), p	0	0	0	0	0	0
Murphy (Braves), rf	1	0	0	0	1	0
Franco (Reds), p	0	0	0	0	0	0
Bedrosian (Phillies), p	0	0	0	0	0	2
eGuerrero (Dodgers)	1	0	0	0	0	0
L. Smith (Cubs), p	1	0	0	0	0	2
S. Fernandez (Mets), p	0	0	0	0	0	0
O. Smith (Cardinals), ss	2	0	0	0	3	0
Brooks (Expos), ss	3	1	1	0	1	2
Scott (Astros), p	0	0	0	0	0	0
aGwynn (Padres)	1	0	0	0	0	0
Sutcliffe (Cubs), p	0	0	0	0	0	0
McGee (Cardinals), cf	4	0	0	0	2	0
Totals	46	2	8	2	39	18

Americans	AB.	R.	H.	RBI.	PO.	A.
Henderson (Yankees), cf..	3	0	1	0	0	0
McGwire (Athletics), 1b...	3	0	0	0	7	0
Mattingly (Yankees), 1b..	1	0	0	0	10	0
Seitzer (Royals), 3b	2	0	0	0	0	0
Boggs (Red Sox), 3b	3	0	0	0	0	3
Langston (Mariners), p	0	0	0	0	0	0
Plesac (Brewers), p	0	0	0	0	0	0
dBaines (White Sox)	1	0	0	0	0	0
Righetti (Yankees), p	0	0	0	0	0	0
Henke (Blue Jays), p	0	0	0	0	0	1
fParrish (Rangers)	1	0	1	0	0	0
Howell (Athletics), p	0	0	0	0	0	0
gTabler (Indians)	1	0	0	0	0	0
Bell (Blue Jays), lf	3	0	0	0	1	0
Nokes (Tigers), c	2	0	0	0	8	0
Winfield (Yankees), rf-lf..	5	0	1	0	2	0
Ripken (Orioles), ss	2	0	1	0	0	5
T. Fernandez (B. Jays), ss	2	0	0	0	1	3
Kennedy (Orioles), c	2	0	0	0	3	1
Evans (Red Sox), rf	2	0	2	0	2	0
Randolph (Yankees), 2b..	1	0	0	0	0	1
Reynolds (Mariners), 2b..	3	0	0	0	4	4
Saberhagen (Royals), p	0	0	0	0	0	0
bTrammell (Tigers)	1	0	0	0	0	0
Morris (Tigers), p	0	0	0	0	0	0
cPuckett (Twins), cf	4	0	0	0	1	0
Totals	42	0	6	0	39	18

National League	000	000	000	000	2—2
American League	000	000	000	000	0—0

Nationals	IP.	H.	R.	ER.	BB.	SO.
Scott	2	1	0	0	0	1
Sutcliffe	2	1	0	0	1	0
Hershiser	2	1	0	0	1	0
Reuschel	1⅓	1	0	0	0	1
Franco	⅔	0	0	0	0	0
Bedrosian	1	0	0	0	2	0
L. Smith (W)	3	2	0	0	0	4
S. Fernandez (S)	1	0	0	0	1	1

Americans	IP.	H.	R.	ER.	BB.	SO.
Saberhagen	3	1	0	0	0	0
Morris	2	1	0	0	1	2
Langston	2	0	0	0	0	3
Plesac	1	0	0	0	0	1
Righetti	⅓	1	0	0	0	0
Henke	2⅔	2	0	0	0	1
Howell (L)	2	3	2	2	0	3

Game-winning RBI—Raines.

aGrounded out for Scott in third. bReached first base on error for Saberhagen in third. cGrounded out for Morris in fifth. dPopped out for Plesac in eighth. eLined out for Bedrosian in tenth. fSingled for Henke in eleventh. gStruck out for Howell in thirteenth. E—Scott, O. Smith, McGwire. DP—Nationals 2. LOB—Nationals 6, Americans 11. 2B—Dawson, Winfield. 3B—Raines. SB—Raines. CS—Schmidt. SH—Reynolds, T. Fernandez, Nokes. U—Denkinger (A.L.) plate, Stello (N.L.) first, Voltaggio (A.L.) second, West (N.L.) third, Cousins (A.L.) left, Davidson (N.L.) right. T—3:39. A—49,671.

It was the year when home runs were being hit in startling numbers, with claims being made that the ball was livelier than ever. Indeed, home runs were leaving ball parks with amazing frequency—and being dispatched to greater distances as well. So when the game's top hitters gathered for the 58th All-Star Game at the Oakland-Alameda County Coliseum on July 14, expectations were high for a bruising battle of long balls.

Baseball, however, proved once again it is a game that goes its own way, thwarting expectations and following no patterns. The 1987 affair was dominated by superb pitching.

The game between Mets Manager Davey Johnson's National Leaguers and Red Sox skipper John McNamara's Americans began in the late afternoon, and for several innings the moving shadow patterns created visibility problems for the batters. But as the game moved scorelessly forward inning after inning, there were no more excuses; instead, there was a reason—great pitching.

The game began with two former Cy Young Award winners facing each other—Kansas City's Bret Saberhagen (1985 recipient) of the American League and Houston's Mike Scott (1986 winner) of the National.

Saberhagen, 15-3 at the All-Star break, breezed through the first three innings, allowing only one hit, a first-inning double by the Cubs' Andre Dawson.

Scott worked the first two innings, and in the bottom of the second came close to being scored upon. The Yankees' Dave Winfield, the only man on either squad to play the entire game, opened by lashing a double down the left-field line. The Orioles' Cal Ripken then lined sharply toward right field, but first baseman Jack Clark of the Cardinals leaped and brought it down, then fired to St. Louis teammate Ozzie Smith, who doubled up Winfield. The play loomed larger and larger as the innings rolled by.

The Cubs' Rick Sutcliffe, another former Cy Young Award winner (1984), took the mound for the Nationals in the third inning and continued spinning goose eggs. He was followed by the Dodgers' Orel Hershiser in the fifth. Hershiser delivered two more shutout innings before being succeeded by the Pirates' Rick Reuschel, who pitched a scoreless seventh.

The American League pitchers were keeping pace. Detroit's Jack Morris followed Saberhagen with two scoreless innings, and then Seattle's Mark Langston hurled two more.

Milwaukee's Dan Plesac blanked the Nationals in the top of the eighth, while Reuschel and Cincinnati's John Franco combined for a scoreless bottom of the eighth. It was the longest scoreless game in All-Star history—the first game of 1962 and the 1970 classic were 0-0 contests through five innings—and it would get longer.

In the Nationals' ninth, Montreal's Tim Raines singled off the Yankees' Dave Righetti. Raines broke for second on Righetti's motion, but the lefthander threw to first and Raines appeared to be a sure out as he sprinted for second. But Oakland rookie first baseman Mark McGwire (who went into the game with 33 home runs) threw wildly and Raines went to third, with just one out.

With the count 1-2 on the Phillies' righthanded-hitting Juan Samuel, McNamara brought in Toronto righthander Tom Henke. Samuel lifted a ball to medium right field, where the cannon arm of Boston's Dwight Evans kept Raines—the first player in the game to reach third base—glued to the bag. The Giants' Jeffrey Leonard then fouled out to Tigers catcher Matt Nokes, ending the game's most promising scoring opportunity.

The Americans made a rush at winning in their half of the ninth, however. With Steve Bedrosian of the Phillies now pitching, Winfield opened by drawing a base on balls. Toronto's Tony Fernandez sacrificed and Evans walked. Seattle's Harold Reynolds then grounded to first, where the Mets' Keith Hernandez, far off the bag, scooped up the ball and fired to second, forcing Evans. The return throw to Bedrosian covering was not in time and Bedrosian, late in getting to the bag, had to make a diving grab of the ball.

Winfield, always aggressive on the bases, rounded third on the play and headed toward home with the potential winning run. Bedrosian's throw to Atlanta's Ozzie Virgil at the plate was in time, although Virgil had to survive a thundering collision with Winfield to make the out.

"I knew I was going to have to be ready," Virgil said. "I had to stand in there and take the hit. He's a big man to run into. It was bam-bam."

The pitchers remained in control until the 13th, Henke and then Oakland's Jay Howell pitching effectively for the Americans and the Cubs' intimidating Lee Smith doing likewise for the Nationals.

The National League finally broke through against Howell. Virgil opened the 13th with a single to center and watched as Lee Smith struck out trying to bunt. Montreal's Hubie Brooks singled Virgil to second. After the Cardinals' Willie McGee flied out, Raines drilled his third hit of the game, a two-run triple to left-center, bringing in the game's only runs.

For Raines, who missed nearly a month of the season as a result of his free-agent quest, the 3-for-3 night ended an All-Star Game "slump." Previously, he had gone 0 for 7 in six classics.

"I've proven myself as a player," said 1986 N.L. batting champion Raines, placing no great significance on his outstanding All-Star performance.

The Mets' Sid Fernandez, the final player on the National League roster to see action, shut down the Americans in the last of the 13th, sealing his team's 2-0 victory. The triumph boosted the Nationals' series lead to 37-20-1.

It was the eighth extra-inning game in All-Star Game history and the eighth time the National League had won in overtime.

In the Year of the Home Run, the 1987 All-Star extravaganza proved to be the Game of the Pitchers.

Tim Raines' ninth-inning steal of second base was aided by Mark McGwire's bad throw to Tony Fernandez.

Harold Reynolds displays the ball after preventing Mike Schmidt's fourth-inning attempt to steal second base.

Ozzie Virgil foils Dave Winfield in ninth.

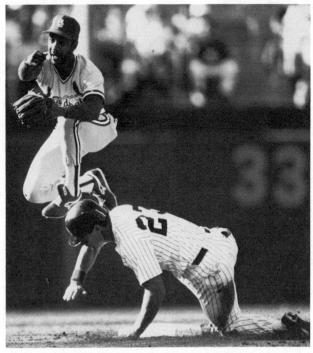

Ozzie Smith forces Don Mattingly at second.

ALL-STAR GAME ELIGIBLES, 1933 THROUGH 1987

Note: These lists include all players named to All-Star squads, except for honorary members. An asterisk (*) preceding a player's name indicates he never played in an All-Star Game for either league, while an asterisk after a year indicates a player was eligible for that game but did not play. The number two in parentheses (2) indicates the player was eligible for the two games played in each year from 1959 through 1962; when this occurs, one asterisk is shown within parentheses for each game in which a player did not appear. A dagger (†) before a player's name indicates he was eligible in both leagues.

American League

Player, Years Eligible and Club
†Aaron, Henry, 1975 Milwaukee
Aase, Donald, 1986 Baltimore
Agee, Tommie, 1966-67 Chicago
Aguirre, Henry, 1962 (2*) Detroit
Allen, John, 1938 Cleveland
†Allen, Richard, 1972-74 Chicago
Allison, W. Robert, 1959* Washington; 1963-64 Minnesota
Alomar, Santos, 1970 California
Alvis, R. Maxwell, 1965-67 Cleveland
Andrews, Michael, 1969 Boston
Aparicio, Luis, 1958-59 (2)-60 (2*)-61-62 (2) Chicago; 1963 Baltimore; 1970 Chicago; 1971 Boston
Appling, Lucius, 1936-39*-40-41*-43*-46-47 Chicago
Armas, Antonio, 1981 Oakland; 1984* Boston
†Arroyo, Luis, 1961* New York
Averill, Earl, 1933-34-36-37-38 Cleveland
Avila, Roberto, 1952-54-55 Cleveland
Azcue, Jose, 1968 Cleveland
Bagby, James Jr., 1942-43* Cleveland
Baines, Harold, 1985-86-87 Chicago
Bando, Salvatore, 1969-72-73 Oakland
Bannister, Floyd, 1982 Seattle
Barber, Stephen, 1966 Baltimore
Barfield, Jesse, 1986 Toronto
Barker, Leonard, 1981 Cleveland
Battey, Earl, 1962 (2)-63-65-66 Minnesota
Bauer, Henry, 1952-53-54 New York
Baylor, Donald, 1979 California
Belanger, Mark, 1976 Baltimore
Bell, David G., 1973 Cleveland; 1980-81-82-84 Texas
Bell, Gary, 1960 (2)-66* Cleveland; 1968* Boston
Bell, George, 1987 Toronto
Bell, Roy, 1937 St. Louis
Benton, J. Alton, 1941*-42 Detroit
Berra, Lawrence, 1948*-49-50-51-52-53-54-55-56-57-58-59 (2*)-60 (2)-61 (2*)-62 New York
Berry, A. Kenneth, 1967 Chicago
Blair, Paul, 1969-73 Baltimore
†Blue, Vida, 1971-75 Oakland
Bluege, Oswald, 1935 Washington
Blyleven, Rikalbert, 1973 Minnesota; 1985 Cleveland
Bochte, Bruce, 1979 Seattle
Boddicker, Michael, 1984 Baltimore
Boggs, Wade, 1985-86-87 Boston
†Bonds, Bobby, 1975 New York
Bonham, Ernest, 1942-43* New York
Boone, Raymond, 1954-56 Detroit
†Boone, Robert, 1983 California
Borowy, Henry, 1944 New York
Boudreau, Louis, 1940-41-42-43*-44*-47-48 Cleveland
Bouton, James, 1963 New York
Bradley, Philip, 1985 Seattle
Brandt, Jack, 1961 (2*) Baltimore
Bressoud, Edward, 1964 Boston
Brett, George, 1976-77-78-79-81-82-83-84-85 Kansas City
Brewer, Thomas, 1956 Boston
Bridges, Everett, 1958 Washington
Bridges, Thomas, 1934*-35*-37-39-40* Detroit
Brinkman, Edwin, 1973 Detroit
Brissie, Leland, 1949 Philadelphia
Brunansky, Thomas, 1985 Minnesota
Buford, Donald, 1971 Baltimore
Bumbry, Alonza, 1980 Baltimore
†Bunning, James, 1957-59-61 (2)-62 (2*)-63 Detroit
Burgmeier, Thomas, 1980 Boston
Burleson, Rick, 1977-79 Boston; 1981 California
Burns, R. Britt, 1981 Chicago
†Burroughs, Jeffrey, 1974 Texas
Busby, James, 1951 Chicago
Busby, Steven, 1974*-75 Kansas City
Byrne, Thomas, 1950* New York
Campaneris, Dagoberto, 1968-72*-73-74-75 Oakland; 1977 Texas
Campbell, William, 1977 Boston
Canseco, Jose, 1986 Oakland
Carew, Rodney, 1967-68-69-71-72-73-74-75-76-77-78 Minnesota; 1980-81-83-84 California
Cash, Norman, 1961 (2)-66-71-72 Detroit
†Cardenas, Leonardo, 1971* Minnesota
Carrasquel, Alfonso, 1951-53-54-55 Chicago
Casanova, Paulino, 1967 Washington
Case, George, 1939*-43 Washington
Caudill, William, 1984 Oakland
Cerv, Robert, 1958 Kansas City
Chalk, David, 1974-75* California
Chambliss, C. Christopher, 1976 New York
Chance, Dean, 1964 Los Angeles; 1967 Minnesota
Chandler, Spurgeon, 1942-43*-46*-47* New York
Chapman, Benjamin, 1933-34-35 New York; 1936 Washington
Chapman, Samuel, 1946 Philadelphia
Clancy, James, 1982 Toronto
Clear, Mark, 1979 California; 1982* Boston
Clemens, W. Roger, 1986 Boston

Clift, Harlond, 1937 St. Louis
Coates, James, 1960 (2*) New York
Cochrane, Gordon, 1934-35* Detroit
Colavito, Rocco, 1959 (2) Cleveland; 1961 (2)-62 (2) Detroit; 1964 Kansas City; 1965-66 Cleveland
Colborn, James, 1973 Milwaukee
Coleman, Gerald, 1950 New York
Coleman, Joseph, 1948 Philadelphia
Conigliaro, Anthony, 1967 Boston
Consuegra, Sandalio, 1954 Chicago
Cooper, Cecil, 1979-80-82-83-85 Milwaukee
Corbett, Douglas, 1981 Minnesota
Cramer, Roger, 1935 Philadelphia; 1937*-38-39-40* Boston
Cronin, Joseph, 1933-34 Washington; 1935-37-38-39-41 Boston
Crosetti, Frank, 1936-39* New York
Crowder, Alvin, 1933 Washington
†Cuellar, Miguel, 1970*-71-74* Baltimore
Cullenbine, Roy, 1941 St. Louis; 1944* Cleveland
†Culp, Raymond, 1969 Boston
Daley, Buddy, 1959 (2*)-1960 (2*) Kansas City
Davalillo, Victor, 1965 Cleveland
Davis, Alvin, 1984 Seattle
Davis, Ronald, 1981 New York
DeCinces, Douglas, 1983 California
DeMaestri, Joseph, 1957 Kansas City
Dent, Russell, 1975 Chicago; 1980-81 New York
†Diaz, Baudilio, 1981 Cleveland
Dickey, William, 1933*-34-36-37-38-39-40-41-43*-46 N.Y.
Dillinger, Robert, 1949 St. Louis
DiMaggio, Dominic, 1941-42*-46-49-50-51-52 Boston
DiMaggio, Joseph, 1936-37-38-39-40-41-42-46*-47-48-49-50-51* New York
Dobson, Joseph, 1948 Boston
Dobson, Patrick, 1972 Baltimore
Doby, Lawrence,1949-50-51-52-53-54-55* Cleveland
Doerr, Robert, 1941-42*-43-44-46-47-48-50-51 Boston
Donovan, Richard, 1955* Chicago; 1961 (2*) Washington; 1962 (2*) Cleveland
Dotson, Richard, 1984 Chicago
Downing, Alphonso, 1967 New York
Downing, Brian, 1979 California
Dropo, Walter, 1950 Boston
Duncan, David, 1971 Oakland
Duren, Ryne, 1958*-59 (2*)-61* New York
Dykes, James, 1933-34* Chicago
Early, Jacob, 1943 Washington
Eckersley, Dennis, 1977 Cleveland; 1982 Boston
Engle, R. David, 1984 Minnesota
Estrada, Charles, 1960 (2*) Baltimore
Etchebarren, Andrew, 1966-67* Baltimore
Evans, Dwight, 1978-81-87 Boston
Evers, Walter, 1948-50 Detroit
Fain, Ferris, 1950-51-52* Philadelphia; 1953 Chicago
†Fairly, Ronald, 1977 Toronto
Farmer, Edward, 1980 Chicago
Feller, Robert, 1938*-39-40-41-46-50 Cleveland
Fernandez, O. Antonio, 1986-87 Toronto
Ferrell, Richard, 1933-34*-35*-36 Boston; 1937*-38*-44* Washington
Ferrell, Wesley, 1933 Cleveland; 1937* Washington
Ferriss, David, 1946 Boston
Fidrych, Mark, 1976 Detroit
†Fingers, Roland, 1973-74-75*-76* Oakland; 1981-82 Milwaukee
Finigan, James, 1954* Philadelphia; 1955 Kansas City
Finney, Louis, 1940 Boston
Fisher, Eddie, 1965 Chicago
Fisk, Carlton, 1972-73-76-77-78-80 Boston; 1981-82-85 Chicago
Flanagan, Michael, 1978 Baltimore
Ford, Edward, 1954-55-56-58*-59-60 (2*)-61 (2*)-64 New York
Fornieles, J. Miguel, 1961 Boston
†Forsch, Kenneth, 1981 California
Fosse, Raymond, 1970 Cleveland
Fox, Ervin, 1944 Boston
Fox, J. Nelson, 1951-52*-53-54-55-56-57-58-59 (2)-60 (2)-61 (2*)-63 Chicago
Foxx, James, 1933*-34-35 Philadelphia; 1936-37-38-39*-40-41 Boston
Francona, John, 1961 Cleveland
Freehan, William, 1964*-65-66-67-68-69-70-71-72-73*-75* Detroit
Fregosi, James, 1964 Los Angeles; 1966-67-68-69-70 California
Garcia, Damaso, 1984-85 Toronto
Garcia, E. Mike, 1952*-53 Cleveland
†Garcia, Philip, 1976 Oakland
Garver, Ned, 1951 St. Louis
Gedman, Richard, 1985-86 Boston
Gehrig, H. Louis, 1933-34-35-36-37-38 New York
Gehringer, Charles, 1933-34-35-36-37-38 Detroit
Gentile, James, 1960 (2*)-61 (2*)-62 (2) Balti-

more
Gomez, Vernon, 1933-34-35-36*-37-38-39* New York
Goodman, William, 1949-53 Boston
Gordon, Joseph 1939-40-41-42-43*-46 New York; 1947-48-49 Cleveland
Goslin, Leon, 1936 Detroit
†Gossage, Richard, 1975-76* Chicago; 1978-80-82* New York
Grant, James, 1963* Cleveland; 1965 Minnesota
Gray, Theodore, 1950 Detroit
Greenberg, Henry, 1937*-39-40 Detroit
Grich, Robert, 1972-74-76 Baltimore; 1979-80-82 California
Griffin, Alfredo, 1984 Toronto
Grim, Robert, 1957 New York
Gross, Wayne, 1977 Oakland
Grove, Orval, 1944 Chicago
Grove, Robert, 1933 Philadelphia; 1935*-36-37*-38-39* Boston
Guidry, Ronald, 1978-79-82* New York
Gumpert, Randall, 1951 Chicago
Gura, Lawrence, 1980 Kansas City
Hall, Jimmie, 1964-65 Minnesota
Hansen, Ronald, 1960 (2) Baltimore
Harder, Melvin, 1934-35-36-37 Cleveland
Hargan, Steven, 1967 Cleveland
Hargrove, D. Michael, 1975 Texas
Harper, Tommy, 1970 Milwaukee
Harrah, Colbert, 1975*-76 Texas; 1982* Cleveland
Harrelson, Kenneth, 1968 Boston
Harris, Maurice, 1946 Boston
Hayes, Frank, 1939*-40-41-44 Philadelphia; 1946 Cleveland
Haynes, Joseph, 1948 Chicago
Heath, J. Geoffrey, 1941-43 Cleveland
Hegan, James, 1947*-49*-50-51-52* Cleveland
Hemsley, Ralston, 1935-36* St. Louis; 1939*-40 Cleveland; 1944 New York
Henderson, Rickey, 1980-82-83-84 Oakland; 1985-86-87 New York
†Hendrick, George, 1974-75 Cleveland
Henke, Thomas, 1987 Toronto
Henrich, Thomas, 1942*-47-48-49*-50 New York
Herbert, Raymond, 1962 Chicago
Hernandez, Guillermo, 1984-85-86* Detroit
Higgins, Michael, 1934*-36 Philadelphia; 1944 Detroit
Higuera, Teodoro, 1986 Milwaukee
Hildebrand, Oral, 1933 Cleveland
Hiller, John, 1974 Detroit
Hinton, Charles, 1964 Washington
Hisle, Larry, 1977 Minnesota; 1978 Milwaukee
Hoag, Myril, 1939 St. Louis
Hockett, Oris, 1944 Cleveland
Hoeft, William, 1955 Detroit
Holtzman, Kenneth, 1972*-73 Oakland
Honeycutt, Frederick, 1980* Seattle; 1983 Texas
Horlen, Joel, 1967 Chicago
Horton, Willie, 1965-68-70-73 Detroit
Hough, Charles, 1986 Texas
Houtteman, Arthur, 1950 Detroit
Howard, Elston, 1957*-58*-59*-60 (2*)-61 (2)-62 (2*)-63-64-65* New York
Howard, Frank, 1968-69-70-71 Washington
Howell, Jay, 1985*-87 Oakland
Howell, Roy, 1978 Toronto
Howser, Richard, 1961 (2*) Kansas City
Hrbek, Kent, 1982 Minnesota
Hudson, Sidney, 1941-42* Washington
Hughson, Cecil, 1942*-43-44 Boston
Hunter, G. William, 1953 St. Louis
Hunter, James, 1966*-67 Kansas City; 1970-72*-73-74 Oakland; 1975-76 New York
Hurst, Bruce, 1987 Boston
Hutchinson, Fred, 1951 Detroit
Jackson, Reginald, 1969-71-72-73-74-75 Oakland; 1977-79-80-81 New York; 1982-84 California
Jacoby, Brook, 1986 Cleveland
Jensen, Jack, 1952 Washington; 1955-58 Boston
†John, Thomas, 1968 Chicago; 1979*-80 New York
Johnson, Alexander, 1970 California
†Johnson, David, 1968-70 Baltimore
Johnson, Robert, 1935-38-39-40*-42 Philadelphia; 1943 Washington; 1944 Boston
Johnson, William, 1947 New York
†Jones, Ruppert, 1977 Seattle
Joost, Edwin, 1949-52* Philadelphia
Josephson, Duane, 1968 Chicago
Joyner, Wallace, 1986 California
Judd, Oscar, 1943 Boston
Kaat, James, 1962*-66 Minnesota; 1975 Chicago
Kaline, Albert, 1955-56-57-58-59 (2)-60 (2)-61 (2)-62-63-65-66-71-74 Detroit
Keegan, Robert, 1954 Chicago
Kell, George, 1947-48*-49-50-51 Detroit; 1953 Boston; 1956-57 Baltimore
Keller, Charles, 1940-41-46 New York
Kellner, Alexander, 1949 Philadelphia

Continued

American League

Continued

Player, Years Eligible and Club

Kelly, H. Patrick, 1973 Chicago
Keltner, Kenneth, 1940-41-42-43-44-46-48 Cleveland
Kemp, Steven, 1979 Detroit
Kennedy, L. Vernon, 1936-38* Detroit
†Kennedy, Terrence, 1987 Baltimore
Keough, Matthew, 1978 Oakland
Kern, James, 1977-78 Cleveland; 1979 Texas
Key, James, 1985 Toronto
Killebrew, Harmon, 1959 (2*) Washington; 1961 (2*)-63-64-65-66-67-68-69-70-71 Minnesota
Kittle, Ronald, 1983 Chicago
Knoop, Robert, 1966 California
Knowles, Darold, 1969 Oakland
Kralick, John, 1964 Cleveland
Kramer, John, 1946-47* St. Louis
Kreevich, Michael, 1938 Chicago
Kubek, Anthony, 1958*-59-61 New York
Kucks, John, 1956 New York
Kuenn, Harvey, 1953-54*-55-56-57-58*-59 Detroit; 1960 (2) Cleveland
Laabs, Chester, 1943 St. Louis
Landis, James, 1962 Chicago
Landreaux, Kenneth, 1980 Minnesota
Langston, Mark, 1987 Seattle
LaRoche, David, 1976* Cleveland; 1977 California
Lary, Frank, 1960 (2)-61 Detroit
Latman, A. Barry, 1961 Cleveland
Lazzeri, Anthony, 1933 New York
Lee, Robert, 1965 Los Angeles
Lee, Thornton, 1941 Chicago
Lee, William, 1973 Boston
LeFlore, Ronald, 1976 Detroit
Lemanczyk, David, 1979 Toronto
Lemon, Chester, 1978-79 Chicago; 1984 Detroit
Lemon, James, 1960 (2*) Washington
Lemon, Robert, 1948*-49*-50-51-52-53*-54 Cleveland
†Leonard, Emil, 1940*-43-44* Washington
Leppert, Donald, 1963 Washington
Lewis, John, 1938-47 Washington
Lindell, John, 1943 New York
Loes, William, 1957 Baltimore
Lolich, Michael, 1969*-71-72 Detroit
Lollar, J. Sherman, 1950* St. Louis; 1954*-55*-56-58*-59 (2)-60 (2) Chicago
Lonborg, James, 1967 Boston
Lopat, Edmund, 1951 New York
Lopez, Aurelio, 1983 Detroit
Lumpe, Jerry, 1964 Detroit
Lyle, Albert, 1973-76*-77 New York
Lynn, Fredric, 1975-76-77-78-79-80 Boston; 1981-82-83 California
Lyons, Theodore, 1939 Chicago
Mack, Raymond, 1940 Cleveland
Malzone, Frank, 1957-58-59 (2)-60 (2)-63-64* Boston
Mantle, Mickey, 1952*-53-54-55-56-57-58-59 (2)-60 (2)-61 (2)-62 (2*)-64-67-68 New York
Mantilla, Felix, 1965 Boston
Manush, Henry, 1934 Washington
Maris, Roger, 1959 Kansas City; 1960 (2)-61 (2)-62 (2) New York
Marrero, Conrado, 1951 Washington
Martin, Alfred, 1956 New York
Martinez, Felix, 1983 Baltimore
Masterson, Walter, 1947-48 Washington
Mattingly, Donald, 1984-85-86-87 New York
Maxwell, Charles, 1956*-57 Detroit
May, Carlos, 1969-72* Chicago
May, David, 1973 Milwaukee
Mayberry, John, 1973-74 Kansas City
McAuliffe, Richard, 1965-66-67 Detroit
McBride, Kenneth, 1961*-63 Los Angeles
McDougald, Gilbert, 1952-56*-57-58-59 New York
McDowell, Samuel, 1965-68-69-70 Cleveland
McGlothlin, James, 1967 California
McGregor, Scott, 1981 Baltimore
McGwire, Mark, 1987 Oakland
McLain, Dennis, 1966-68-69 Detroit
McLish, Calvin, 1959 Cleveland
McNally, David, 1969-70*-72 Baltimore
McQuinn, George, 1939*-40*-42*-44 St. Louis; 1947-48 New York
McRae, Harold, 1975-76-82 Kansas City
Melton, William, 1971 Chicago
†Messersmith, John, 1971* California
Michaels, Casimer, 1949 Chicago; 1950 Washington
Milnar, Albert, 1940 Cleveland
Mincher, Donald, 1967 California; 1969 Seattle
Minoso, Orestes, 1951-52-53-54-57-60 (2) Chicago; 1959 (2*) Cleveland
Mitchell, L. Dale, 1949-52 Cleveland
*Mize, John, 1953 New York
Molitor, Paul, 1985 Milwaukee
Monbouquette, William, 1960 (2*)-62*-63* Boston
†Monday, Robert, 1968 Oakland
Money, Donald, 1974*-76-78 Milwaukee
Monge, Isidro, 1979 Cleveland
Moore, Donnie, 1985 California
Moran, William, 1962 (2) Los Angeles
Morris, John, 1981-84-85-87 Detroit
Moseby, Lloyd, 1986 Toronto
Moses, Gerald, 1970 Boston
Moses, Wallace, 1937 Philadelphia
Mossi, Donald, 1957 Cleveland
Mullin, Patrick, 1947*-48 Detroit

Muncrief, Robert, 1948 St. Louis
Munson, Thurman, 1971-73-74-75-76-77 New York
†Murcer, Bobby, 1971-72-73-74 New York
Murphy, John, 1937-38*-39* New York
Murray, Eddie, 1978*-81-82-83-84-85-86* Baltimore
Myer, Charles, 1935-37* Washington
Narleski, Raymond, 1958 Cleveland
Nelson, David, 1973 Texas
†Nettles, Graig, 1975-77-78-79-80 New York
Newhouser, Harold 1942*-43-44-46-47-48 Detroit
Newman, Jeffrey, 1979 Oakland
Newsom, Louis, 1938* St. Louis; 1939*-40 Detroit; 1944 Philadelphia
†Niekro, Philip, 1984* New York
Nokes, Matthew, 1987 Detroit
Noren, Irving, 1954 New York
Norris, Michael, 1981 Oakland
O'Dell, William, 1958-59 Baltimore
Odom, Johnny, 1968-69 Oakland
O'Donoghue, John, 1965 Kansas City
Oglivie, Benjamin, 1980-82-83 Milwaukee
Oliva, Pedro (Tony) 1964-65-66-67-68-70 Minnesota
Oliver, Albert, 1980-81 Texas
Orta, Jorge, 1980 Cleveland
Otis, Amos, 1970-71-73-76 Kansas City
Paciorek, Thomas, 1981 Seattle
Page, Joseph, 1944*-47-48* New York
Paige, Leroy, 1952*-53 St. Louis
Palmer, James, 1970-71-72-75*-77-78 Baltimore
Pappas, Milton, 1962 (2)-65 Baltimore
Parnell, Melvin, 1949-51 Boston
Parrish, Lance, 1980-82-83-84-86 Detroit
†Parrish, Larry, 1987 Texas
Pascual, Camilo, 1961-62 (2*)-64 Minnesota
Patek, Freddie, 1976-78 Kansas City
Pattin, Martin, 1971 Milwaukee
Pearson, Albert, 1963 Los Angeles
Pearson, M. Monte, 1936-40* New York
Pepitone, Joseph, 1963-64-65 New York
†Perry, Gaylord, 1972-74 Cleveland
Perry, James, 1961* Cleveland; 1970-71* Minnesota
Pesky, John, 1946 Boston
Peters, Gary, 1964*-67 Chicago
Peterson, Fred, 1970 New York
Petrocelli, Americo, 1967-69 Boston
Petry, Daniel, 1985 Detroit
Pierce, W. William, 1953-55-56-57-58*-59*-61* Chicago
Piersall, James, 1954-56 Boston
Piniella, Louis, 1972 Kansas City
Pizarro, Juan, 1963-64* Chicago
Plesac, Daniel, 1987 Milwaukee
Porter, Darrell, 1974* Milwaukee; 1978-79-80 Kansas City
Porterfield, Ervin, 1954 Washington
Powell, John, 1968-69-70 Baltimore
Power, Victor, 1955-56 Kansas City; 1959 (2)-60 (2*) Cleveland
Presley, James, 1986 Seattle
Puckett, Kirby, 1986-87 Minnesota
Quisenberry, Daniel, 1982-83-84* Kansas City
Radatz, Richard, 1963-64 Boston
Radcliff, Raymond, 1936 Chicago
Ramos, Pedro, 1959 Washington
Randolph, William, 1977-80-81-87 New York
Raschi, Victor, 1948-49-50-52 New York
Remy, Gerald, 1978 Boston
Reynolds, Allie, 1949*-50-52*-53 New York
†Reynolds, G. Craig, 1978* Seattle
Reynolds, Harold, 1987 Seattle
Rice, James, 1977-78-79-83-84-85-86 Boston
Richardson, Robert, 1957*-59*-62 (2)-63-64-65-66 New York
Richert, Peter, 1965-66 Washington
Righetti, David, 1986-87 New York
Ripken, Calvin, 1983-84-85-86-87 Baltimore
Rivers, John, 1976 New York
Rizzuto, Philip, 1942*-50-51-52-53 New York
Robinson, Aaron, 1947 New York
Robinson, Brooks, 1960 (2)-61 (2)-62 (2)-63-64-65-66-67-68-69-70-71-72-73-74 Baltimore
†Robinson, Frank, 1966-69-70-71 Baltimore; 1974 California
Robinson, W. Edward, 1949 Washington; 1951-52 Chicago; 1953 Philadelphia
Rodriguez, Eliseo, 1969 Kansas City; 1972* Milwaukee
†Rojas, Octavio, 1971-72-73-74* Kansas City
Rolfe, Robert, 1937-38*-39 New York
Rollins, Richard, 1962 (2) Minnesota
Romano, John, 1961 (2)-62 (2*) Cleveland
Rosar, Warren, 1942* New York; 1943* Cleveland; 1946-47-48 Philadelphia
†Roseboro, John, 1969 Minnesota
Rosen, Albert, 1952-53-54-55 Cleveland
Rowe, Lynwood, 1935-36 Detroit
Rudi, Joseph, 1972-74-75 Oakland
Ruffing, Charles, 1934-38*-39-40-41*-42* New York
Runnels, James, 1959 (2)-60 (2)-62 Boston
Russell, Jack, 1934 Washington
Russo, Marius, 1941 New York
Ruth, George, 1933-34 New York
†Ryan, L. Nolan, 1972*-73-77*-79 California
Saberhagen, Bret, 1987 Kansas City
†Sain, John, 1953* New York
Scarborough, Ray, 1950 Chicago
Scheinblum, Richard, 1972 Kansas City

Schrom, Kenneth, 1986 Cleveland
Schwall, Donald, 1961 Boston
Score, Herbert, 1955*-56 Cleveland
Scott, George, 1966-77 Boston; 1975 Milwaukee
Seitzer, Kevin, 1987 Kansas City
Selkirk, George, 1936-39 New York
Sewell, J. Luther, 1937 Chicago
Shantz, Robert, 1951*-52 Philadelphia; 1957* New York
Shea, Francis, 1947 New York
Siebern, Norman, 1962 (2*)-63* Kansas City; 1964 Baltimore
Siebert, Richard, 1943 Philadelphia
Siebert, Wilfred, 1966 Cleveland; 1971* Boston
Sievers, Roy, 1956-57*-59 (2*) Washington; 1961 Chicago
Simmons, Aloysius, 1933-34-35 Chicago
†Simmons, Ted, 1981-83 Milwaukee
Simpson, Harry, 1956 Kansas City
†Singer, William, 1973 California
Singleton, Kenneth, 1977-79-81 Baltimore
Skowron, William, 1957-58-59-60 (2)-61* New York
Slaton, James, 1977 Milwaukee
Smalley, Roy F. III, 1979 Minnesota
Smith, Alfred, 1943 Cleveland
Smith, Alphonse, 1955 Cleveland; 1960 (2) Chicago
Smith, Edgar, 1941-42* Chicago
†Smith, C. Reginald, 1969-72 Boston
Sorensen, Lary, 1978 Milwaukee
Spence, Stanley, 1942*-44-46-47 Washington
Spencer, James, 1973 Texas
†Staley, Gerald, 1960 (2*) Chicago
Stanhouse, Donald, 1979 Baltimore
Stanley, Robert, 1979-83 Boston
†Staub, Daniel, 1976 Detroit
Stenhouse, David, 1962 (2*) Washington
Stephens, Vernon, 1943-44-46 St. Louis; 1948-49-50*-51 Boston
Stieb, David, 1980-81-83-84-85 Toronto
*Stigman, Richard, 1960 (2**) Cleveland
Stirnweiss, George, 1946 New York
Stone, D. Dean, 1954 Washington
Stone, Steven, 1980 Baltimore
Stottlemyre, Melvin, 1965*-66-68-69-70 New York
Sullivan, Franklin, 1955-56* Boston
Sundberg, James, 1974*-78 Texas; 1984 Milw.
†Sutcliffe, Richard, 1983* Cleveland
Tabler, Patrick, 1987 Cleveland
Tanana, Frank, 1976-78* California
Tebbetts, George, 1941*-42 Detroit; 1948-49 Boston
†Temple, John, 1961 (2) Cleveland
Tenace, F. Gene, 1975 Oakland
*Terry, Ralph, 1962 (2**) New York
Thomas, J. Gorman, 1981 Milwaukee
Thomas, J. Leroy, 1962 (2) Los Angeles
†Thompson, Jason, 1977*-78 Detroit
Thornton, Andre, 1982-84 Cleveland
Tiant, Luis, 1968 Cleveland; 1974-76 Boston
Trammell, Alan, 1980-85-87 Detroit
†Travers, William, 1976* Milwaukee
Travis, Cecil, 1938*-40-41 Washington
Tresh, Thomas, 1962 (2*)-63 New York
Triandos, Augustus, 1957*-58-59 Baltimore
†Trillo, J. Manuel, 1983 Cleveland
Trout, Paul, 1944-47* Detroit
Trucks, Virgil, 1949 Detroit; 1954 Chicago
Tucker, Thurman, 1944 Chicago
Turley, Robert, 1954* Baltimore; 1955*-58 New York
Vernon, James, 1946-48-53-54-55 Washington; 1956 Boston; 1958 Cleveland
Versalles, Zoilo, 1963-65 Minnesota
Vosmik, Joseph, 1935 Cleveland
Wagner, Harold, 1942* Philadelphia; 1946 Boston
Wagner, Leon, 1962 (2)-63 Los Angeles
Wakefield, Richard, 1943 Detroit
Walker, Jerry, 1959 Baltimore
Ward, Gary, 1983 Minnesota; 1985 Texas
†Washington, Claudell, 1975 Oakland
Wert, Donald, 1968 Detroit
Wertz, Victor, 1949-51-52* Detroit; 1957 Cleveland
West, Samuel, 1933-34-35*-37 St. Louis
Whitaker, Louis, 1983-84-85-86 Detroit
White, Frank, 1978-79-81-82-86 Kansas City
White, Roy, 1969-70* New York
White, Samuel, 1953 Boston
Whitt, L. Ernest, 1985 Toronto
†Wilhelm, J. Hoyt, 1959 (2*)-61 (2*) Baltimore
Williams, Theodore, 1940-41-42-46-47-48-49-50-51-54-55-56-57-58-59 (2)-60 (2) Boston
†Wilson, James A., 1955* Baltimore; 1956 Chicago
Wilson, Willie, 1982-83 Kansas City
†Winfield, David, 1981-82-83-84-85-86-87 New York
Witt, Michael, 1986-87* California
Wood, Wilbur, 1971*-72-74* Chicago
Woodling, Eugene, 1959 Baltimore
Wright, Clyde, 1970 California
Wyatt, Johnathan, 1964 Kansas City
Wynegar, Harold, 1976-77 Minnesota
Wynn, Early, 1947* Washington; 1955-56-57 Cleveland; 1958-59 (2)-60 (2*) Chicago
Yastrzemski, Carl, 1963-66*-67-68-69-70-71-72-74-75-76-77-79-82-83 Boston
York, Rudolph, 1938-41-42-43-44* Detroit; 1946 Boston; 1947* Chicago
Yost, Edward, 1952 Washington
Young, Matthew, 1983 Seattle
Yount, Robin, 1980-82-83 Milwaukee
Zarilla, Allen, 1948 St. Louis
Zisk, Richard, 1977 Chicago; 1978 Texas

National League

Player, Years Eligible and Club

†Aaron, Henry, 1955-56-57-58-59 (2)-60 (2)-61 (2)-62-63-64-65 Milwaukee; 1966-67-68-69-70-71-72-73-74 Atlanta
Adams, Ace, 1943 New York
Adcock, Joseph, 1960 (2) Milwaukee
†Allen, Richard, 1965-66-67 Phila.; 1970 St. Louis
Alley, L. Eugene, 1967 Pittsburgh
Alou, Felipe, 1962 San Francisco, 1966*-68 Atlanta
Alou, Mateo, 1968-69 Pittsburgh
Altman, George A., 1961 (2)-62 Chicago
Andrews, Nathan, 1944 Boston
Andujar, Joaquin, 1977*-79 Houston
Antonelli, John A., 1954-56-57* New York; 1958*-59 (2*) San Francisco
Arnovich, Morris, 1939 Philadelphia
†*Arroyo, Luis, 1955* St. Louis
Ashburn, Richie, 1948-51-53-58* Philadelphia; 1962 (2*) New York
Atwell, Maurice, 1952 Chicago
Bailey, L. Edgar, 1956-57-60 (2*) Cincinnati; 1961*-63 San Francisco
Baker, Eugene, 1955 Chicago
Baker, Johnnie, 1981-82 Los Angeles
Banks, Ernest, 1955-56*-57-58-59 (2)-60 (2)-61-62 (2)-65-67-69 Chicago
Bartell, Richard, 1933 Philadelphia; 1937 New York
Bass, Kevin, 1986 Houston
Beckert, Glenn, 1969-70-71-72 Chicago
Bedrosian, Stephen, 1987 Philadelphia
Bell, David R., 1953-54-56-57 Cincinnati
Bench, Johnny, 1968-69-70-71-72-73-74-75-76-77-80-83 Cincinnati
Benedict, Bruce, 1981-83 Atlanta
Berger, Walter, 1933-34-35-36* Boston
Bibby, James, 1980 Pittsburgh
Bickford, Vernon, 1949 Boston
Billingham, John, 1973 Cincinnati
Blackwell, Ewell, 1946-47-48-49-50-51 Cincinnati
Blanton, Darrell, 1937 Pittsburgh; 1941* Philadelphia
Blasingame, Donald, 1958 St. Louis
Blass, Stephen, 1972 Pittsburgh
†Blue, Vida, 1978-80*-81 San Francisco
Bolling, Frank, 1961 (2)-62 (2) Milwaukee
†Bonds, Bobby, 1971-73 San Francisco
†Boone, Robert, 1976-78-79 Philadelphia
Bowa, Lawrence, 1974-75-76-78-79 Philadelphia
Boyer, Kenton, 1956-59 (2)-60 (2)-61 (2*)-62 (2)-63-64 St. Louis
Branca, Ralph, 1947*-48-49* Brooklyn
Brecheen, Harry, 1947-48* St. Louis
Brenly, Robert, 1984 San Francisco
Brett, Kenneth, 1974 Pittsburgh
Brewer, James, 1973 Los Angeles
Brock, Louis, 1967-71-72*-74-75-79 St. Louis
Brooks, Hubert, 1986-87 Montreal
Brown, J. Christopher, 1986 San Francisco
Brown, James, 1942 St. Louis
Brown, Mace, 1938 Pittsburgh
Buckner, William, 1981 Chicago
Buhl, Robert, 1960 (2*) Milwaukee
†Bunning, James, 1964-66 Philadelphia
Burdette, S. Lewis, 1957-59 (2*) Milwaukee
Burgess, Forrest, 1954 Philadelphia; 1955 Cincinnati; 1959 (2*)-60 (2)-61 (2)-64* Pittsburgh
†Burroughs, Jeffrey, 1978* Atlanta
Callison, John, 1962 (2)-64-65* Philadelphia
Camilli, Adolph, 1939 Brooklyn
Campanella, Roy, 1949-50-51-52-53-54-56 Brooklyn
Candelaria, John, 1977 Pittsburgh
Cannizzaro, Christopher, 1969 San Diego
Capra, Lee, 1974 Atlanta
†Cardenas, Leonardo, 1964-65-66-68 Cincinnati
Carlton, Steven, 1968-69-71* St. Louis; 1972-74*-77*-79-80*-81*-82 Philadelphia
Carroll, Clay, 1971-72* Cincinnati
Carter, Gary, 1975-79-80-81-82-83-84 Montreal; 1986-87 New York
Carty, Ricardo, 1970 Atlanta
Cash, David, 1974-75-76 Philadelphia
Cavarretta, Philip, 1944-46-47 Chicago
Cedeno, Cesar, 1972-73-74-76 Houston
Cepeda, Orlando, 1959 (2*)-60 (2)-61 (2)-62 (2)-63*-64 San Francisco; 1967 St. Louis
Cey, Ronald, 1974-75-76-77-78-79 Los Angeles
Cimoli, Gino, 1957 Brooklyn
Clark, Jack, 1978-79 San Francisco; 1985-87 St. Louis
Clemente, Roberto, 1960 (2)-61 (2)-62 (2)-63-64-65-66-67-69-70-71-72* Pittsburgh
Colbert, Nathan, 1971-72-73 San Diego
Collins, James, 1935-36 St. Louis; 1937 Chicago
Concepcion, David, 1975-76-77-78-80-81-82 Cincinnati
Conley, D. Eugene, 1954-55 Milwaukee; 1959 (2*) Philadelphia
Cooper, Morton, 1942-43 St. Louis; 1946* Boston
Cooper, W. Walker, 1942-43-44 St. Louis; 1946-47-48 New York; 1949* Cincinnati; 1950* Boston
Coscarart, Peter, 1940 Brooklyn
Crandall, Delmar, 1954*-55-58-59 (2)-60 (2)-62 (2) Milwaukee
Crowe, George, 1958 Cincinnati
Cruz, Jose, 1980*-85 Houston
Cuccinello, Anthony, 1933 Brooklyn; 1938* Boston
†Cuellar, Miguel, 1967 Houston
†Culp, Raymond, 1963 Philadelphia

Cunningham, Joseph, 1959 (2*) St. Louis
Cuyler, Hazen, 1934 Chicago
Dahlgren, Ellsworth, 1943 Philadelphia
Danning, Harry, 1938*-39*-40-41 New York
Dark, Alvin, 1951-52*-54 New York
Darling, Ronald, 1985 New York
Davenport, James, 1962 (2*) San Francisco
Davis, Charles, 1984-86 San Francisco
Davis, Curtis, 1936 Chicago; 1939* St. Louis
Davis, Eric, 1987 Cincinnati
Davis, Glenn, 1986 Houston
Davis, H. Thomas, 1962 (2)-63 Los Angeles
Davis, Jody, 1984-86 Chicago
Davis, William, 1971-73 Los Angeles
Dawley, William, 1983 Houston
Dawson, Andre, 1981-82-83 Montreal; 1987 Chicago
Dean, Jerome, 1934-35-36-37 St. Louis
Demaree, Frank, 1936-37 Chicago
Derringer, Paul, 1935-38*-39-40-41 Cincinnati
†Diaz, Baudilio, 1987 Cincinnati
Dickson, Murry, 1953 Pittsburgh
Dierker, Lawrence, 1969 Houston
Dietz, Richard, 1970 San Francisco
DiMaggio, Vincent, 1943-44 Pittsburgh
Dravecky, David, 1983 San Diego
Drysdale, Donald, 1959 (2)-61*-62-63-64-65-67-68 Los Angeles
Durham, Leon, 1982*-83 Chicago
Durocher, Leo, 1936 St. Louis; 1938-40* Brooklyn
Easler, Michael, 1981 Pittsburgh
Edwards, C. Bruce, 1947 Brooklyn; 1951* Chicago
Edwards, C. Bruce, 1943-64-65* Cincinnati
Elliott, Robert, 1941-42-44 Pittsburgh; 1948-51 Boston
Ellis, Dock, 1971 Pittsburgh
Ellis, Samuel, 1965 Cincinnati
Ellsworth, Richard, 1964 Chicago
Elston, Donald, 1959 (2*) Chicago
English, Elwood, 1933 Chicago
Ennis, Delmer, 1946-51-55 Philadelphia
Erskine, Carl, 1954 Brooklyn
Evans, Darrell, 1973 Atlanta; 1983 San Francisco
Face, ElRoy, 1959 (2)-60 (2*)-61 (2) Pittsburgh
*Fairly, Ronald, 1973 Montreal
Farrell, Richard, 1958 Philadelphia; 1962 (2*)-64-65 Houston
Fernandez, C. Sidney, 1986-87 New York
Fette, Louis, 1939 Boston
†Fingers, Roland, 1978 San Diego
Fletcher, Elburt, 1943 Pittsburgh
Flood, Curtis, 1964-66-68 St. Louis
Foiles, Henry, 1957 Pittsburgh
Foster, George, 1976-77-78-79-81 Cincinnati
†Forsch, Kenneth, 1976 Houston
Franco, John, 1986*-87 Cincinnati
Frankhouse, Fred, 1934 Boston
French, Lawrence, 1940 Chicago
Friend, Robert, 1956-58-60 (2*) Pittsburgh
Frey, Linus, 1939-41-43 Cincinnati
Frisch, Frank, 1933-34-35* St. Louis
Fryman, Woodrow, 1968 Philadelphia; 1976* Montreal
Furillo, Carl, 1952-53* Brooklyn
Galan, August, 1936 Chicago; 1943-44 Brooklyn
†Garner, Philip, 1980-81 Pittsburgh
Garr, Ralph, 1974 Atlanta
Garrelts, Scott, 1985 San Francisco
Garvey, Steven, 1974-75-76-77-78-79-80-81 Los Angeles; 1984-85 San Diego
Gaston, Clarence, 1970 San Diego
Gibson, Robert, 1962 (2*)-65-67-68*-69-70-72 St. Louis
Gilliam, James, 1956* Brooklyn; 1959 Los Angeles
Giusti, J. David, 1973 Pittsburgh
Gooden, Dwight, 1984-85*-86 New York
Goodman, Ival, 1938-39 Cincinnati
Gordon, Sidney, 1948*-49 New York
†Gossage, Richard, 1977 Pittsburgh; 1984-85 San Diego
Grabarkewitz, Billy, 1970 Los Angeles
Griffey, G. Kenneth, 1976-77*-80 Cincinnati
Grimsley, Ross, 1978 Montreal
Grissom, Lee, 1937 Cincinnati
Grissom, Marvin, 1954 New York
Groat, Richard, 1959 (2)-60 (2)-62 (2) Pittsburgh; 1963-64 St. Louis
Grote, Gerald, 1968-74 New York
Grubb, John, 1974 San Diego
Guerrero, Pedro, 1981-83-87 Los Angeles
Gustine, Frank, 1946-47-48 Pittsburgh
Gwynn, Anthony, 1984-85-86-87 San Diego
Haas, Berthold, 1947 Cincinnati
Hack, Stanley, 1938-39-41-43 Chicago
Haddix, Harvey, 1953*-55 St. Louis
Hafey, Charles, 1933 Cincinnati
Hallahan, William, 1933 St. Louis
Haller, Thomas, 1966*-67 San Francisco; 1968 Los Angeles
Hammaker, C. Atlee, 1983 San Francisco
Hamner, Granville, 1952-53-54 Philadelphia
Harrelson, Derrel, 1970-71 New York
Hart, James, 1966 San Francisco
Hartnett, Charles, 1933-34-35-36-37-38* Chicago
Hatton, Grady, 1952 Cincinnati
Hearn, James, 1952 New York
Helms, Tommy, 1967-68 Cincinnati
†Hendrick, George, 1980-83* St. Louis
Henry, William, 1960 (2*) Cincinnati
Herman, William, 1934-35-36-37-38-39-40 Chica-

go; 1941-42-43 Brooklyn
Hernandez, Keith, 1979-80 St. Louis; 1984-86-87 New York
Herr, Thomas, 1985 St. Louis
Hershiser, Orel, 1987 Los Angeles
Hickman, James, 1970 Chicago
Higbe, W. Kirby, 1940* Philadelphia; 1946 Brooklyn
Hoak, Donald, 1957 Cincinnati
Hodges, Gilbert, 1949-50*-51-52*-53-54-55-57 Brooklyn
Hoerner, Joseph, 1970 Philadelphia
Holland, Alfred, 1984 Philadelphia
Holmes, Thomas, 1948 Boston
Hooton, Burt, 1981 Los Angeles
Hopp, John, 1946 Boston
Horner, J. Robert, 1982 Atlanta
Howe, Steven, 1982 Los Angeles
Hoyt, D. LaMarr, 1985 San Diego
Hubbard, Glenn, 1983 Atlanta
Hubbell, Carl, 1933-34-35*-36-37-38*-40-41* New York
Hume, Thomas, 1982 Cincinnati
Hundley, C. Randolph, 1969 Chicago
Hunt, Ronald, 1964-66 New York
Jablonski, Raymond, 1954 St. Louis
Jackson, Grant, 1969 Philadelphia
Jackson, Lawrence, 1957-58-60 (2*) St. Louis; 1963 Chicago
Jackson, Ransom, 1954-55 Chicago
Jackson, Travis, 1934 New York
Jansen, Lawrence, 1951 New York
Javery, Alva, 1943-44* Boston
Javier, Julian, 1963-68 St. Louis
*Jay, Joseph, 1961 (2**) Cincinnati
Jenkins, Ferguson, 1967-71-72* Chicago
†John, Thomas, 1978* Los Angeles
†Johnson, David, 1973 Atlanta
Johnson, Donald, 1944 Chicago
Jones, Cleon, 1969 New York
Jones, Randall, 1975-76 San Diego
†Jones, Ruppert, 1982 San Diego
Jones, Samuel, 1955 Chicago; 1959 San Francisco
Jones, Willie, 1950-51 Philadelphia
Jurges, William, 1937 Chicago; 1939* New York
Kasko, Edward, 1961 (2*) Cincinnati
Kazak, Edward, 1949 St. Louis
†Kennedy, Terrence, 1981-83*-85 San Diego
Kerr, John, 1948 New York
Kessinger, Donald, 1968-69-70-71-72-74 Chicago
Kiner, Ralph, 1948-49-50-51-52* Pittsburgh; 1953 Chicago
Kingman, David, 1976 San Francisco; 1980 Chicago
Klein, Charles, 1933 Philadelphia; 1934 Chicago
Kluszewski, Theodore, 1953-54-55-56 Cincinnati
Knepper, Robert, 1981 Houston
Knight, C. Ray, 1980 Cincinnati; 1982 Houston
Konstanty, C. James, 1950 Philadelphia
Koosman, Jerry, 1968-69 New York
Koufax, Sanford, 1961 (2)-62*-63*-64*-65-66 Los Angeles
Kranepool, Edward, 1965 New York
Krukow, Michael, 1986 San Francisco
Kurowski, George, 1943*-44-46-47 St. Louis
Labine, Clement, 1956*-57 Brooklyn
LaCoss, Michael, 1979 Cincinnati
Lamanno, Raymond, 1946 Cincinnati
Lanier, H. Max, 1943 St. Louis
Larker, Norman, 1960 (2) Los Angeles
Lavagetto, Harry, 1938*-39*-40-41 Brooklyn
Lavelle, Gary, 1977-83* San Francisco
Law, Vernon, 1960 (2) Pittsburgh
Lawrence, Brooks, 1956 Cincinnati
Lea, Charles, 1984 Montreal
Lee, William, 1938-39 Chicago
Lefebvre, James, 1966 Los Angeles
Leiber, Henry, 1938 New York
†Leonard, Emil, 1951* Chicago
Leonard, Jeffrey, 1987 San Francisco
Litwhiler, Daniel, 1942 Philadelphia
Lockman, Carroll, 1952 New York
Logan, John, 1955-57*-58-59* Milwaukee
Lombardi, Ernest, 1936*-37*-38-39-40 Cincinnati; 1942 Boston; 1943 New York
Long, R. Dale, 1956 Pittsburgh
Lopata, Stanley, 1955-56* Philadelphia
Lopes, David, 1978-79-80-81 Los Angeles
Lopez, Alfonso, 1934 Brooklyn; 1941 Pittsburgh
Lowrey, Harry, 1946 Chicago
Luzinski, Gregory, 1975-76-77-78 Philadelphia
Madlock, Bill, 1975 Chicago; 1981-83 Pittsburgh
Maglie, Salvatore, 1951-52* New York
Mahaffey, Arthur, 1961 (2*)-62 Philadelphia
Maloney, James, 1965 Cincinnati
Mancuso, August, 1935-37 New York
Marichal, Juan, 1962 (2)-63*-64-65-66-67-68-69*-71 San Francisco
Marion, Martin, 1943-44-46-47-49*-50 St. Louis
Marshall, Michael A., 1984 Los Angeles
Marshall, Michael G., 1974-75* Los Angeles
Marshall, Willard, 1942-47-49 New York
Martin, Hershel, 1938 Philadelphia
Martin, John, 1933-34-35-37* St. Louis
Martin, Stuart, 1936 St. Louis
Masi, Philip, 1946-47-48 Boston
Mathews, Edwin, 1953-55-56*-57-58*-59 (2)-60

Continued

National League